Flourishing in Babylon

Flourishing in Babylon

Black British Agency and Self-determination

Joe Aldred

scm press

© Joe Aldred 2024

Published in 2024 by SCM Press
Editorial office
3rd Floor, Invicta House
110 Golden Lane
London EC1Y 0TG, UK

www.scmpress.co.uk

SCM Press is an imprint of Hymns Ancient & Modern Ltd
(a registered charity)

Hymns Ancient & Modern® is a registered trademark of
Hymns Ancient & Modern Ltd
13A Hellesdon Park Road, Norwich,
Norfolk NR6 5DR, UK

All rights reserved. No part of this publication may be reproduced, stored in a retrieval system, or transmitted, in any form or by any means, electronic, mechanical, photocopying or otherwise, without the prior permission of the publisher, SCM Press.

Joe Aldred has asserted his right under the Copyright, Designs and Patents Act 1988 to be identified as the Author of this Work

Scripture quotations marked (NIV) are taken from The Holy Bible, New International Version (Anglicised edition) copyright © 1979, 1984, 2011 by Biblica (formerly International Bible Society). Used by permission of Hodder & Stoughton Publishers, an Hachette UK company. All rights reserved.

Bible extracts marked (KJV) are from the Authorized Version of the Bible (The King James Bible), the rights in which are vested in the Crown, are reproduced by permission of the Crown's Patentee, Cambridge University Press.

British Library Cataloguing in Publication data
A catalogue record for this book is available
from the British Library

ISBN 978-0-334-06506-7

Typeset by Regent Typesetting

Contents

Acknowledgements

The journey to this publication has been challengingly long and arduous, yet enjoyable and fulfilling. The most relieved person now is Novelette, my wife and friend, who has endured my incessant preoccupation with how Jeremiah's letter to Jewish exiles has influenced our own lives and how it might be a source of information and inspiration to Black British people like us. My thanks to you, Nov, for your unconditional love, including at times when I am a challenge. My indispensable nuclear familial support network also includes Marsha, Genelle, Alethea, Krystal, Arooj, Luke, Ellis, Marcus and Kamaal; my siblings James, Hosea, Paul, Timothy, Cynthia, Gloria, Ruth, Jerry and Winsome, all of whom contribute to a healthy co-existence of support.

Thanks to colleagues at Roehampton University and Queen's Foundation who have allowed me to test some of my outlandish ideas unconditionally and I am sorry not to be able to make better use of your outstanding intellectual and academic challenges. I am thankful too to a small core of friends who indulge me, the Fab Six plus one: Jackie and George, Vassel and Carol (Novelette and I), and Carver. Your friendships have been indispensable accompaniments on my salmon-like upstream journey.

Finally, thanks to all at SCM Press for your generosity in affording me this publication. Special thanks to David Shervington whose role has gone above and beyond that of Commissioning Editor. To everyone who has contributed to this book in any conceivable way, I thank you!

And thank God who through us makes things possible.

1

Introduction

This book is written within a Black British diaspora context and is my pastoral response to dealing with the challenges and opportunities faced by this ethnic group. This is a long opinion piece, a polemic against anti-agency and anti-self-determining constructs. By Black I mean those who are the progeny, in whole or part, of African and/or Caribbean lineage. In referring to them as 'Black' I am aligning myself with its ethnic-geographic designation for people of African heritage, diverging from 'black' as a political term for oppressed people in contradistinction to 'white' that designates oppressor people and systems. The political use of 'black' includes black African people but can also include white Europeans who are poor or oppressed or who are in solidarity with oppressed people. While I understand the use of 'black' as a political term for oppressed people and a tool to challenge oppressive constructs and practices, I do not use the term in that way here, although some of my citations do so. Also, when I use the term 'white' with reference to ethnicity, I mean those of European heritage, or Caucasian.

My critique draws upon my own experience of living in Britain since the late 1960s, in addition to what is generally known about this community, through research and other observable insights. There are ongoing narratives concerning how this community attempts to progress and I argue for much greater emphasis upon the essential nature of self-agency and self-determination in this process. It is a desire for human flourishing that is mainly responsible for the presence in post-colonial Britain of communities who are descended from subjects of its former empire, drawn to it by better economic prospects, and the truism that we are here because you were there (Sanghara 2021, pp. 67–87). As we observe or are part of people movement around the globe – due to colonial hangover, natural disasters, persecution or wars – we might see life through the lens of a lesson from our Sunday School days: the earth belongs to God and humans are co-stewards and co-inhabitors, not selfish owners of our planet (Psalm 24).

I frame the dilemma faced by the Black diasporic community as one of how to flourish in Britain (or Babylon). In this book I propose 'flourishing in Babylon' as a metaphor for how Black British people in diaspora can live optimally. This calls for a self-realization both that they are a people in diaspora and that they are part of humanity made in the divine image and likeness. I believe it is time to change how we speak and act if Black British people are to flourish. Flourishing is not dependent upon the absence of ill-will but happens in spite of it. The battle between good and evil is an existential and infinite one. Descendants of those who historically exploited humans and natural resources in faraway lands are now faced with the need to coexist with descendants of those same people as neighbours. The gains of the former British empire made at the expense of their former colonies mean there are opportunities to flourish in Britain, notwithstanding many challenges and ever-present racism. Current approaches to Black British flourishing are inadequate, apparently pursuing some unspecified idealism or utopia. I use the Old Testament prophet Jeremiah's letter to Jewish exiles as a biblical antecedent to discuss flourishing rooted in agency and self-determination in this exilic context, arguing for a new practical and theological approach mediated through *imago Dei*, not through suffering and illusive liberation.

I have been part of this Black British community since 1968, when I and my siblings joined our parents, who were economic migrants from Jamaica in the Caribbean, a former Spanish and British slave colony. Our family settled in the West Midlands and were part of what is commonly referred to as the Windrush Generation, migrating after World War Two from the Commonwealth including the Caribbean. I arrived in Britain with an understanding of God; I had grown up in a Christian Pentecostal faith that emphasizes power to overcome challenges. Yet, overcoming the poverty prevalent in the deep rural community in which I grew up in Jamaica relied mainly on people's ability to leave for urban areas on the island or to travel abroad for better economic prospects elsewhere, including Britain. I learned that God was not Santa Claus delivering people's wish lists, but a God who helps those who help themselves through initiative-taking. This idea of a God/human partnership, labourers together with God (1 Cor. 3), grew in my consciousness over time. It was clear, for example, that those who left my district to work abroad would return richer and that the district benefited from their newfound if relative wealth as they built or refurbished their houses. It was assumed that those who travelled to Britain and elsewhere sought to make a better life for themselves and their family. This was what my parents did, and soon they would send for me to join them in an economically better place. If the power taught in Pentecostalism has been effective in changing people's social, economic and political situation, it has not been so by some magic money tree in the clouds, but rather by people travelling to where economic resources were. It is clear to me now that more intentional and strategic thinking by the people of my district about how to develop our local and wider area for the uplifting of the community, might usefully have been part of the Pentecostal prayer meetings. Distant powers – religious or political – tended to be indifferent, exploitative or malevolent.

In Britain, I have become aware of the extent to which the eventual freedom from chattel enslavement of Africans in the Caribbean and elsewhere occurred due to the relentless deployment of agency on the part of enslaved people, never accepting their status as slaves and always seeking ways to free themselves, more than by the pity or benevolence of their captors, oppressors or benign sympathizers (Dunkley 2012, p. 169). Previously I had understood liberation as about an other-worldly eternal salvation available in the hereafter through the suffering, death and resurrection of Jesus. Now I became aware of the human need for freedom from oppressive hegemonic forces, of empire for example, which means that even after independence my native Jamaica and her citizens remained mainly in subsistence living, except for a privileged few. I had already seen signs as a child growing up in Jamaica that the lighter the skin, the more privileges seemed accessible. As a child of enslaved African forebears under white oppression and brought up in the long shadow of colonialism, I began to understand what my ethnic type meant for my life. While my awareness of socio-cultural and political matters in Jamaica may have been low and slow, as Bakan shows, 'racism as a predominating ideological feature of society, however, continued to linger with a tenacity far greater than any structural correlation between race and class', but self-evidently, the effects of colonialism in all facets of life continue in perpetuity (Bakan 1990, p. 7).

One of my earliest memories upon coming to the UK is of being called a 'coloured boy' by a white woman. This was done without obvious malice but raised my youthful curiosity about my identity and belonging in Britain. It became apparent that in the place to which I had come, a person's skin colour determined wholly or in part their life chances, as was the case where I had come from. I learned too that categories like class, gender, religion or faith influenced prospects of flourishing in Britain. Here, mainstream news about people who looked like me tended to highlight negative aspects and disparities, and stereotyping grouped disparate people together as near indistinguishable apart from their being 'other' than the white norm. If I were to flourish in Britain there were evidently 'many rivers to cross' to get there, in the words of a popular song by Jimmy Cliff. It would therefore be an error of judgement to make my flourishing in Britain conditional on what other – malevolent – people might do, whether past, present or future.

A stark reality is that descendants of Britain's former colonial subjects are attempting to settle and make progress in the context of an antagonistic historical relationship between empire and subjects, and this situation seems unalterable. Protests, campaigns and legislation against racism and for racial justice over the past half a century have brought about amelioration in the white expression and Black British experience of racism;

however, there remains little or no sign that it is about to be eliminated. Against a popular mainstream background that labels Black British people as failures, there have been attempts to showcase success (McCalla 2003; Byfield 2008; Wade 2005; Williams and Amalemba 2015; Johnson-Fisher 2008). Success or failure must be understood by contextual realities. According to the Commission on Race and Ethnic Disparities (2021), the picture is changing, but the popular public narrative remains one of disparities affecting the Black British community negatively and the largely uncontested causation is linked to systemic or institutional racism and, to a lesser degree, class. Worryingly for me as a pastor, what appears scarcely engaged in is an acknowledgement of Black British success in spite of racism, and discussion about how this group can flourish if racism cannot be eradicated from British society. What are Black British people to do when racism appears to be permanently etched into the fabric of life in western European societies? Treating racism as a cancer in an otherwise healthy body may unhelpfully provide false hope that its eradication is both possible and a panacea for Black British flourishing; as though were we to apply chemotherapy, rid the body of cancer and hey presto, all would be well!

An important point of departure for me concerns how Black British people flourish in Britain – a popular public understanding assumes party-political left-leaning politics are the answer (Reddie 2014) but it is critically important that no political party can legitimately assume the Black British vote; rather, a high price should be put on every vote aligned with individual and group interests. In my experience, while some Black British people align themselves with British political parties, a majority align with left-of-centre, centrist and right-of-centre politics, embracing social justice and economic empowerment, looking after self and neighbour simultaneously. As I write, Jamaica's governing party is the right-of-centre Jamaica Labour Party, while the governing party of Barbados is the social democratic Barbados Labour Party which although politically left of centre is centrist compared to the Democratic Labour Party it replaced in the 2022 General Elections (https://en.wikipedia.

org/wiki/2022_Barbadian_general_election). I recall too that the much-maligned former UK Conservative Prime Minister Margaret Thatcher was loved and admired by many Black British people, not least for policies that allowed them to get on the property ladder. To insist only left-leaning politics are appropriate for Black British people ignores also the fact that the British Conservative Party, the Labour Party and the Liberal Democrats all have their share of Black British politicians and followers, with several in government or shadow government posts. In the expression of Black British selfhood all shades of theological, social and political persuasions have their legitimacy, and so too should those who agitate on their behalf and seek to empower them. The just creation and ethical use of capital and labour after all is a pan-human pursuit; socialism without capital is a dysfunctional opiate; capitalism without conscience is heartless profiteering, for both are addressable through democratic and righteous pursuit of a society in which all contribute to human flourishing (Streeter et al. 2002). In my experience, Black British people exhibit overall broad and eclectic tendencies, mixing concern for others with self-help, thriftiness with generosity, and are both home owners and renters. This breadth of belonging is true too in the area of religion and faith, where although 'black' and Pentecostal popularly go together the reality is that African and Caribbean people in Britain belong to the widest cross-section of faiths and denominations within faiths, especially Christianity. In both politics and religion it seems appropriate that Black British people wear their 'party' affiliation lightly, putting their need to flourish above ideological interests!

Simopoulos reminds us that no interpretation is disinterested; all interpretations are, rather, reflections of the lenses through which we see and experience ourselves, the world and God (Simopoulos 2007, pp. 63–73). It is crucial that the way Black British life is interpreted reflects the views and aspirations of the people themselves, varied and complex as such may be. Mine is not the only perspective, but I am particularly interested in how Black British people might benefit from a change of tack concerning how they view and understand God, liberation, race and racism, disparities and life in general. Key to this pastoral message is that the flourishing of Black British people rests on the agency and determination of the people. In an article examining the need for a procedure to be used by the United Nations to openly manage and resolve self-determination in Africa, Ikeanyibe et al. provide a helpful perspective. In theory, while one might resort to violent or non-violent means to enforce one's right to self-determination, yet simultaneously one must consider the potential for infringement upon another's territorial integrity, literally or philosophically (Ikeanyibe et al. 2021, pp. 123–48). In this work, agency and self-determination is posited as an inherent quality and right of every human being and something that in a diasporic and fallen world is constantly under threat, yet should be exercised unapologetically while watching out for the interests of all.

Jeremiah's letter to Jewish exiles was to a people in a hostile foreign place, with their motherland under occupation, challenging their ability to exercise their agency and determination. My conviction is that living in the power of God-given agency, a community can flourish in a hostile place, even in exile, as in the words of the Psalmist, 'You prepare a table before me in the presence of my enemies' (Psalm 23.5). At home or in diaspora, it can be assumed that occupiers' and colonizers' interests are not the salvation of the colonized but rather their own prosperity (Brazelton et al. 1918). Responsibility for Black British people's flourishing, therefore, must be understood by them as being in their hands alone, even when that means extracting it from the fabric of a hostile empire. To introduce this discourse further, I will briefly explore three important facets involved in discussing flourishing in Babylon: i) Black British people; ii) Jeremiah's letter to Jewish exiles, and iii) Black Theology.

Black people in Britain

Black British people are multi-ethnic human beings, made in the image and likeness of God as are all humans, and are no Johnny Come Lately to British soil either, since an African community has existed in Britain for centuries (Fryer 1984; Olusoga 2016; Dabydeen, Gilmore and Jones, eds. 2007). Williams and Amalemba offer seven key 'waves' of African immigration into Britain up to the 1960s: i) from the cradle of civilization when Africans migrated from central east Africa across the globe; ii) Iberian Celts, *circa* 8000 BC; iii) Roman occupation of Britain, *circa* AD 79; iv) Moors ruling in Spain and present in Britain also, *circa* AD 700, possibly introducing both morris dancing in England and bagpipes in Scotland; v) in Tudor times incoming free and enslaved Africans, around the fifteenth and sixteenth centuries; vi) Africans who fought in the American War of Independence settled in Britain in the eighteenth century; vii) World War One, World War Two and the Windrush economic migration brought thousands of migrants from the Caribbean and Africa to live in Britain, around the mid-twentieth century (Williams and Amalemba 2015, pp. xii–xiv). Since the mid-1940s, the Black community has achieved a sort of critical mass while remaining a small ethnic minority in Britain, registering 4% of the overall population in the 2021 census. There has therefore been a historic African presence in Britain over millennia with the economic migration of the (mainly Caribbean) Windrush Generation. Further waves of social, economic, political and environmental unsettlements have brought about a much greater visible and widespread African and Caribbean presence as people move in search of better to Britain and elsewhere. As Perry argues, to understand this gravitational pull and the historical genealogies of the claims upon British belonging for such as the Windrush Generation during the post-war era, 'it is important to situate them within a broader history of race, empire, and competing conceptions of emancipation, imperial belonging, and citizenship via subjecthood' (Perry 2016, p. 25).

It is claimed that 'the Black man was the original man of Britain' and that the 'Moors were, beyond a shadow of a doubt, African people who had played a vital role in the colonisation of Western Europe and especially Britain' (Rashidi 2011, pp. 99–100). Van Sertima suggests that the identity of the 'Moor' is complex and broadly reflects several people groups emanating from North Africa, but can accurately be called Africans (Van Sertima 1985, p. 141). Afri-centric historians such as Rashidi and Van Sertima make clear that there have been concerted and successful efforts by European white historians to write the African presence out of Western history. Scobie, in a scathing attack upon 'imperialists, enslavers, colonisers ... imprisoned in their fog of white supremacy', says that African history, including their presence in Europe/Britain, 'has been distorted in the writings of European historians with half-truths, omissions, and outright lies' (Scobie 1994, pp. 13–14). According to historian Olusoga, 'The people of the British Isles and the people of Africa met for the first time when Britain was a cold province on the northern fringe of Rome's intercontinental, multi-ethnic and multi-racial empire' (Olusoga 2016, p. 29). Although there does not appear to be consensus on the presence of Africans in Britain, my contention here is that there are strong hints of an African presence in Britain for centuries, and probably for millennia. Fryer and Olusoga among others agree that according to historical records Africans have become more evident in British society since the period of the transatlantic slave trade, both World Wars and particularly since the Windrush era starting in the mid-twentieth century. All of these factors have contributed to a Black diaspora in Britain. Usually, these are not taken as migrants acting out of choice to live in diaspora, since there were and are extenuating factors, from kidnap, to being sold and enslaved, to pursuing economic improvement to stave off deprivation. Yet, it is the case that within these enforced people movements, those involved always viewed themselves as human and exercised their humanity to the extent they could.

We are reminded that the tale of the hunt always glorifies the hunter until the lion writes (Reddie 2007) and we can be sure that the tale of Babylonian exiles, the transatlantic slave trade, chattel slavery and more have been told by the 'hunters'. In modern times, based on people I know, a majority of migrants had a common objective: securing better life prospects for their families than had been available back home in the British colonies, current and former. A mainly religious people, they knew that although Scripture says, 'the love of money is a root of all kinds of evil' (1 Tim. 6.10), it also says, 'money meets every need' (Eccl. 10.19). I have had numerous such conversations and heard testimonies of this reasoning over the years. The colonies of Britain's empire were mined for human and material resources that benefited Britain but left those countries and regions poor and underdeveloped (Rodney 1988). The overwhelming majority of the population of former slave colonies like Jamaica were condemned to peasantry, and the adventurous took the opportunity to migrate to the 'motherland' of empire, and elsewhere – not out of patriotism, but self-interestedly to better themselves and with hope of returning to their homelands in five to seven years, the richer for their odyssey. The post-World War Two émigrés are now in their fourth generation as Black British, as evidenced in my nuclear family where I, of the second generation, now have children and grandchildren born in Britain (Aldred 2015). Like thousands of others, my father, a subject of the British Empire, possessor of a British passport, travelled to England in 1955. Pushed by economic necessities and pulled by opportunities for economic betterment, with a sense of adventure he left the familiar for the unfamiliar with its uncertainties, finding cold weather and indifferent people. The question of how the Black British community remains true to the focus of economic empowerment through 'resistance, self-reliance, inventiveness, innovativeness and creativity in their historic relationship' with white people is what is at stake (Williams and Amalemba 2015, p. 2).

Africans in Britain, before and particularly since the transatlantic slave trade and chattel slavery, could have had little doubt about the nature of the relationship between themselves and Britain. As Williams and Amalemba state, 'One would think that after the cruel treatment which Africans suffered during the "Trans-Atlantic Enslavement Trade", they would stay clear of Europe and whites' (Williams and Amalemba 2015, p. xiii). Instead, increased numbers gravitated to Britain in search of a better life, and at the height of the transatlantic slave trade 'There is evidence of cohesion, solidarity, and mutual help among African people in Britain. They had developed a lively social life. And they were finding ways of expressing their political aspirations' (Fryer 1984, p. 67). Whether migration happened by force or choice, and while some may have thought they were going to a land that flowed with 'milk and honey', as the biblical story portends, there could have been little doubt that the land had 'giants' and hostile opposing forces (Exod. 3). From the early fifteenth to the late nineteenth century, Spain, Portugal, Holland, France, Germany, Italy, Belgium and Britain began exploring areas of the globe previously unknown to them for potential commercial purposes. This led inexorably to great swathes of the planet coming under European colonial dominion (Aldrich and Stucki 2023, p. 17). A key aspect of this dominion has been forced people movement in the attempt to subject Africans to a racist infrastructure based upon 'white' superiority and 'black' inferiority, ushering in the racism known well today (Yeboah 1997; Gregory and Sanjek 1994; Hannaford 1996). In Africa, the Americas, the Caribbean and Europe, African people, with European allyship, resisted and eventually succeeded in legally ending the transatlantic slave trade, chattel slavery, colonialism and imperialism through various means, from bloody uprisings to diplomatic negotiations and religious fervour – but not before some 12 million Africans had been trafficked (Dick 2002; Morrison 2014). In addition to the ending of the transatlantic slave trade, there has been the end of apartheid in Africa, the end of Jim Crow laws and establishing of civil rights in the USA, and in Britain, anti-racism legislation to punish racist perpetrators.

Over 200 years after the passing of the Abolition of the Transatlantic Slave Trade Act in the British Parliament in 1807, and almost 200 years since chattel slavery was abolished in British colonies in 1838, it is self-evident that progress has been made toward liberation of historically oppressed people (Reddie 2007). However, it appears that subsequent to these victories of the past, a liberation narrative persists but without clarity concerning what 'black liberation' actually means and for whom. This results in an ideological cul-de-sac, with uncertainty for 'white' people and systems and for 'black' people too concerning precisely what steps need to be taken to deliver the 'liberation' of Black British and other 'oppressed' people. Nebulous freedom demands therefore become something of a stumbling block to making progress towards a better place. To call for justice requires clarity concerning what justice looks like, otherwise we end up with a scenario where white people cannot deliver it and Black British cannot take it, because no one really knows what 'it' is. It seems that much of today's liberation discourse amounts to an appeal to oppressive 'white' people's sense of guilt concerning specific evils of the past and less specific evils in the present, though with the onus on 'white' people to deliver 'black' liberation (Bhopal 2018, p. 22; DiAngelo 2018). It is my view that the campaigns to end the transatlantic slave trade, chattel slavery, apartheid and Jim Crow laws, had clarity of determination in contrast to a foggy demand to 'end racism'. As a result, Black British people are at risk of permanent uncertainty about their destination and are unable to answer the question, 'What does freedom look like?' After the victories mentioned and the passing of anti-racism laws and other regulations in Britain, maybe the time has come for Black British people to acknowledge battles won, the nature of empire that even after its apparent end it retains a sceptical often hostile attitude to its former subjects. What it means to be free or liberated should consider Black British existence within the nebulousness of the ongoing ideological and material infrastructure of empire (Aldrich and Stucki 2023). Liberation requires specific and designated goals that when attained provide the launching pad from which the liberated remove the self beyond the gravitational hold of the imperial epicentre.

People came to Britain for economic empowerment, aware that anti-African racism existed here and in western Europe but came anyway and later brought their families too. Their descendants should beware of mission creep that seeks to replace pursuit of economic empowerment with eliminating racism from British society. There is a significant similarity here with what I believe is a misguided preoccupation in attempts to reform the British Home Office following the 2018 Windrush scandal that saw some who were entitled to citizenship denied status and some deported for being unable to prove they were British. The fallout from this fracas resulted in the Wendy Williams Review (https://www.gov.uk/government/publications/windrush-lessons-learned-review) which showed that the hostile environment that caused the problem was a direct result of governmental legislation, the repeal of which would make a difference (Gentleman 2019). However, instead of pursuing legislative change, the community pursued reform of the Home Office.

The economic mission of post-World War Two migration was based upon focused and sacrificial lifestyles by a people travelling to colder climes, adapting their diet to the food available in a foreign land; something believed to possibly contribute to today's high risk, even prevalence, of diabetes in the Black British community (Trueland 2014). Jimmy, one of the 'voices' in a work by Matthews, mentions 'struggle' repeatedly as a word symptomatic of the social and political experience of Black migrants, including eating the bland food which the British cooked (Matthews 2018, p. 60). King, who travelled from Jamaica in 1944 to join the RAF during World War Two, served as an aircraft engineer, returned to Jamaica, then came back to Britain on the iconic MV *Empire Windrush* in 1948, and became mayor of Southwark in 1983–84, tells of widespread hardships such as overcrowded housing, the unavailability of mortgages and other financial services denied to Black migrants. He says, 'West Indian immigrants were viewed as uneducated country bumpkins but were innately resilient, with high hopes' (King 2004, p. 115).

Although the Windrush Generation may not have got the balance exactly right between resistance and mission, it is because of them that many hardships have been ameliorated by hard-won changes in law, practice and attitudes and Black British people should now seek realignment with their parents' original entrepreneurial and self-interested vision. Their parents knew that the transatlantic slave trade and chattel slavery was over and that they had won their freedom, yet the empire persisted, and their quest was to exploit it from within or without for their economic betterment. What lay ahead was not a fight for liberation already gained, but to answer the questions related to freedom and flourishing in diaspora. It was always going to be a challenge for descendants of enslaved and colonized Black people to coexist with descendants of white enslavers and colonialists, a challenge magnified once the original short stay became a long stay. Life is there to be shaped for future generations, but a decision has to be made whether to stay faithful to the original mission of economic empowerment and well-being in 'Babylon' or become distracted by intractable racial contestation. Rediscovering the economic mission is both desirable and necessary and should not become victim to the improbable task of dismantling and expunging racism from the fabric of Western society and culture. There are laws in place in Britain to protect the rights of Black British people – they do not require others to love you, and being dependent upon that is to exhibit a neediness that is unseemly, suggesting insecurities. The Black British response to racism is best understood as rooted in resistance, resilience, self-interest; protecting the self against principalities and powers (Eph. 6.12, KJV). And for those who wonder if self-interest is consistent with Christian principles, I remind them of Jesus' maxim 'love your neighbour as yourself' (Mark 12.31). Only as one loves, nurtures and protects the self can one hope to do the same for neighbour, and if we will the end, we must will the means (Weaver 2002).

Black British people should not betray the history of bitter experience and knowledge of the past half millennium of Western mal-racial attitudes and actions towards people of African descent. They should not somehow behave as though they have learned nothing and have expectations of loving cordiality inconsistent with that history; when it comes it is likely to be the exception, not the rule. The extent to which Black British people fail to relate historic European antipathy and lack of love towards them may be a demonstration of cognitive dissonance (Harmon-Jones 2019). While there will be some white allies, Black British people should as a precursor inoculate and protect themselves in empire while pursuing their goals of well-being, utilizing their inherent humanity and the force of laws designed to discourage and punish offenders, building relationships based on strength. Where such laws do not exist, Black British people should work to bring them into being. If the elimination of racism from Western society is anyone's burden, surely it is 'European people's burden', not 'African people's burden'. Black British people need to shun the notion that eliminating racism from society equates to 'a theory of everything' upon which their flourishing depends, supposing that nothing short of the overthrow of empire and obliteration of its infrastructure can hope to lead to a world in which they flourish. Imperial subjects should either take themselves out of the orbit of empire or find ways to thrive within its orbit. It is foolhardy to anticipate a time when every racist will be dead or expunged from British and other Western societies, after which we enter a post-racial era of 'non-racial' human existence (Gilroy 2000, p. 2). Indeed, in pursuit of flourishing, the key reason for which Windrush pioneers came to Britain, Black British people should be willing to use the nuclear option to terminate their presence. To leave the plantation of empire to a different Afri-centric space is in some circumstances the only credible option left, and refusal to embrace this as an option may demonstrate a degree of black dependency on Britain's hold over former subjects. My pastoral instincts suggest that it is more productive to expend valuable and finite energy on building one's own kingdom rather than attempting to dismantle another's. As Nehl suggests, Africans in diaspora do well to spend time exploring the diverse ways they relate to their history and each other grounded on authenticity, continuity and roots, which I believe is more profitable than a preoccupation with pleasing or appeasing a system imbued, seemingly irredeemably, with anti-African sentiments (Nehl 2016, p. 81).

A key strength of a diasporan community like Black British people is their connectivity with each other and with their homelands, as can be discerned in the situation of Jews in exile in Jeremiah 29. There are dangers in rupturing the ties that bind diaspora with homeland peoples. Such a rupture would result in shallow or no relationships between diaspora and homelands and that would force diasporans to fill the vacuum by uncritically adopting the majority culture or attempt to create a new identity *ab initio*. In the absence of historic ties desperate claims to majority cultural identity lead to fraught and unedifying discourse concerning identity and belonging. Given their common historic roots, it is unwise to view African and Caribbean identities in Britain as separate, so I am arguing here for an amalgamation of both into a Black British exilic paradigm, fashioning an agency-led and self-determining approach to flourishing (Reid-Salmon 2014, p. 8; Aldred 2005). It is important that Black British people lay their aspirations for flourishing alongside those of their people in diaspora and back in their historic homelands. Indeed, Black British people 'back home' in Africa and the Caribbean are under the influence of the same colonial forces that are at work in Britain, retaining social, economic and political influence in both. During a sabbatical break in Jamaica in 2016, I came across writing by former Prime Minister Michael Manley where he described Jamaica's struggles as a former colony of the British Empire trying to chart its own way in the world of international development as like trying to get to the second floor of a building on a 'down escalator' (Manley 1983). Black British people in their back-a-yard and diasporic existence have much to gain by being connected and supportive in the common battle for flourishing against the force of empire. Such holistic unity and shared interests and concerns call for changes in the identity narrative of Black British people.

A recent example of the way the narrative might change occurred in December 2022 when Ngozi Fulani, founder and chief executive of Sista Space, an anti-domestic abuse charity, had an encounter with Susan Hussey, at the time a lady-in-waiting to the late Queen Elizabeth II, at a charity appreciation event at Buckingham Palace. Fulani, a Black British woman, reported what happened, and her recollection of events has not been disputed by Hussey, a white woman. According to Fulani, Hussey asked her, persistently, 'Where are you from?' As Fulani's response clearly did not match Hussey's expectation, she followed up with, 'But where are you really from?' Fulani interpreted Hussey's line of questioning as hostile, intimidating and racist, assuming she was not British but African. Fulani publicized the encounter on social media which led to a national uproar across the press and media, and the resignation of Hussey from her royal duties. Eventually the two met, and Hussey apologized for the offence taken, which she said was unintended. Fulani accepted her apology and all seemed set well. Some in the Black British community expressed disgust that such an apology was accepted.

I confess to being perplexed at a Black British person being traumatized by this sort of encounter, whatever the motive of the questioner – malign or benign conversation-making. 'Where are you from? Yes, but where are you really from?' is a universal conversation starter that has become a tool of racial offence, as a microaggression, for apparently implying that a Black British person is not British (Mukwashi 2020). A challenge for Black British people may be to arrive at a point where this kind of encounter and question ceases to hold potential to cause offence. Instead, 'Where are you really from?', asked by a white person, could be answered informedly and generously, followed by another question, this time from the African British person to the white person: 'So, where are *you* from?' The answer may be, let's say, Dudley. 'Yes, but where are you really from?' Here the Black British person might pursue the question, without antipathy, to discover where historically the white person is from right back to the West Germanic tribes of the Angles, Saxons, Jutes and Frisians. I ask people of various ethnicities often, 'Where are you from?', and, 'Where are you really from?' It is a good conversation piece that should not become victim to this kind of so-called microaggression. This flips the narrative from a place of victimhood and inferiority to one of assumed human equality, from taking offence about being quizzed about identity and belonging to proudly owning African heritage alongside which British identity and belonging sits. And since we know everyone's identity and belonging is complex, rather than closing down the debate, life can become much more interesting and mutual. Microaggression risks sucking the oxygen out of healthy co-relationships, conversely communication from a position of co-humanity and equality pumps oxygen into co-existence. Cabral describes microaggressions as small or subtle behaviours occurring in casual encounters of verbal or nonverbal actions that 'judge, accuse, demean, marginalize, or show prejudice toward someone' based on their identities such as age, ethnicity, or gender (Cabral 2020, p. 107). One of the challenges of microaggression is its subjectivity that depends upon the intent of the speaker versus the meaning attributed by the hearer as well as the undercurrents and overcurrent of malintent, misunderstanding and more. In sum, microaggression is thought to create discriminatory psychological dilemmas for marginalized individuals and groups (Torino et al. 2019). The elephant in the room here, however, is the war of attrition mired in a lack of cultural competence, as well as in identity insecurities, and suspicions based on claims and counter-claims linked to British and African heritages. Black British people do well to be wary of being sucked into the gravitational mire of microaggressions.

'Babylon' in this book, while plucked directly from the biblical text and the story of the empire of that name around the sixth century BC which colonized and exiled Judeans, is adopted for today's Black British people. I apply the term to Britain's complicity in enslaving, colonizing, exiling or diasporizing Black British people and their ancestors. Metaphorically, Babylon is a complex imperial space that spawns simultaneously oppression, exploitation and opportunities for those caught within its orbit. Afari, from the perspective of Rastafari, describes Babylon as the 'Western system and its agents of colonialism, slavery and international injustice' (Afari 2007, p. 323). Babylon alludes beyond national boundaries to a broader systemic 'down-pression' of European supremacy resulting in outcomes of social, economic, political and spiritual evils and corruption, according to Afari. The Babylon system operates in its own interests and benefits to which end its subjects are the raw material to be used as Babylon deems best. Such use includes brain-draining its colonies and extracting resources for the benefit of the centre of empire, to weaken them and strengthen imperial power. The amassing of human and other resources in empire acts as a magnet to the colonized even as conditions tend to be antagonistic to them when they live there. Britain represents herein a modern 'Babylon'. Even with a waning empire its gravitational pull continues and this is the principal reason that explains why people like me are in the UK.

Babylon has become a powerful metaphor for sites of oppression, as Seymour points out. He notes that the metaphor of the Babylonian captivity was 'less horrific and far smaller in scale than the effects of the Atlantic slave trade it has come to symbolize, yet that symbolism has remained of paramount importance' (Seymour 2014, p. 168). And from my Christian faith culture it has been long established that this world is a type of Babylon in which Christians live in constant displacement as 'in the world but are not of it' (John 17). And yet, this double-consciousness can render believers 'so heavenly minded they become of no earthly good', as a saying goes. Living in an 'other worldly' mindset has to align itself with the imperative of flourishing now and working towards God's will for justice and peace on earth as in heaven (Matt. 6). Somehow then, Black British people need to discover ways of flourishing in a metaphorical and literal Babylon. Living in Britain, Black people should take ownership of their destiny, not looking to others as though salvific powers to flourish lies elsewhere. They must refuse to be distracted, looking to self and their inherent strength and integrity rooted in their own God-endowed agency and self-determination, never forgetting where they are, what to expect, and where their roots are.

Jeremiah's letter to Jewish exiles

The second introductory premise upon which this book is based is my use of Jeremiah's letter to Jewish exiles in sixth-century Babylon which I made an initial attempt to unpack in a peer-reviewed article (Aldred 2022). My attraction to Old Testament prophet Jeremiah's letter to the exiles is rooted in my conviction that it has much to teach us today. I take into account that the representation of Jeremiah as a prophet who courageously confronts the power structures with a genuine, but unpopular, word from Yahweh is a product of the many oral and literary contributories that shape the book that bears the prophet's name (Nogalski 2018, p. 79). Though scribed long ago, the exilic background of the text and its practical proposal for coping in exile along with its theological moorings of a people of God responding to circumstances is a fecund exemplar. As Katho suggests, the book of Jeremiah and the circumstances concerning Judah it exposes, demonstrate similarities with the complex realities of African diaspora peoples experiencing devastating poverty, injustice and war, as well as the need to exercise imagination, and dare to dream past the present and into a future where God is known and humans flourish (Katho 2021). Probably a luxury item, but I find it affirming that a historical–biographical and theological work on Jeremiah by Adamo demonstrates the many citations of Africa in the book, as indeed in the Old Testament, showing the prophet was acquainted with Africa and Africans, including Ebed-Melech, the Cushite who rescued Jeremiah from a pit in which he had been dumped to die (Adamo 2018). The plan contained in Jeremiah's 'Letter to the Exiles', sent to deported Judeans in sixth-century Babylon, is used here as a biblical antecedent for how Black British people might flourish in Britain today. Utilizing biblical texts in this manner can carry challenges for interpretation and application, including an acknowledgement that texts such as Jeremiah emerge from cultural contexts that are less critical of power dynamics such as gender and colonial subjectivities than we are today (Maier and Sharp 2015). My approach is that of a Black British theologian from a Pentecostal tradition. By utilizing this text, I make no claim to a direct parallel between sixth-century Judeans in Babylon and twenty-first-century Black British people. A common feature between the two situations, however, is the exile or diaspora experience and what to do about it.

Texts like Jeremiah are, in my American Caribbean British Pentecostal tradition, quintessentially part of the Bible, the authoritative 'Word of God' (Heb. 1.1; 2 Tim. 3.16), and the community utilize it to reflect on aspects of life in the here and now. We do not take every line of the Bible literally and apply them unthinkingly; instead, the community practise what may be termed 'rhetorical hermeneutics' where the Bible constitutes a book of tools to be appropriated by skilled craftspersons in the use of rhetoric to critique society and bring hope to hearers, especially those in desperate need of it, and to inform actions (Fisher 2018), or as Coleman suggests, it is a way of telling a people's story using biblical texts as a main resource (Coleman 2000). My tradition of Pentecostalism is known from its genesis in Azusa Street USA under the inspired leadership of the one-eyed son of enslaved parents William Seymour, to take seriously the pneumatic presence of God as Holy Spirit in and among the people (Acts 1.8). Bartleman, an eyewitness to the genesis of the Pentecostal movement, emphasizes their understanding of 'power' among adherents that permeated all their activities, hopes and aspirations (Bartleman 1980, pp. 23, 33, 54). At a time of rampant racism, they even believed the 'color line' was washed away in the blood (of Jesus). It is the said Holy Spirit that empowers the people inspired by the preaching of the Word to develop means of flourishing in Babylon, and Jeremiah's letter to the exiles provides a helpful template.

When I looked for a biblical antecedent for Black British diaspora, I needed one that addresses upward mobility consistent with the concept of Pentecostal power. Beckford points to ways in which perceptions of power can be misconstrued by assuming that challenges faced are cosmic phenomena and therefore the response is to pray and expect that God will fight our battles leaving us with nothing more to do. Jeremiah's letter to the exiles as antecedent suggests something quite different because it addresses what can and should be done by utilizing God-given human capabilities in the power of the Spirit. Beckford continues by arguing for a duality of 'resisting systems of White supremacy as well as developing a political and social structure that is capable of challenging the domestic neo-colonial situation faced by Black people' (Beckford 1999). In this way, Black British people resist past and present oppositional powers, yet do not omit to build their own infrastructure to flourish, thereby asserting their God-given humanity, transcending imposed circumstances in Babylon! Jeremiah does not call upon the exiled Jews to pretend their situation was what they might have hoped, or to respond to it as though it defined them, but instead to treat it as an episode in an intergenerational existence.

In my church tradition there is deep love of Old Testament personalities like the patriarchs and matriarchs, judges and pre- and post-exilic prophets and prophetesses. As we read prophets such as Jeremiah, we find therein an interpretative basis to stand on the shoulders of those gone before. Hence the Bible remains the most authoritative resource for Black Pentecostal Christians the world over (Baker-Fletcher 2009, p. 11). I grew up listening to repeated sermons based on the sayings and oracles of these biblical luminaries. Maybe their popularity also has something to do with resonance with the agrarian and oral contexts in which Old Testament personalities operated. Orality allows for some latitude while still working with the Bible as the Word of God. For example, it is believed that Jeremiah's letter to the exiles is contained in chapter 29 that has been subject, in a dominant oral culture, to transmission, repeated edits or redaction, but this matters little as what survives is believed to be the Word of God (Davidson 2011, p. 138). I say this cognizant that there is an academic Pentecostal tradition, but one that scarcely touches the people in the church pew, particularly in the Pentecostal church community I belong to. Until recently, none of the preachers, pastors or teachers had academic training in theology, ministry or biblical studies, as knowledge within the community emerges through an oral tradition that developed its own interpretative canon. This academic and intellectual deficit has begun to change in recent years and yet, as mentioned above and as Sturge reminds us, the Black Pentecostal Church in Britain continues to have a high view of Scripture (Sturge 2005, p. 132; see also Tomlin 2019).

And yet, pastors beware! When I completed my master's degree in theology and ministry, I was a pastor and even as I glowed in my success a member told me after a sermon, 'Pastor, I preferred your preaching before you went to college!' Mbiti has long highlighted the significance and concerns of the oral tradition in African theology and Bible preaching, and some still grudgingly watch out for any erosion of that intersection between orality – which some call preaching or speaking or praying from the heart – and written presentation (Mbiti 1969, p. 52). Generally, preachers in Black British churches do not place the same value on exegesis or hermeneutics as would meet the academic and intellectual expectations of hermeneutical purists. Utilizing the text is a matter of faith, not science, in my Pentecostal tradition (Gossai 2009, p. 98). Admittedly, applying biblical texts premised upon faith first in contemporary settings runs a danger of misapplication, overapplication, romanticizing or idealizing it, and Pentecostals need always to have creative tension between faith and practice, formal and informal, oral and literary. My use of Jeremiah 29 aims to borrow this historic text, note its original purpose and to make contemporary use of it for the here and now (Punt 2009, p. 276). I bear in mind also that biblical texts are not innocent and that they reflect the cultural, religious, political and ideological interests and contexts out of which they emerge, as do contemporary attempts at hermeneutics – there are no neutral or a-contextualized situations (Sugirtharajah 2002, p. 78).

Written in the context of imperial rule in Judah, Babylon and further afield, this Jeremiah text comes unavoidably imbued with imperial assumptions about human and divine operatives, with God depicted as the supreme colonialist. As one whose ancestors suffered at the hands of the cruel exercise of imperial powers, sometimes with African complicity, in the transatlantic slave trade, chattel slavery, colonialism and racism, I deploy a hermeneutic of suspicion concerning any and all attempts by friend and foe alike to interpret matters of history, faith and theological praxis, including for example the assertion in Jeremiah's letter that Jewish exiles were being punished for sins committed against God. The text intimates that a section of the Judean people was in exile as punishment by God for their unfaithfulness within the covenant relationship. God's people, having failed to do justice to their fellow humans, and having failed to worship God alone, incurred divine wrath that led to the co-option of the Babylonian king in carrying out the divine judgement. Vellem shows that the discipline of Black Liberation Theology intentionally 'unthinks' Western theological understandings, displacing them with its own independent conceptual and theoretical foundations (Vellem 2017). Even as this holds true, at least as an aspiration, there should continue to be suspicion of all forms of attempts at interpretation since the issue of hermeneutics can never be simply black or white, or West versus the rest. Hermeneutical suspicion operates well only by inter-contextual vigilance. While the Old Testament uses the rhetoric of human sin and divine punishment, it is possible to set the text within the context of human greed for power and control over others, thereby perpetrating suffering upon their subjects. Indeed, the covenant relationship within which this sin/punishment paradigm operates, contains redemption and the constant presence of God that mediates the effects of punishment that is in the end redemptive.

Green suggests that it may be best to understand this 'extraordinary and likely fictive document' in Jeremiah's name, most probably developed in exile, through the multigenerational promise given, backed by the searing divine commitment, '"I know the plans I have for you," declares the LORD, "'plans to prosper you and not to harm you, plans to give you hope and a future"' (Jer. 29.11, NIV; B. Green 2013, p. 113). These are not the words of a fifth columnist, unless intended to lull the exiles into a false sense of future hope thereby rendering them subdued in the immediate time. In light of some of the content of Jeremiah's letter, it may be reasonable to question the author's real identity and objective. Was Jeremiah an imperial agent, a political or a religious operator, or all three; and who stood to benefit from his intervention? His appearance in the text is of a well-connected cleric with access to power that facilitated his communication with the exiled Jews. Jeremiah wrote claiming divine authority, something difficult to gainsay since a mortal cannot challenge the immortal and invisible. His dismissal of false prophets who purported to speak for God may be regarded as one-upmanship by a man with direct access to Judean and Babylonian powers, the exiles of all ranks, from royalty to artisans, which in turn gave him a certain hegemony among his prophetic contemporaries. Such unopposed access to a vulnerable people cannot be underestimated for its influence upon recipients and as a signifier to others.

By utilizing the 'royal mail' system the contents of the letter were observable to the powers, verifying that there was no cause of concern to King Nebuchadnezzar or his vassal King Zedekiah in Judah. Intentionally or unintentionally, subversively or in collusion, Jeremiah's naming of people and ranks mediated transparency, and reminded and assured the exiles of their identity as Jews, a people in relationship with God; their status had not changed in diaspora. But if the Babylonian powers were in doubt about who they had captured, Jeremiah just told them. Based on contemporary feminist and postcolonial ethics, Jeremiah undoubtedly poses questions concerning the patriarchal and colonial practices and assumptions that go unchallenged in the book; however, I credit Jeremiah's pastoral concern for the sixth-century exiles' survival and flourishing (Maier and Sharp 2015; Davidson 2011). This warranted or unwarranted scepticism towards Jeremiah is indicative of the attitude that should apply to today's 'prophets' speaking into the affairs of Black British people and others elsewhere.

I view Jeremiah 29 through the lens of the needs of Black British people rather than through a spiritualized conception of covenant, obedience and promise between God and his people (Gossai 2018, p. 258; Jackson 2021). Jeremiah's letter can be understood as the political manoeuvring of a skilled, wily practitioner, himself avoiding deportation to Babylon while acting as pacifier of the powerful by maintaining calm and order among the foreign prisoners. But the letter can also be understood as coming from a pastor of his people who recognized that their survival and flourishing in foreign captivity required a certain attitude that better enabled their welfare for the intergenerational odyssey that lay ahead of them. That empires exist means that those caught within their ambit seek ways of securing beneficial outcomes through the construction of new ontological designs, or new ways of conceptualizing the self, for captors and captives (Boer 2009). Here, in a new way of thinking, the hegemonic power structure is engaged with a sense of shared humanity whereby the former victim becomes partner in the imperial context – working towards a better shared existence. This book attempts a counterintuitive narrative based on prophetic pragmatism that seeks partnership engagement built upon strength within empire, working towards human mutuality not by permission but by God-given *imago Dei* and the agency and self-determination that flows from it.

Against this somewhat challenging background, I find Jeremiah's text helpful for the argument I pose in this book: that in spite of exile, for whatever reason it occurs, and in spite of the existence and power of empire, people in diaspora can flourish through the efficacy of their God-imaged humanity and agency. Therefore, I do not read Jeremiah as telling his fellow Jews in Babylonian captivity to capitulate, indigenize, assimilate and submit to the imperial power. I read Jeremiah as telling them to strategize, embrace a plan of action to survive and flourish first by looking to and depending upon the God-empowered self, not the imperial other that does not wish you well; by making the self strong, and from a position of stake-holding strength, brokering mutuality and interdependence with the imperial power (Brueggemann 1991; Elliott 2012). This positioning leaves open possibilities of an eventual return home or making exile/diaspora home on mutual terms.

Black British theology – beyond suffering towards flourishing

People of African descent have for centuries been racialized by Europeans as 'black' and inferior to themselves whom they racialized as 'white' and superior, legitimizing their right to dehumanize and use them as though they were beasts of burden (Yeboah 1997). For me, the central point of reference for dealing with this challenge is theological, countering inferiorization by insisting that all humanity is made in the image and likeness of the Creator God. The discipline of Black Theology however attempts to counter such racialized inferiorization by using the European designation 'black' and synonymizing it with 'oppressed', aligning with European praxis. A Black Theology of liberation posits God as liberator, based upon biblical events such as the freeing of the Jews from Egypt and the identifying of Jesus with poor and oppressed people (Cone 1975). The discipline then broadens the scope of black beyond its traditional meaning of African heritage people to include all oppressed people and those who support liberation struggle. The concept of 'Black Theology' in this book therefore refers to that academic theology discipline and the above meaning, while the theological theory is referred to as Black British Theology.

Black British Theology addresses itself to the breadth of this people's human experience historical, contemporary and future aspirations in relation to God. In this discourse, European oppression is acknowledged in all its demonic devastation, but is not a defining agency for Black people who are defined instead by a self-understanding of an identity rooted not in the words or actions of an oppressor but through self-naming and a determination to flourish in 'Babylon', that is, Britain. In common with all theologies, I understand Black British Theology as a contextual theology, specific to the African heritage continuum, does not limit itself to critiquing Europe, imperialism, racism, colonialism and other evils wreaked upon the non-European world. This goes beyond a theology understood as 'the radical re-interpretation of the revelation of God in Christ, in light of the struggles and suffering of Black existence in order that de-humanised and oppressed Black people might see in God the basis for their liberation' (Jagessar and Reddie 2007b, p. 1). Instead, Black British people need a theology concerned with their whole life, emerging from their sense of *imago Dei*, a theology on their terms not one dictated by a response to European misdeeds. I proffer a differently premised theological focus to address Black identity and experience, one not restricted to being defined by one's oppressor and the circumstances they create, into which Black British people can all too easily be entrapped. As Louw suggests, 'the "victim" must cease defining themselves by the categories of the coloniser' (Louw 2017).

As a pastor, I believe that central to my function is helping to empower those I support to live sustainably, that is, the ultimate aim of pastoring is protecting the flock by enabling and empowering the flock to protect themselves. I am disquieted by a Black Theology that exists only in response to Black pain rather than as an aid to live fully in the humanity created in the image and likeness of God. Lartey warns of being trapped by western imaginations in conceptions of God, the colonized mimicking the colonizer, and suggests that '[African Caribbean] practical theology must pursue and engage in the activities of post-colonialising God' (Lartey 2015, p. 129). In his work, an expression of a postcolonial God is a God that accompanies and empowers, not one that promises to one day liberate – as I believe Western theology has promoted and taught to the detriment of Black British people, leaving them still waiting for their miracle in a post-colonial by and by. A being-with God, not a doing-for God, better describes the God they have come to know. As Louw posits, 'postcolonialism' is not a utopia for the complexity of creating a fair and just society on the basis of democracy – a society without class, race and discrimination. There is need to move beyond postcolonialism, from the paradigm of resisting imperialism and oppression to a paradigm of peaceful coexistence within the discrepancies and schismatic divisions in society (Louw 2017). This focus on looking within and beyond the struggle to what Black flourishing free from the European gaze may be, is precisely one of the issues Black British Theology must embrace and engage. If theology's only purpose is to throw off European oppressors, it begs the question of what happens to that theology when that mission is complete; and if that is all God is interested in, what of God before and after oppression is overthrown? Black British Theology relates to the God present from the beginning, during the history of African peoples, not showing up at times of deliverance from oppression, otherwise where was God during all other times?

Black British Theology must provide theological ballast for Black British people's understanding of and response to their place in the world and the racism they face, so that it does not become the all-consuming preoccupation of this community. Black British Theology should instead be a tool for flourishing, overcoming, transcending. The origins of Black Theology lie in the frustration first of enslaved Africans, then African Americans before spreading to other spheres where people of African heritage needed an interpretative tool to make sense of their historical and current context of suffering (Jagessar and Reddie 2007b). The focus mentioned above is not in my view unrelated to the fact that the main practitioners of Black Theology belong to Western mainstream churches drawing on a European liberal culture that has become alienated from a mainly conservative Black British Christian community. That theology is therefore in urgent need of decentring Western liberal theological values. By refocusing upon African heritage people, Black British Theology by intent is a discipline not prepared to be a talking shop, however elegant, but addresses itself to the humanity, agency and self-determination of the Black British community. Self-evidently, the better place from which Black British Theology ought to be done is Black British churches, not from the compromising context of the 'master's house' of white mainstream churches.

A consequence of what I describe here is a turning away from a preoccupation with containment protest against oppression, historic and contemporary, actual and perceived, as an ongoing engagement, with palpably inadequate focus upon the power of Black British agency and self-determining liberative and flourishing action. Such agency might construct and maintain hegemonic infrastructure that exists independent of western power. So long as Black Theology is being done from a room within the master's house as an ongoing conversation, talk of liberation will forever be 'still comin'', but never actually arrives (Davis 1990). Lorde's much referenced 'The Master's Tools Will Never Dismantle the Master's House' has, in my view, encouraged wrongly premised sentiments on the matter of liberation and flourishing, since it is patently clear that liberative tools can be effective wherever they come from; what is undermining to such use is the proximity and indebtedness of the user to the master's house (Lorde 2018). When Black British fortune is tethered to white controlling power, the consequence acts as a moderating agent upon flourishing aspiration and self-determination. For Black British theologizing to be effective in actualizing black liberation, it has to be a tool more in the hands of the 'field negroes' than the compromised-by-proximity 'house negroes' as Malcolm X famously described them (X 1963), or 'misguided middle-class negroes' (X 1965, p. 83). The current trajectory of Black Theology amounts to an appeal to White oppressive powers to be reasonable, to see they are hurting oppressed people and desist; when what is needed is a theological praxis predicated on the intrinsic power of the humanity of Black British people made in the image and likeness of God that drives agency and self-determination as a motor for flourishing and effective counter to all opposing forces; social, spiritual, economic and political. However, a theology that does this must be rooted in holistic African consciousness that is linked to free thinking and acting Black British people and their organizations, uprooted from the ivory tower entrapments of the West (Buffel 2010, pp. 470–80).

I describe this work as a 'Black British Contextual Theology' that sees the world through the lens of holistic African centric personhood, not prioritizing Eurocentric lens (Aldred 2005, p. 20). While I accept the excavatory work of Black Theology as a tool for exploring the oppression/liberation dialectic with respect to the past half-millennium of Africa/Europe relations, that primordial work while it continues needs to be expanded both historically and futuristically. It is a fundamental mistake to believe that critiquing Eurocentrism and finding some European allies along the way will ever deliver the end of European imperialism and empire hangovers. What is needed is a resort to engaging with the more fundamental issue of the nature of humanity and enduring empire and how to flourish in coexistence. Allyship is likely to be a mixed blessing such as in Stowe's influential novel in the nineteenth century that on the one hand offered a 'vigorous critique of the institution of slavery' while simultaneously portraying the weak submissiveness to tyranny and indignities of the African hero of the story in Uncle Tom (Stowe 1995, p. ix). The Black British must not be located in perpetuity as a hand outstretched supplicant asking or sometimes even demanding that white people and systems acknowledge them as human beings, rather than asserting Black British humanity as a pre-existent reality that cannot and must not be denied. African humanity is not negotiable but is a creation order reality.

We already know that a historically European anti-African racism casts African people, and Africanness generally, as not counting as human life (Watson, Hagopian and Au 2018). Also, the Christian faith has been used as an instrument to instil an ideology that it is the divine will for African people to be oppressed and suffer, with the faith as the single most persuasive tool in convincing Europeans of their superiority and Africans of their inferiority (Singleton 2012). This means too that the Black British Christian should beware Western forms of Christianity and theology, lest they compromise Black British people's humanity and spirituality. Black British Theology therefore has to avoid the subtlety of perpetuating these myths, becoming seduced into facilitating suffering and oppression in perpetuity, uncommitted to overthrowing and overcoming obstacles in the power of God in whose image African humanity is made, committed only to the theological art of critique.

In my experience those Black British people who appear least appreciative of the personal agency of the masses of their fellows fall into three overlapping categories: 'Black middle class' (Rollock 2015); the 'Talented Tenth', a term coined by W. E. B. Du Bois in 1903 to describe affluent, cultured, well-educated Africans (Johnson-Fisher 2008); and the 'afristocracy', a term used by conservative African Americans to describe such as African American politicians, pundits, professors, performers and preachers (Michelle 2022). These are evident characteristics in the Black British context too. The theology that emerges from this cohort tends to undervalue African agency and self-determination, infantilize them as their protector of the helpless, and look to euro-saviourism through dependence upon white allyship as essential to the cause of liberation. Increasingly, such white support is validated not by merely doing and saying they are 'not racist', but by being actively 'anti-racist', which can lead to a performative allyship. An understated yet critical thread that is a key element to my thesis of 'flourishing in Babylon' is the role of allyship. In 'Babylon' the exile must depend first upon their own agency while recognizing the role of others in enabling effective agency. This too the person in diaspora/exile must take control of, deciding which ally they want depending upon their need. It is never the place of the ally to decide to be your ally, it is always your decision.

The theology advocated in this book breaks with this consensus that only an elite among Black British people can liberate masses who must be eternally grateful, except that disparity statistics remain essentially the same. Black British Theology seeks to empower Black British people to stand on their own feet in the power of their God-given humanity with dignity, agency and self-determination in clear, demonstrable ways. Those Black British people who believe their 'class' sets them apart and above their peers should heed Rollock's warning that shows the way limiting racial factors interplay with progress, so that those Black British people who attain middle-class status find themselves differently inflected by race and racism that is endemic in the British space, negating their class (Rollock 2015, p. 118).

The articulators of Black Liberation Theology's central tenets retain a laser-like focus on the anti-imperial and anti-hegemonic struggle against European 'white' and imperial racist tendencies (Jagessar and Reddie 2007a). This is even as it becomes apparent that such preoccupation does little more than preoccupy its practitioners. To be effective, a methodology of empowerment needs to be articulated to that end. As a member of a church I pastored long ago said, after reading my denomination's list of rules-based teachings, 'Well, Pastor, I can see what this church is against, what is it for?' I have been involved in developing 'Black Theology in Britain', which for me has always focused on the whole experiential history of African heritage people and how to express their humanity in any and every situation, not singularly or primarily upon the sordid European encounter with Africans. Theology must do more than damn the Africans' oppressors, and move on to 'thus says the Lord' concerning their flourishing. God-talk must do more than preoccupy a people with talk-and-wait tactics, since as Tha God says, opportunity comes to those who create it (Tha God 2017). The default therefore of Black British people, a people of diaspora, must be a preoccupation with the flourishing of the group self that overflows into wider flourishing that is the foundation upon which justice and peace is realized. No one will give it, it must be taken – in the power of God.

Positing theology as God-Talk means that when Black British people talk about God, they do so from strength of identity. They are the creation of God, of African descent, with a history as old as humanity itself. Black British people are here as a consequence of forced and voluntary transplantations from Africa, the Caribbean and from diaspora around the world. When they talk about God, therefore, they do so as people of long standing and challenging relations with the Creator in the context of African history before the Arab and Western transatlantic slave trade, the genocidal trade of African chattel enslavement, colonialism and neo-colonialism. In other words, their theology engages with the question of what Black British people are to make of God's presence in African life and experience historically and to this day, since the past must dialogue with the present, and inform the future (Erskine 1998, p. 38). My deliberations lead me to conclude that restricting their theology to a critique of their experience of European oppression, as espoused in an oppression/liberation dialectic, is inadequate since although there are serious theological questions concerning the past half a millennium, African life lived in the presence of God predates this period. And importantly the African was human made in the image of God from the beginning and therefore theology should engage with the humanity of the African that existentially is beyond the encounter with European people. The theology I proffer therefore puts African humanity and their relationship with God before and above their encounter with European people, and engages in God-Talk through the prism of their historic and contemporary humanity. Such God-Talk however must do more than talk, it must translate into empowerment rooted in the dignity of Black British humanity in the *imago Dei* (Henry-Robinson 2017).

As mentioned above, the answer to flourishing in Babylon is mainly a theological one; not first about material things but about God-ordained African humanity and agency and their divine right, privilege and responsibility to pursue human flourishing. This is the opposite of European 'white' theology that Cone says he developed an intense dislike for, because it avoided the really hard problems of African life while talking about revelation, God, Jesus and the Holy Spirit (Cone 1993, p. 43). What is needed for the Black British people is a theology that affirms their humanity and agency, understands the history and nature of Eurocentricity, expresses a God that makes sense of a liberated life and is committed to flourishing. For Black British people this is a life lived as a people in diaspora in Britain, centre of the former empire and its remains (Akala 2018).

I find a helpful example of living in one's agency and self-determination in the actions of nineteenth-century ex-enslaved turned abolitionist Frederick Douglass in his autobiography. Douglass, born into enslavement in the USA, after submitting himself to regular cruel beatings by slave masters and mistresses, 'resolved to fight' back when his master set about attempting to tie him to beat him again. Douglass knows only that 'the spirit' came upon him in a moment of self-discovery of his humanity and agency that saw him overcome his master and became the turning point in his life as a 'slave'. That day the embers of freedom were kindled and a sense of his 'own manhood' was revived (Douglass 1995, p. 43). With insight that his supposed master, Mr Covey, was human too, Douglass vowed never again to submit to being beaten by a white man, and never to consider himself a slave. Douglass' theological understanding that his destiny was in his own determination led to his physical freedom from enslavement. It is a theological enlightenment that teaches the African person to look to self, empowered by the Spirit, to procure liberation and flourishing. Douglass' example and that of others introduces us to the concept of a God of liberation, empowerment and accompaniment, since the examples we have of liberative acts by oppressed peoples have been carried out by humans inspired by the Divine (Morrison 2014; Reid-Salmon 2012). Theologizing and campaigning against racism in this time has of necessity to embody theoretically and practically a deep understanding of the relationship between one's humanity, the humanity of others, the imperial nature of our habitat and a pathway to flourishing free of dependency, though not of allyship, firmly rooted in agency and self-determination. In empowering Black British people to liberate themselves, dependent upon themselves and God, theology has a role in negating European society's assertion that it has the power to take African dignity and identity, and to affirm in its stead a consciousness of their humanity made in the *imago Dei* with an irremovable God-given dignity and identity that at worst needs reviving, but is never dead (van Aarde 2016, pp. 1–9). Only from a place of dignity and assumed freedom can the descendants of formerly enslaved and oppressed African people engage in respectful partnership with white people. Shifting the racialized narrative away from its preoccupation with European behaviour towards African peoples and towards the flourishing of all, help to move on from pinning hopes on solving the theory of the 'bad apples' as it ignores the systemic and institutional nature of the problem (Altman 2020, p. 36).

Cone, recognized as the father of Black Theology, long ago accepted that a strategic error was made by him and other early pioneers of the discipline in the USA. As he says, 'We allowed our definition of Black theology to be too much a reaction to racism in White churches and society' (Cone 1992, p. 86). A consequence of this preoccupation is still with us today as seen in the belief that because God despises racism, until its eradication there can be no liberation for African people. This preoccupation works to African people's detriment since it turns this product of empire into a perverse dependency by which Black British people cannot see or imagine a world worth living in where racism continues to exist, and yet they cannot see a way to ridding the world of it either. Theology in this book is not tethered to European determination, but is rooted instead in the sum of African historical and contemporary ontology. In the early days of the development of Black Theology in Britain, Lartey states in the first issue of the original journal *Black Theology in Britain: A Journal of Contextual Praxis* that it seeks to 'make known what black people in Britain are thinking, feeling, saying and expressing about their experience of God' (Lartey 1998, pp. 7–9). In other words, the journal aims to interpret black experience in a holistic manner. A people's theological starting point, then, is their humanity rooted in God in whose image and likeness they are made.

Since 'black' has unhelpfully become synonymous with 'white' oppression, it is right to assert that African 'black' existed before such oppression and will exist after it, because the past 500 years is only a part of, not the whole, historical experience of African people who were royalty long before they were enslaved (R. Walker 2006). African 'black' people are made in the image and likeness of God, endowed with agency, ethno-religious identity and a diaspora experience of roots and routes; they cannot afford to be made subject to oppression and racism. As Black people in diaspora in Britain engage in God-talk they should do so against the background of their divine humanity as a riposte to enemies and an invite to allies, as they endeavour to flourish in Britain and beyond. Borrowing a phrase from Cornel West, African American philosopher, this work deploys a 'prophetic pragmatism' by speaking clearly into the trying situation and aspiration to flourish of Black British people and applying what is deemed best for them even when the solution may appear counterintuitive and to some plain wrong (West 1999, p. 147). I enquire into what diaspora is and how Black British people might deal with it by being clear about and embracing their ethnic religious identity as people in Britain of African descent. This work proceeds by developing my argument based on the outline of Jeremiah's plan for Jewish exiles as I address the question of the flourishing of Black British people. Black British Theology is my main philosophical frame. My auto-ethnographic approach allows me to speak as an insider (Aldred 2005, p. 28). In Chapter 1, I have laid out an introduction to the book, discussing the three premises upon which the work is predicated; the people, the letter, and theology. In Chapter 2, I discuss exile and diaspora with reference to Jeremiah 29.1–4. In Chapter 3, I explore how by applying *imago Dei* and agency, Black British people can settle, build and grow, with reference to Jeremiah 29.5–6. In Chapter 4, I examine seeking peace, prosperity, prayer and shared interests towards improving conditions for everybody in the imperial context, with reference to Jeremiah 29.7. In Chapter 5, I explore false prophets and the way their rhetoric poses challenges for the diaspora, based upon Jeremiah 29.8–23. In Chapter 6, I discuss what a life of flourishing might look like for Black British people, with reference to Jeremiah 29.10–14.

Questions for intergenerational discussions

- Do Old Testament prophets like Jeremiah teach us anything? If so, what?
- How do you identify yourself – African, Caribbean, British, Black? Or as composite?
- Black British Theology versus Black Theology – discuss.

2

Exile/Diaspora

> This is the text of the letter that the prophet Jeremiah sent from Jerusalem to the surviving elders among the exiles and to the priests, the prophets and all the other people Nebuchadnezzar had carried into exile from Jerusalem to Babylon. (This was after King Jehoiachin and the queen mother, the court officials and the leaders of Judah and Jerusalem, the skilled workers and the artisans had gone into exile from Jerusalem.) He entrusted the letter to Elasah son of Shaphan and to Gemariah son of Hilkiah, whom Zedekiah king of Judah sent to King Nebuchadnezzar in Babylon. It said: This is what the LORD Almighty, the God of Israel, says to all those I carried into exile from Jerusalem to Babylon. (Jer. 29.1–4, NIV)

Introduction

Jeremiah's letter, sent from the Jewish homeland of Judah and Jerusalem to his kinfolks who had been forcibly exiled to Babylon, I view as a pastoral attempt to settle them in view of counter prophecies being made by others claiming, as he did, to speak in the name of God (B. Green 2013, p. 114). At the heart of Jeremiah's letter, I find a concern for the hurt and, quite probably vengeful, cohort of exiled Jewish people in need of discovering ways to live in exile and retain links with the homeland and the rich heritage that sustained their people over centuries in adversities, including their belief in a providential and ever-present God. A point of Jeremiah's letter was a survival plan, which I argue was a plan to flourish in Babylon since they were in for a long stay. Some of Jeremiah's contemporaries, Shemaiah for example, contested Jeremiah's prophecies concerning the nature of the odyssey, viewing Jeremiah's intervention that the exiles should not expect a quick return home as 'unwelcomed and counterintuitive advice' (Allen 2008, p. 17), rather than sympathizing with the positive exhortation contained in Jeremiah's 'letter of hope' (Navigators 2018, p. 28).

Hill argues that in the quest to resist empire there is need for prophetic rage to course through the veins of those, like Jeremiah and others, who work for renewal and transformation, seeking to establish spheres of peace, justice, reconciliation, hope and redemption (Hill 2013, p. 10). As a descendant of enslaved Africans, with chattel slavery, colonialism and racism as part of my history, there is definitely anger in me against perpetrators and their benefitting descendants that drive my thoughts and actions concerning life in Britain. Beckford helpfully argues that vengeance can be redemptive when channelled towards 'returning evil with good' (Beckford 2001, p. 38). Returning evil with good, as well as being a sound biblical mandate, is made possible when the wronged realizes that nothing the perpetrator does can rob them of their humanity, agency and self-determination. This realization does not seek to diminish the actions of perpetrators, or their effects upon victims; rather, it categorizes and contextualizes such actions in ways that show deep understanding that African humanity is the equal in every way to European and other ethnic types in the human family created in the image and likeness of God, full of creativity and ingenuity, never mere victims.

In sixth-century Babylon as today in exile/diaspora, displaced people live in danger of fragmenting into disenfranchisement due to internal disputes and external pressure contributing to complex anxieties and experiences that need contextualizing. Jeremiah's letter to the exiles, and the book itself, sought to help 'make sense of their tragedy, recover their identity, and move toward the future as God's beloved community' (Newsom et al. 2012, p. 269). I believe the Jewish exilic situation resonates with and can inform the diasporic one of Black British people; and that the complexities of exile, the relationship between home and away, the role of God in empire, the hope of return and more all contribute to navigating one's way home from home. Above all a sense of lived transcendence is conveyed in Jeremiah's text so that while one cannot undo the past, they can certainly transcend the past's present effects and live not in the shadow of evil but out of the depth of self-realization. Drawn from the first few verses of Jeremiah 29, four themes come under discussion in this chapter. First, what might be the meanings and implications then and now of being in exile or diaspora, what home might mean, how ethno-religious identity is affected, and the God and Nebuchadnezzar dynamics.

Exile/diaspora

Black British people are part of an African diaspora living in the Western world, sometimes referred to poignantly as exiles or, less so, diaspora. The term 'exiles' was probably first used with reference to the Jews who were deported against their will in the sixth century BC into Babylonian captivity, but has meaning beyond that precise period, people and experience (Ackroyd 1968, p. 243). Jeremiah was clear that the Jews would be in Babylon intergenerationally, a period of time marked by '70 years', then return to their ancestral homeland, although we know this happened only in a diffused manner and not in totality. 'Diaspora' may first have appeared with reference to the Jewish people scattered beyond Palestine and has wide applicability for people dispersed from the country or region of their historic heritage, a reality that spawns almost all human experience. Brueggemann has noted that exile carries with it an expectation of a return to normalcy, whereas diaspora suggests a state of being far away without any realistic expectation of a return to normalcy (Brueggemann in Beach 2015, p. 11). According to sociologist Gilroy, 'diaspora is a concept that problematizes the cultural and historical mechanics of belonging' (Gilroy 2000, p. 123), and for Hall it raises questions about historical and contemporary 'locations of residence and locations of belonging' (D. Hall 2021, p. 124). However, in this work, both terms are used interchangeably, although diaspora is preferred in regard to Black British people, including descendants of ancestors who were once forcibly removed from their homelands, enslaved and colonized, but are in Britain, though circumstantially, of their own volition.

Trafford reminds us that at its peak 'Britain ruled over 100 colonies, protectorates and dominions, with 52 forming the later Commonwealth', involving 'the annexation of lands, settler colonialism, chattel slavery, extraction, genocide and expansionist commerce' (Trafford 2020, p. 3). With reference to Black diaspora since the Windrush Generation, Bentley Cunningham, a veteran of that community, uses the phrase 'the tyranny of distance' to describe the devastating effects of migration that removes people from one adopted home to another far away, a transaction in which they are objects of empire (from a tweet 11.11.2022). While it may not be possible to undo the damage caused to many Windrush diasporeans, including me, it is now possible to mitigate the worst excesses of distance tyranny by new technological advances, such as the internet, or the expansion of aviation. Even in complex and multi-layered situations, such as diaspora or exile, the desire for liberation and a place to call home 'binds people together in a common demand for freedom and justice ... as they seek ways forward for the human family in overcoming the stagnating and destructive forces of nihilism and empire' (Hill 2013, p. 11). Gilroy reckons diaspora is something of an illusion since people movement is such an established human expression that we are all part of one big diaspora (Gilroy 2000). People movement is multi-caused and we note for example, that through a combination of voluntary and involuntary realities many were 'glad to leave behind a Caribbean riven by social and political strife, unemployment and a stagnant, hyperinflation economy ... [there being] little to work or hope for in the colony' (Kufour 1999, pp. 352–60).

A form of de-stabilizing leading to exile is found in the trade in Black bodies by Arabs, Europeans and African slave traders. As Kelly and others show, slave trading was a well-practised commercial activity around the world including in Africa, and so the activities that resulted in the capture and transport of approximately 12 million Africans was an ongoing development before the Europeans became involved (Kelly 1997). We know now, for example, that some African kings and rulers bought and sold their own people as slaves, trading among themselves and with Trans-Sahara Arabs (Aderibigbe 2016). So even as Europeans became involved in the inhumane trade in Black humanity, some African brothers and sisters needed only to extend their market to include white buyers of their sordid goods. We might take as read that those African dealers prosecuted their business with eyes wide open, taking their profits to benefit themselves in similar manner to the European traders, all entrepreneurs. It would be bordering on infantilizing African leaders to suppose they were merely pawns in a European game of buying and selling enslaved people, creating their displacement. We learn too that in plying their enslavement business through kidnapping unsuspecting Africans and trickery, Europeans also traded in goods like firearms, trinkets and other material in exchange for human stock en route to slave markets in the Caribbean and Americas (Equiano 1995, p. 47).

A popular story told in diaspora says, 'When the White man came to our country he had the Bible and we Blacks had the land. The White man said to us, "let us pray". After the prayer, the White man had the land and we Blacks had the Bible' (West 2018). The question for the African on the homeland and in exile/diaspora is how to retake the land, where 'land' is emblematic of wider life. I believe theologians have consistently used the Bible to perpetuate a Western hegemony by situating the African as the inferior, oppressed, done-to 'other' at the mercy of their oppressor, needing to submit to concepts of the innocence and neutrality of the Bible, yet advancing the idea that one group and its culture is better than others and has the divine right to control the other – a form of bewitchment by which all Black British people can do is suffer and protest but never throw off the oppressor and live in their own dignity (Senokoane 2022). The narrative suggests that white power is normative and this is instead of deploying a biblical hermeneutic rooted in the *imago Dei* empowered to overcome white hegemony and flourish in the world. The 'African experience' on the whole, not just the 'African experience of oppression and exploitation', should provide the epistemological lens through which to perceive the God of the Bible as the God of liberation, a concept I question. This is because in the Bible and in Black experience God may be said to *accompany* exilic peoples far more than he can be said to deliver them from oppression. Mosala warns that this kind of hermeneutic risks succumbing to the danger of collaborating with the Bible's dominant ruling class ideology since it denies the African person's ability to thrive beyond centring whiteness (Mosala 1989, pp. 14–42). Therefore, I view Jeremiah's letter as an exercise in preservation and transfer of social/spiritual capital between homes; it highlights overcoming rather than victimhood.

Speed and Kulichyova, in a study about harnessing and developing refugee talent, highlight what I consider an indirect protégé of Jeremiah's ministry to Jewish exiles, as his communication shows the role of 'agents of human development' in helping the displaced deal with the challenges a new place brings (Speed and Kulichyova 2021). The value of such a contribution from home to those Judeans exiled by the military force of Nebuchadnezzar's empire should not be underestimated for a displaced people in need of additional support and direction. When we contrast the Judah/Babylonian situation with the Africa/Caribbean and Americas of the transatlantic slave trade era, we notice that the distance and circumstances that apply to the latter militated against a letter from home to bewildered African exiles. Yet exiles and diaspora people imposed upon by colonial forces found ways to exercise their human agency by taking their legacies with them between homes – including their sense of faith and mission (Moyo 2017). Also, enslaved Africans made use of their multiple cultures and languages that contributed to the etymological basis for the creoles that facilitated resistance communication between diverse peoples in exile (Görlach and Holm et al. 1986, p. 133). Some transportation occurred too by malevolent and deceptive operatives of cultural vandalism, theft and transfer (Van Sertima et al. 1986). Bangura reminds us that there was in the nineteenth century cross-fertilization including deliberate attempts by

European powers to return chosen free Africans as reverse colonizers and missionaries in the West's self-interest, with Sierra Leone and Liberia being two examples of this development (Dumbuya 2016).

Finding myself in diaspora, in a foreign land away from my place of birth in Jamaica and heritage in Africa, I want to know how I came to be here and what my culture brings for successfully living here and sharing with others. I understand the historic circumstances that have led to my being in Britain and should now deploy and make best use of the prophetic praxis that can impact where I am. Understanding how the divine will appears to have collaborated with malevolent human 'pharaohs' and their oppressive hegemonic systems that brought me here makes me wiser when positioning myself for life in diaspora. While I cannot hand on heart say it is the will of God that I am in England, nor do I believe it is a result of a curse, I readily accept that in finding myself in diaspora I must come to terms with the known and discoverable contributory circumstances, appropriately learn from them, attribute blame and praise, but most of all take charge of my destiny.

A challenge for people in diaspora with their roots elsewhere is to view themselves, not just as immigrants, refugees or asylum seekers as they may be popularly identified by the majority culture, but as human beings made in the image and likeness of God, belonging to the human race, having single or multiple ethnic and religious identities, with creative abilities and the power of reasoning. Even those brought against their will do not lose their personhood but remain someone's father, mother, son, daughter, sibling, child, extended family or friend. People in diaspora cannot afford to be unaware that empire has always used those brought under their subjugation as chattels, subjects to be used and abused for the benefit of empire, an example of which is the totalizing and selfish design of American empiricism during the twentieth century (Bogues 2010, p. 67). People exiled and caught in the grip of empire have to make rational decisions about the level of cooperation to give, whether to resist and to what extent, whether to risk an escape attempt or situate themselves ready to act at an opportune time. Black British people, consciously or unconsciously, make decisions whether to continue living in Britain or emigrate, something many I know have done by re-emigrating to Canada or the United States, and especially in recent times, moving to Africa from whence their ancestors came and the Caribbean from whence their parents came.

My father may have been a statistic to statisticians and historians, but he was really a man making decisions about himself and his family. When he returned to Jamaica after five years as planned, he soon discovered that the small amount of money he had managed to save was not enough and so he returned, settled down, brought some of the family over before returning to Jamaica in retirement and dying in his homeland. In a similar vein, Christians arriving and discovering that their denomination was not active in Britain set about founding them, hence the existence of today's African Caribbean, or Black, British churches. Equally those who found the denominations they belonged to from their homelands but were made to feel unwelcome responded by making decisions to stay in the face of overt and subtle racism, while some left mainstream churches and joined the Black British churches. It is important for Black British people to remember they are living, breathing, thinking humans with capacity to reason how to make progress with their complex lives, clear that they do not exist at the whim of mainstream society. Black British people might do well to take a look at the Christian Church in a post-Christendom epoch, challenged to understand itself in exile as displaced and needing to discover or rediscover tools that allow it to respond to changing culture while retaining a sense of its Christ-centred self and identity; so Black British communities do well to embrace their core being while coexisting and flourishing in diaspora (Beach 2015, p. 160). As the Jews remained Jews in Babylon, so Black British ontology rooted in African beingness may find themselves in different parts of the globe, yet must always be aware that the roots of a tree do not change and the tree always remains connected to its roots even when transplanted from its natural habitat. Whether the context of Black British people is described as 'exile' or 'diaspora' is a moot point; what is irrefutable is that for someone like me, a combination of choice and circumstance is at play.

Home

Black British people face a dilemma concerning where home is. Is it Britain where they find themselves or more historically where their parents and ancestors are from in the Caribbean and Africa? 'Home', it is popularly said, is where the heart is, yet for people in diaspora there is the ever-present wrestling between one's ancestral home and current location (Reid-Salmon 2012, p. 6). The Jews in exile had been violently and forcibly removed from home in Judah and were being told by Jeremiah, in God's name, to make Babylon home, not for ever, but for '70 years', that is, intergenerationally. The exile's sense of displacement is complex, multi-homed and calls for 'creativity in crisis' (Gossai 2018, p. 264). In a two-part BBC Radio 4 programme series in 2018, *Caribritish: Children of Windrush*, one contributor (Hugh Muir) commented that until you know what is behind you, you cannot push forward, and another emphasizes the genealogical connectivity between one's parents and history that retreats further and further, leaving them questioning, 'Should I be here or there?', in a bittersweet ongoing dilemma. Implicit here is the possibility of the exile's historical homeland retreating into the past while the centre of oppressive empire becomes home by its imminence; this is similar to the danger faced by the Christian retreating from the earthly home as they gravitate towards a promised heavenly home. A preferable situation is to understand home incarnationally, and inculcate an ability to relate to and live simultaneously in both or multiple homes, as the literal and philosophical merge. Home is more than a house and Jeremiah's letter fuses wider concerns such as multinational boundaries and jurisdictions as from Judah and Jerusalem he extends his pastoral reach to his people in Babylon.

In the church where I grew up, we sang sentiments such as 'This world is not my home, I'm only passing through'

... 'we'll soon be done with troubles and trials' ... 'trouble won't last always' ... 'Someday I'll go where Jesus is' ... all rooted in biblical understandings of the transient nature of life on earth and the struggle to establish an earthly home against the background promise of the glory of the heavenly home towards which the faithful sojourn (Rom. 8.18; 2 Cor. 5.1). This other-worldly understanding has had deep spiritual meaning that cuts both ways, positively and negatively. Such a mindset allows for resisting whatever life throws at you, an indomitable spirit that reminds you that if you persevere you will be saved from present troubles. That mindset tends also to allow for an unhelpful level of non- or part-engagement with the affairs of life that easily become self-fulfilling prophecies of doom, neither exploiting opportunities nor confronting challenges. Stone, in a study of Pentecostalism in Britain, a strong influence in the Black British community religious life in particular, highlights a tension between 'pneumatic dualism' and 'pneumatic integralism'. The former understands the power of the Holy Spirit as impacting their personal or group religious piety, healing and comfort while the latter understands the embodiment of the Spirit to effectively address human and societal challenges be they social, economic, political resulting in poverty, injustices of race, class and gender (Stone 2021). Pneumatic integralism holds out the possibility of engaging both challenges and opportunities so that Black British people need not choose between the here and the hereafter, or between Britain and Caribbean, or between Caribbean and Africa. This integrative approach to home enables them also to maximize opportunities and challenge oppositional forces within and beyond the religious, or Christian, or Pentecostal context and the secular world. This way of lived empowerment by the Creator allows the diaspora to develop new concepts of making and being at home.

To wrestle with issues of home as a diaspora people calls for proactivity, not indifference, in the now. I find that in exile as at home, addressing how to handle what one writer calls 'the "in-between" and "liminal" home away from home' situation, Western Christianity and theology emphasize pastoral care as something done to you, whereas the spirit of what I am discussing prioritizes self-care that precedes other care (Magezi 2019). Encouraging or facilitating the abrogation of self-care, especially in exile, ignores the need to be strong as a unit (personal, family or community), that you have the capacity to help yourself, and help others. This is all the more necessary in exile since exile is subject to higher powers and home is subject to their jurisdiction, leaving questions of flourishing and freedom problematic. In my experience, sometimes the situation of African-descended people in diaspora are made worse by feelings of shame, displacement and ultimate alienation (Clark 2012, p. 16). Jeremiah wanted the exiles to know that this uprooting from home was not just earthly Babylon's doing, it was also God's doing, in which heavenly and earthly interests coincided, meeting the will of the Babylonian Empire and the Kingdom of God. This writer knows precisely what it feels like to live with uncertainties about where exactly home is: the UK? the Caribbean? or Africa? With an unresolved question of who is responsible for my odyssey, I need to take charge of affairs in authority and in the power of God's name. It is spiritually and psychologically draining to be caught in the crossfire between human and divine will and purpose – it increases my uncertainty and vulnerability. People in exile or diaspora need not give in to their worst fears about displacement and dilemmas about where really home is since, in keeping with Psalm 24.1, 'the earth is the LORD's', and as Jeremiah's action hints, the Jews were one people irrespective of where they were; home or away from home, they could take care of business, grow and flourish. Challenges and opportunities were also to be found in multiple places and spaces.

By the time of the Windrush era, and since the 1940s, challenging social-economic factors in the former colonies meant that Britain, the centre of empire, was a more likely place to find employment opportunities and an alternative home. Aldwyn Roberts (self-named Lord Kitchener, after the British field marshal and war secretary), a Trinidadian who sailed on the MV *Empire Windrush* that docked at Tilbury in June 1948, encapsulates the mood of many subjects of empire with his calypso song, 'London is the place for me', written on board the *Windrush* (Pareles 2000). How London transforms itself in the minds of the descendants of enslaved people, those oppressed by its imperialism, into becoming eulogized as the 'place for me', that is, home, remains an interesting osmosis. In an age of improving travel and communication, subjects and former subjects of empire have been able to travel and communicate more freely, thereby further blurring the question of where home is. Yet, the forces mediating if not mandating migration are imperial ones, and the systems that extracted free slave labour also extract resources and wealth, and concentrate the outcomes in the home of empire to which the sons and daughters of their formerly enslaved ancestors needily wend their way to work and live.

Yet, as Serequeberhan reminds us, the European space to which Africans have come has long held that all that the African brings into the Western space is viewed as from the primitive other (Serequeberhan 2015, p. 39). However, the person in diaspora need not accept external designations – it is up to the Black British person to put value on their history and heritage. Moving from home to diaspora is always accompanied by a sense of being, culture and spirituality that engage in interchanges with prevailing existences in the new setting (Walters 2005). Means of transportation and communication between home and exile largely determine what you carry, but some things are in your heart, soul, character and history; they accompany you whether the journey is a caravan taking months, a ship taking weeks, or a jet taking hours; whether communication is done by messengers on foot, on horseback, or by satellite telecommunications.

Some of the ways by which Black British people have attempted to make home from home are quite evident. Essentially, people create or recreate facets of life from their history and put to use to make liminality more homely, culturally and spiritually, as Black Britons strive to carve out their own identity and place in an often-hostile society (Owusu 1999). It is self-evident that in diaspora or exile people make an effort to establish the norms that make home, home – whether that is a way of speaking dialect or language, art, religion and more. We even dream of the reality we would like to bring alive in the new setting, and 'when life in the here is hell, one longs for there' (Erskine 2008, p. 82). In the spheres of music, Africa has exported Afrobeat, the Caribbean has exported Calypso, Ska and Reggae, while Black America has given Black British society R&B and Gospel, and the Black British community has in situ developed Lover's Rock. In linguistics, the Caribbean has contributed patois that Black British people use as a common alternative language, as a mark of solidarity and as switching to allow for communicating in the presence of others who do not understand patois (Tomlin 2019, p. 52). Some believe the most popular word on the street in London is Jamaica patois-based. In cuisine, Africa and the Caribbean have contributed to the national menu with food such as curry patties, ginger beer, chicken rice and peas, jerk, and much more. The Caribbean takeaway is now legendary in urban communities in Britain. None of this can obliterate the dilemmas of belonging and non-belonging, a test of the in-betweenness of a life of the mind over the body as the person born or having roots in one place physically while mentally, spiritually and philosophically relating to other locations, or the realization that home is always elsewhere (D'Aguiar 1999). In economics, Black British people imported the 'pardna' as a form of a communal savings programme that has developed into fully fledged credit unions. The extended family and sense of the interrelated and interdependent connection – that is, *Ubuntu* – has also impacted Black British communities, creating social housing and respite services in health and education. We can see, too, black exports from the homelands to the Black British community in sports, arts and other areas, with probably the most impactful being the transfer of African and Caribbean Christian worship that is evident in vibrant Black British churches and a presence in mainstream churches too, most noticeably in urban areas (Gerloff 1992). These and more have enriched the lives of Black British communities, making more homely a naturally hostile place, and spilling over into mainstream life and experience in Britain. In her seminal research on the Black church movement in Britain, Gerloff identifies this prophetic voice of God calling the British nation back to the faith as a signature cause, alongside the economic one, for people to move to the country at the centre of empire. She remarks that 'They were carried by zeal and driven by the Holy Spirit' to represent the Christian gospel they once travelled abroad to preach back to them (Gerloff 1992, pp. 55–7). Core to this religious faith is the understanding of the Christian as a pilgrim on a mission, having no permanent home on earth, therefore having both a worldly and an other-worldly relationship with the concept and reality of home. One of the clearest exponents of this voice of God is Guyanese missionary Mohabir: 'I distinctly heard Jesus say, "Leave all, and become a missionary"' (Mohabir 1988, p. 37). As Smith puts it, 'The African Caribbean-led churches should be appreciated for putting the fire back into Britain's religion' (Smith 1989, p. 109).

Brought up by my mother, it is mainly from her homemaking skills that I have a sense of home. Matriarchy has a deep and abiding influence on my sense of home, made the more so since patriarchy in my home was largely absent apart from the faltering presence of elder brothers, yet church leadership was peculiarly patriarchal, even as it was clear that matriarchy ran the show. For me, home was real when mother was there with her children and friends around, yet she would say, 'Anywhere is home if Christ is there', and that is pretty much anywhere and everywhere! Grant reminds us that, in general, we live in a world dominated by patriarchy, in which women bear disproportionately trauma, disaster and seek survival, at home and in exile, yet African women can easily be obscured and have had to fight for 'an active role in naming themselves and their experiences' as a step towards liberation. Such naming, however, situates itself within the present realities with resonance beyond them (Grant 1989, p. 13). In diaspora, Black British people cannot afford to silence any part of their society; all voices are valid and needed. A key lesson is that Black British people should keep open lines of communication with their homelands by all means, so that historic wisdom, and insight that sustains the motherland, can appropriately contribute through various means to the building and sustaining of home away from home. It seems that it is only as Black British embrace Africa as their ancestral home that the riches of the motherland can become an asset in diaspora (Clark 2012, p. 50).

Insights and resources from diaspora also may contribute to improving life back home, by remittances and lessons learned from being close to the centre of white economic and political power and control. The wisdom to be gleaned from experiences in that space if true connection is made between exile and homeland cross-referring interpretations of (for example) the wisdom of the elders, prophets, women and what future the young desire and expect, can be enriching for the homeland. God had no qualms about sending his people Israel from their home into exile, or preventing those at home from being occupied by enemy forces, so this may indicate that God's understanding of what constitutes home did not accord with theirs. If home is where we feel most comfortable and creative, those in exile/diaspora may need to embrace a deeper, wider and more profound concept of home by sharing in the realities of home for others.

Identity

Another point I draw from the introduction to Jeremiah's letter to Jewish exiles is the significance of an assured ethnic identity in diaspora, and as a Christian I understand ethnic identity and diversity as part of the beautiful creation of God (Tarus and Lowery 2017). Living in Britain almost all my life convinces me that ethnic identity is critical in this space even as it is important that we avoid ethnic essentialism and ethnocentrism since no ethnic identity can claim exclusivity or that they are better than any other. In this racialized and inferiorizing context, minority ethnic identity rooted in historic belonging can provide the stability needed. Drever defines 'identity' as having 'the character of persisting essentially unchanged' which for Black British people, like Jewish exiles in Babylon, points to an innate part of their humanity set against historic and contemporary attempts to crush them (Drever 1966, p. 128). The Jews in exile were an extension of those they left behind in Judah and, with the main body of exiles perhaps numbering in the tens of thousands, settled in the border area between Assyria and Babylonia (Coogan 1999, p. 270). The implication is that one's identity transcends movement and location. I am who I am even as I change locations, since who I am is deeply rooted and remains essentially unchanged, though subject to development. Especially in an away-from-home setting, ethnic and religious identity is important for reasons of 'protection, association and recognition' (West 1999, p. 561), as a way of affirming the self as an agent, a subject in history who creates and initiates (West 1999, p. 500). The prophet wrote to his people in Babylon confident they would be identified there as they were identifiable in Judah. Jeremiah called them by name and rank demonstrating the strength and transnational nature of Jewish identity and as a hint to the need to maintain order and shape in exile. The Jews were Jews in Judah and they remained Jews in Babylon. I was African Jamaican in Jamaica and I remained African Jamaican in Britain, only now Jamaica tends to give way to the geographically broader Caribbean identity, to which I add British.

There has been, in my experience, too great a willingness to forego self-naming while allowing categorizing of minority communities by the white ethnic majority through media and literature. The Black British community watched as the mainstream labelled them 'coloured', 'black', and so on, but there can be no justification for perpetuating this practice of passive permissiveness. As mentioned above, in this work I am using Black as a signifier for African Caribbean, followed by 'British' to refer specifically to descendants of African and Caribbean parents and ancestors who now live in Britain. I deem it preferable that over time the narrative moves from colour-coding to geography and culture; 'African Caribbean British' demonstrates this concept and facilitates a decisive shift away from what Anderson calls 'ontological blackness', meaning an identity necessitated by in contradistinction to 'white' supremacy (Anderson 1999). In other words, 'black', having been invented by those who invented themselves as 'white', has been redeployed with an oppositional anti-white purpose in an anti-black world (Warren 2018, p. 27). A helpful principle might be that it is understood that African people originating on the continent remain African anywhere in the world, and after however many generations, as are Chinese, Indian and Pakistani for example. The USA has led the way on this with the designation 'African American'. Black British people could follow suit by dropping 'black' and using geography (that is, African and/or Caribbean British) as a preferred signifier – where necessary sub-ethnicizing to include Indo Caribbean, White Caribbean, and so on (Levy 2009).

Hybrid identity such as 'African Caribbean Black British', though inelegant, is important in Britain since such a compound ethnic designation dispenses with the imposed 'black' while clarifying the journey a people have trod. It refuses to play the European supremacist game by not accepting its false ontology that situates my identity in black as opposed to white or linked to suffering in perpetuity. Neither am I adopting the solo identity either of Africa where my ancestors originate, the Caribbean where, because of the circumstance of my ancestors' displacement, I was born, or Britain where, because of the pull of its globalizing efforts to concentrate economic power, I find myself living. All three constitute my hybridized ethnic identity. None is credible without the other. What is credible is to represent in a diaspora context my identity with its cultural history including the suffering of the past half a millennium and importantly my historic identity as a human being made in the image of God, both sides of enslavement and colonized history. This identity then is incarnational in manner as it simultaneously synthesizes and problematizes a long-journeyed ethnic identity refusing to allow the dominance of the enslavement epoch to define me and other African peoples. I find here an interesting corollary with my Pentecostal tradition where scholars have pointed out the manner in which this Christian tradition has been populated around the world driven by forms of migration, and its construction as a pneumatological imagination in which the Spirit holds together disparate things without compromising each thing's identity and integrity. Pentecostal identity is a construction of multiple contextual voices, informed by them without silencing one voice by conflating it with another (Vondey and Mittelstadt (eds) 2013, p. 79). So, people around the world belong to the one humanity that differentiates itself in its ethnically diverse oneness, of which black (that is, African Caribbean) British are a part.

It is as the different identities fuse into Black British that a true perspective can be rationalized of my place in Britain. If I come empty handed, as though I were created *ab initio* here, to be just British, or if I come as 'black' that is created exclusively in oppression, my place in Britain is incredible. Black British in this context is the only credible identity for a person such as me, and from this template other identities can be crafted. As hinted at above, at times I may wish to emphasize my Jamaican identity and may be African Jamaican British, or just Jamaican British; someone else may be African British, or where appropriate Nigerian British, Ghanaian British, and so on. What ought to be shunned is an identity shorn of its history and which ignores the human identity made in the image of the Creator, and where 'black' is a baby of its white supremacist parent. Erskine says, even in situations of oppression we celebrate the status of *imago Dei*, a privilege predicated not upon human will and determination but based on the grace given through the forgiveness of Jesus Christ (Erskine 2008, p. 158). I go further though, assuming *imago Dei* as a grace given in creation, not something attributed as a result of belief in Jesus.

Mbubaegbu highlights the challenges of identity insecurities and reminds us of the essentiality of being secure in our bodies, identities, and I add presence (Mbubaegbu 2013, p. xvi). The African body has been subjected to so much degradation in Western society that it is understandable that some Africans become insecure in their looks and capabilities in a society where the European features and genius are celebrated as virtuous in beauty and intelligence. West argues that it is power and pressure that decide who get visibility in contested spaces and in the Western world African-descended people generally have little power relative to the European majority

(West 1999, p. 504). Black British people must therefore recognize their contextual power reality with reference to social, economic, political and spiritual spheres, and how they can manipulate them to acquire power that is the agency of visibility, meaning regard, authority and assertive presence while still a minority in a majority culture. It seems to me that a way forward for Black British people is the acquisition of power clearly identifiable as belonging to the group, something unlikely to be achieved by inverting African identity within Britishness. By disconnecting themselves from their historic identity and taking comfort under an 'I am British' identity, the African-heritage person risks disconnecting themselves from their historic heritage while simultaneously failing to connect with the British identity they claim for lack of heritage in that ethno-history. Tomlin, in her book on preaching in the Black Pentecostal tradition, encourages those preachers to engage prophetically with socio-economic challenges, a call echoed by Beckford, and which points to the church as a place to harbour strength to flourish (Tomlin 2019; Beckford 2023). The result of ethnic dissonance is likely to be ethnic statelessness and homelessness. As a pastor, I encourage African-heritage people in Britain never to abandon their historic ethnic and religious identity in diaspora, since even when hybridized, it is a powerful help in the challenging space they occupy in the West.

'Babylon' as a place where exiled people experience constant challenges to their humanity and the abiding danger of being crushed under the weight of oppositional forces, cannot be allowed, unopposed, to determine the exile's identity. Nor should the exiles allow themselves to depend upon the majority culture in a quasi-divine dependency believing that Babylon will miraculously become the benevolent protector of a people it has objectified as an expendable imperial resource. Pentecostal theologian Augustine argues that the Genesis text highlights *imago Dei* as the concept of a shared humanity, a common good, a human capacity for flourishing in relationship with God and with each other (Augustine 2019, p. 48). This speaks to a self-understanding of human identity as a human–human and human–divine relationship, as a foundational basis for ethnic/national identity that cannot be allowed to depend upon the will and determination of another in a fallen sinful, spiteful and selfish world (McFarland et al. 2011, p. 49). 'The fall' is a contested theological idea, but even without it, my experience is that human selfishness and greed means that the majority culture operates in ways that protect the interests of the majority, while those identified as minorities or as inferiors are systematically related to according to their perceived usefulness to the apparatus of state working in the interest of the ethnic majority. Only the people so perceived can be depended upon to have the vested interest and determination to change this, by turning an upside-down world right side up.

The 2021 national census for England and Wales provides a framework for ethnic identity (https://www.ons.gov.uk/peoplepopulationandcommunity/culturalidentity/ethnicity/bulletins/ethnicgroupenglandandwales/census2021#ethnic-groups-in-england-and-wales), with ethnic sets and subsets; however, the statistics say nothing about the contestable relationship between and within ethnic groups. For example, Black English and Welsh comprise 4% of the population, approximately 2.4 million people, an increase on 2011 during which time African identity has increased while Caribbean identity has remained the same, meaning that in England and Wales, Africans outnumber those from the Caribbean by two to one.

Wallerstein says starkly, 'People shoot each other every day over the question of labels' (Wallerstein 1991, pp. 71–85). And sociologist Gilroy highlights further dangers of identifying humans based on racial/ethnic differences, seeing the practice as responsible for many of the conflicts that humanity experiences. Gilroy calls these ways of identifying humans 'vain and mistaken attempts to delineate and subdivide humankind', which are oppositional to the 'planetary humanism' he advocates (Gilroy 2000, pp. 1–2). Ethnic identity, however, points to more than a way of talking about individuality, community and solidarity. It points to 'the interplay between subjective experiences of the world and the cultural and historical settings in which those fragile, meaningful subjectivities are formed' (Gilroy 2000, p. 98). Notwithstanding the complexities and dangers of ethnic differentiation, I believe it is important to embrace one's ethnic location and understand it as contributing to God's creation of a human patchwork of diversity as an inherent nature and strength. It is a tempting distraction to believe that if humanity discards legitimate ethnic difference and sees itself as just one humanity (which we are), but without diversity, we then live in one accord. There is no need for unity if there is no diversity. The work of Christian ecumenism with which I have been professionally associated for decades recognizes that unity is a perennial challenge because of the diverse nature of the Christian Church, and even as unity is hoped and worked for, diversity's richness means it must be protected and preserved, and not compromised by reconciling attempts at unification (Tjørhom 2021). It is not the aim of unity, therefore, to eradicate diversity, but to protect it. Particularly in diverse exilic spaces, minority ethnic people should know their ethnic type, believe it to be God-given equal to all, unequal to none. Theorists may speculate about identities but my lived experience in Britain is that ethnic certitude is better than ethnic vagueness where such identity resonates with a person's cultural and geographic history.

Ethnic identity speaks both to how we perceive ourselves as well as how we are perceived by others. It helps to situate the self in the vastness and complexity of the exilic space in which we live. This contextual identity works best when the people identified as Black British are in sync with the terminology used as a result of self-naming, not because it has been imposed by mainstream writers. In the West, naming the other tends to be an expression of projecting a racial pyramid which situates the European – racialized as 'white' – as superior to all, especially those they racialize as 'black' and in their concepts subordinate in terms of beauty, intelligence and humanity. According to Cone, this is the concept at the heart of white racism (Cone 1969, p. 9), and because Black British people, our parents and ancestors have for centuries been the objects of Eurocentric imperialist empire, we have been conditioned into white hegemony as the norm, leading to self-loathing and European worship. This challenge is made worse as globalization controlled by the white West impacts negatively all poor people particularly in the global South.

While the Jewish exiles in Babylon were clearly a religio-ethnic people, the Black British people do not share a mono-religious identity – in fact, quite the opposite. This community is one of great religious diversity with a presence in almost every faith and religious category that exists, albeit with Christianity clearly enjoying the greatest following. Diverse belonging across faiths is matched by denominational belonging across Christianity with dominant presence of Pentecostals and mainstream British denominations such as Catholic, Anglican, Methodist, Baptist and United Reformed. From my work in interfaith relations in Britain, I know Black British people belong to the nine leading world faiths practised in Britain: Christian, Islam, Sikh, Hindu, Baha'i, Jewish, Buddhist, Jain and Zoroastrian. In addition, faith expressions such as Rastafari and African spiritualities are among several other faith belongings.

However, a starting point in diaspora for faith and theology has to be human identity and the *imago Dei*. There is much contestation concerning what it means for humanity to be made in the image of God, from relative power over creation to creativity, reason, dignity and the ability of humanity to reason and make sound judgements (McRorie 2021). The exercise of moral reasoning, while never perfect, is viewed as an essential part of how humans develop and a fundamental aspect of how societies change over time, drawing upon the image of God (Killen and Dahl 2021). Suffice it to say the main assertion here is that contrary to attempts to suggest that the African is not fully human, the principle of *imago Dei* states that all humanity is made in the divine image and likeness, barring none. As to what this might mean, Cone argues that human beings are free when they see clearly the fulfilment of their being in the image of God as an envisioned self-reality, thus becoming what they should (Cone 1989, p. 39). I believe all God's 'children' inherit God-like characteristics and this humanity rooted in the Creator is the supreme existential common reality concerning the human race. Wherever on planet earth you were born, or live, and whatever your religion or belief, pigmentation or ethnicity, common to all is being made in the image and likeness of God (Tschuy 1997, p. xi). All humans therefore descend from the same source, with a central identity that is their transcendent characteristic as bearer of the *imago Dei*, imbued 'with dignity, equality, and honour' (Grizzle 2021, p. 74).

Glen, in a paper that challenges the epistemological and anthropological basis of Black Theology, posits two bases of understanding about *imago Dei*, a substantive and a relational view, and argues that Black Theology is wedded to the wrong option. The substantive view upon which he suggests Western theology is based and from which Black Theology takes its cue, looks inward for certainty and validity of the *imago Dei*, while the relational view looks outwards to the relationship between human and God as its premise. Glen regards the substantive view as humanistic and although the dominant Christian world view, a weak basis for doing theology. For Glen, *imago Dei* is a result of a relationship between human and God and is not de facto a human quality, and suggests that, given attempted 'white' inferiorization of' 'black' people's intellectual ability, moral decision-making, moral purity, dominion over the earth, rationality and reason, it may be tempting to defend African-heritage people against racialized attacks by resorting to a substantive view of *imago Dei*. Although I have my own challenge with Black Theology, as discussed above, I disagree with Glen's argument largely based on my experience that humans inside and outside of faith-belonging, or particular Christian denominations and ecclesial streams, exhibit substantive essences of the *imago Dei* (Glen 2005). No one argues that one's sex, male or female, is determined by a person's relationship with God, so from a creationist perspective and without implying a literalistic or non-scientific view of creation, it is safe to say all humans are made in the image and likeness of the Creator irrespective of their faith perspective or practice. The parent–child biological tie, like the God–human tie, cannot be undone once done. Becoming a Christian, for example, involves a second birth or born-again experience but this does not undo or annul the first birth in which *imago Dei* is established.

Butler warns that it is possible to affirm the biblical record that makes the claim that human beings have been formed in the image of God, yet there can be a disconnect between the statement of the *imago Dei* and one's self-perception (Butler 2016). I believe that all Christians can take a lead in evidencing deep belief in and understanding of the validity of *imago Dei* as it applies to Black British people so that our actions demonstrate our theological understanding. Cone reminds us that an expression of the image of God in us is the liberation of knowing oneself as the creation of God, capable of living in one's power, which leads to 'a vocation to affirm who I am created to be' (Cone 1975, p. 146). Malignant others may dispute the image of God in Black people but the people should themselves demonstrate that they are in no doubt by living in their agency and self-determination in all matters that concern them. In her work on gender wholeness, Clark discusses how it is that distortions of the concept of *imago Dei*, from Western hegemonic values of beauty to patriarchal practice of gender superiority, has been used to diminish others, rather than uphold the principle that all human beings are bearers of the image of the Creator God, endowed with beauty and strength physically, emotionally, intellectually and spiritually (Clark 2018, p. 4).

Ethnic and religious identities are two major elements of the complex phenomenon that constitutes identity, along with others such as nationality and culture, but the people groups themselves have to show self-belief and not appear dependent upon the affirmation of the 'other' as a way of vouchsafing their God-given humanity. As Hopkins argues, even under the degrading and depraved white practice of enslavement, Africans held deeply to their own self-understanding and reasoning that whereas the white behaviour towards them said differently, they knew they were humans made in the image of God (Hopkins 1993, p. 37). Black British people have been on a long journey of identity recognition – always a work in progress. In recent times, Campbell-Stephens has suggested 'Global Majority' as a way of ridding the community of negative minoritizing, given that Europeans comprise approximately 15% while 'people of colour' comprise 85% of the global population (Campbell-Stephens 2021). I understand the need to avoid negative labelling, yet in the context of Britain there seems a givenness about the minority status of minority ethnic groups! This is contextual: when I am in Jamaica and the wider Caribbean, or in Nigeria and the wider Africa, I am not an ethnic minority, but very much part of the ethnic majority. Stuart Hall (2017, p. 99) suggests that 'Identities are constructed and mobilised through the shifting of signifiers in political struggle' and I argue that in diaspora people need greater surefootedness concerning their primary identity rooted in their social, spiritual and historical as well as present identity. Such strong points of reference relate to blood and belonging, geographic location, language, culture and religion (Tschuy 1997, p. xi). This includes behaviours that are passed down the generations, that may or may not be linked to state boundaries (Wallerstein 1988, pp. 71–85). In the midst of the challenges linked to identity in diaspora, we should affirm the 'autobiographical self' within a reliable framework of history, present and future, as Bell suggests (2013, p. 52). This is the self that is in sync with their full historic and contemporary identity and which as a pastor I encourage people from a similar history to mine to embrace unreservedly the melanin-skinned self as Black British as a sure way to relate to the autobiographical and authentic self in diaspora or in the homeland.

God and Nebuchadnezzar

God and Nebuchadnezzar appear in the opening verses of Jeremiah 29 as co-sovereign, having jurisdiction over the Jews in Judah/Jerusalem and in exile. Both transcend national boundaries in pursuit of their interests: God disciplines the Jews by taking or removing them from their homeland to exile in a foreign land, promising return home after a while; Nebuchadnezzar in the interest of his empire decapitates Judah's leadership as spoils of war for use as resource in Babylon. The one operates as a purifying agent for the good of the people, the other is incurably self-serving. Boer reminds us that because empires tended to suffer shortages of the labour needed to support their expansionist ambitions, deportations – not merely of the ruling classes – were common occurrences in imperial history (Boer 2018, p. 203). Not much seems to have changed when we contrast the Babylonian and the British contexts two millennia apart. Black British people's history is one of being trafficked across the Atlantic Ocean, enslaved as chattel, colonized and racialized yet pulled by powerful gravitational economic and other forces to live and work in Britain, the centre of empire.

Of course, there are stark differences between God and Nebuchadnezzar, although both are behind the exile of part of the Jewish people, with all the death and misery caused by this. On the face of it, exiling causes a loss of security and well-being; however, the Jews were already insecure in that Babylon had blockaded Jerusalem and ran Judah, rendering the country's people subjects of empire, their country a vassal state. God, however, had long had a covenant relationship with the Israelites that while regarding Jerusalem as its spiritual centre, transcending national boundaries in that wherever the people were, the jurisdiction of their God went with them. Then there is the issue of intent. Nebuchadnezzar's seems malign and self-interested, benefitting empire, whereas God's intention on the other hand seems aimed at punishment for sins committed, but as redemptive. As a lifelong Christian, I find it challenging to embrace God as administrator of corporal punishment willing to orchestrate the uprooting and exiling of people, but I am not surprised that human dictators do this. Bertocci suggests a difference between vindictive and non-vindictive punishment – the latter could apply to that perpetrated by God upon the Jews, their exile intended to teach them faithfulness to God and the imperative of administering justice to the people (Bertocci 2004, p. 29). Growing up on a former slave colony, I am familiar with the harsh beatings that were meted out to my peers by their parents (thankfully my father migrated when I was a baby) who, when in later life asked why, would tell them that it was for their good. Referred to by Mbiti as incurably religious, African people over millennia have had a sense of the divine expressed in polytheistic ways, without a covenant relationship with a deity we associate with the Jews and YHWH, leaving issues of fidelity to God/human understanding unclear for Black British and causing them to ask questions about where help comes from except from the people themselves (Mbiti 1969). Laying aside self-flagellation, Black British people can regard the challenges they face in diaspora as caused by their fellow human beings. Notwithstanding prior encounters, the European-led transatlantic slave trade began an epoch of hostile determinism that has led to where we are today with Black British people in diaspora (Thomas 1997). Once African and Caribbean peoples and countries came under the colonial rule of various European countries and their rulers, monarchs, popes and prime ministers and their powerful, wealthy sponsors – whether at home or in diaspora – the hegemonic power and control remained. Matters of who or what was responsible for removal, displacement and resettlement, and where that displacement might take them, were near redundant, as ostensibly the African seemingly had no capacity to exercise agency and self-determination over their lives. Economic and political and racialized colour coding meant the imperial power held sway. This leads inevitably, however, to a question of the role and purpose of God. Does God offer any respite to the cruelty of the life African people have come to know in the past half a millennium? In the unfolding narrative of human history and in our own experience, we do well to settle for the God we find, not the God we wish for.

As discussed elsewhere, 'Black Theology' wishes for a God who liberates 'black people' from oppression, when in reality we find this God neither in the Bible nor in lived experience. Theodicy for African-heritage people is usually linked to suffering in the transatlantic slave trade, chattel slavery, colonialism and racism and is understandably a starting point of theology done by Black people. I argue that God never stepped in to prevent the Jews from going into exile, or to liberate African people from the above atrocities, or millions from many and frequent disasters – that is the God we find. There are therefore no grounds for charging God with being a 'white racist', since it is white racists that are white racists, not God (Jones 1971).

In the Babylonian experience of the Jews, I lean towards a hermeneutic that understands Nebuchadnezzar as the actor, with the Jeremiah tradition spiritualizing the experience to include God as actor too. I therefore start my theology with African humanity rooted in the *imago Dei*, not exclusively upon African suffering and without associating such suffering with God simply because oppressors invoked the name and authority of God to legitimize their racial crimes. The God I find and experience is the accompanier/empowerer, not the determiner, with the occasional divine intervention, in pursuit of fidelity, truth and justice.

In my Pentecostal tradition much is made of God's presence in the form of the Holy Spirit, in the baptism or indwelling of the Spirit. And while there is a tendency to understand the Holy Spirit operating within the Church, there is a deeper sense of the Holy Spirit operating in the cosmos and accompanying humanity in our earthly sojourn (Vondey 2020). God helps by being alongside and within creation and humanity enabling forward progression towards liberation and flourishing, not by *doing for*. Wrongly premised faith in and about God hinders effective human dealings with the vicissitudes of life. Not only is there a danger of an inappropriate expectation of God, but Wariboko highlights that there are other powers at work in the world too, which means we need to be vigilant (Wariboko 2015). By adopting an understanding of God as an accompanier or empowerer, not as an actor in our stead, we liberate ourselves from a hesitancy to act and an expectation of intervention, and free ourselves with the knowledge that we have both responsibility and power to do the will of God. We do not wait on or for God, instead we act in God in whose image and likeness we live. Or do we expect Nebuchadnezzar to behave magnanimously toward the exile unless magnanimity serves the purpose of empire? Black British people should live in their Babylon with eyes wide open to the wiles of empire and respond accordingly, in the interest of their flourishing.

People in diaspora should remember that empires maintain their position not by obedience to a higher benevolent power in the interest of their subjects, but by dominance through the constant threat or maintenance of violence, uncertainties and vulnerabilities, and we see this in the Jeremiah narrative that depicts Nebuchadnezzar and God as willing to displace their subjects forcibly to achieve their ends (Dwyer and Nettlebeck 2017, p. 1). No amount of praying or giving or faithful adherence changes this predisposition. The Jews in exile were faced with making sense of God in their predicament under the tyranny of colonial power, and the prophet who cared enough to write to them made clear that they were there by the will of King Nebuchadnezzar of Babylon and by the will of their God, YHWH. This was a case of wall-to-wall, earth-to-heaven empire, since the same power that forcibly took them from their homeland and brought them to a place of exile, was also in control back in Judah and God was in lockstep with Nebuchadnezzar in occupation of their land and their displacement. What was more, as the earthly king pursued expansionist ambitions as explanation for his actions, God the king of the world was visiting his displeasure upon them because they had failed to dispense justice to their fellows and failed in their monogamous relationship to worship YHWH alone. God's mission of redemption was therefore by means of punishment of the exiles. If they learned lessons, repented and made amends, exile would be redemptive and they would get to return home after several generations (notionally, 70 years) better people than when they came. For now, though, the Jews had to contend with an understanding of God that demanded loyalty to him and justice towards one another, otherwise redemptive punishment in exile would be their lot.

Hill and Hill suggest that the exiled would develop a greater awareness of their identity as the chosen people of God in exile than they did before it (Hill and Hill 2016, p. 22). This highlights that for Black British people the real life prospect of what happens to a people in exile or diaspora, is that they evolve through their experience and must ensure they keep flourishing as central to their preoccupations. The God they knew was willing to co-opt Nebuchadnezzar's selfish ambition to subjugate his people, in order to bend them towards his will and purpose. We know from the biblical text that some of Jeremiah's contemporaries in the Judaic prophetic ministry wanted to sugar-coat God's intention a little by propagating a message of a short stay in exile for which God would bring them swift deliverance from their captors and they would be back in Judah in no time at all – after all, God had delivered his people miraculously before. This idea of God ignored the length of time the Israelites were under the bondage of slavery in Egypt before the great feat of deliverance by Moses, the crossing of the Red Sea, and the provision of manna in the wilderness. The oppositional prophets also ignored the presence of the same power that captured them and occupied their country. This bittersweet God who blessed and punished his people, collaborated with evil oppressive imperial rulers, promised liberation after generations of oppression and servitude was the God Jeremiah preached. Judaeans in exile knew, therefore, that God was not going to be their miraculous deliverer; they would need to help themselves to cope in adversity as they reckoned with the God they experienced, not the God of the imaginations of 'false' prophets offering quick getaways.

An understanding of God as adhering to justice principles that challenge human wisdom was as helpful in Jeremiah's time in the sixth century BC as it is in the twenty-first century AD! Cooperation between God and today's Nebuchadnezzars – the divine and human powers – is evident, as is the competition between schools of prophets offering solutions to the dilemmas faced in diaspora. As was the case then, today discernment is needed to understand in context a God whose ways do not change in the homelands or in diaspora. What might God's word be for today's Black British people? How can we tell the false prophets with their quick fixes from the true prophets who discern the times and know what the community ought to do? In the same way that we go through the day guided by what time it is set against what we need to do when, similar to the day of the week, the week of the month, the month of the year, and the four seasons, so we should be guided by what time it is in our existence in the place of diaspora. What ought this generation in this place to be doing when set in context against history and the future? And given the God we have come to know through direct experience and observation is quantitatively and qualitatively different from the God our faction of faith indoctrinates us with – if you do this as we say, God will do that – how should we live? What time is it on the clock of the God we have come to know?

I surmise that YHWH did not protect the Jewish homeland of Judah or the holy city of Jerusalem with its holy temple from being desecrated by occupation by Nebuchadnezzar's forces; nor did God step in to prevent the decapitation of the leadership by being carried away to Babylon; nor the northern territory of the ten tribes from being overrun and occupied by the Assyrians and its people evolving into Samaritans; nor the holy lands being occupied by oppositional forces including during the time of Jesus whom some hoped would set up an alternative kingdom and drive out the Romans – yet Jesus did no such thing. In my history, God did not prevent the transatlantic slave trade and the millions of my ancestors that were captured, tortured, used as chattel, dehumanized, killed, colonized, racialized; or from the centuries of social, economic and political oppression. What does all this (and much more I could list) say about the God we have come to know and, given that we believe God to be eternal, is the same God with us today?

God's identity does not change because people are in exile or diaspora. This should cause us to ask serious questions of the proponents of theologies that call us to look to God for deliverance in ways that ignore what we know about how God works. My all-time favourite theologian, James Cone (1969), who introduced me to a God in Jesus that looked like me, a dark-skinned African, does not, I have had to admit, really offer me a God who delivers from oppression. Cone offers a God who in Jesus I can identify with, because he identifies with my and my people's suffering. Some have come to see this as a form of Black nihilism since Black Theology critiques the Black condition of the oppressed, critiques the White condition of the oppressor, and aligns both with a God who sides with the oppressed and against the oppressor but leaves the status quo unchanged (unless, that is, the oppressor feels shamed into easing up a little the weight of the knee on the neck of the oppressed victim). What purpose is served by knowing that God understands my pain? What the oppressed need is not divine empathy, but deliverance and life and flourishing; and if theology is not helping that cause in practical and effective ways, that theology is not much more than a placebo, or an opiate. The concept of God that is useful to the oppressed, the exiled, the diaspora people is to understand what God is saying about the situation they are in and to help them throw the oppressor off. Where are we on that journey? What time is it on that journey of liberation? What is God's role in this? What is my role in this?

A challenge for Black British people is that no amount of singing and praying all day or all night, however disciplined or undisciplined, has made any impact to the social, economic or political situation the people find themselves in. The changes that have come have not been by divine intervention without human intervention, rather change happened when the people who believe in God understood that they have within themselves the divine image to reason, think, act, create and do so. Too much time has been and is being spent on our knees, rather than on our feet taking action in the power of God already in us. All past and current experience must be mined for lessons on how to go forward in flourishing in Babylon. Enslavement, empire, colonialism, apartheid, racism, Jim Crow laws and migration elicit different responses requiring critical theological and socio-economic and political reflection, followed by a plan to be pursued towards shalom. Discerning appropriate contextual responses require 'insights into the evil that others often overlook ... that is what creates prophets: the gift of God's grace combined with critical interpretation' (Cone 1992, p. 97).

From the transatlantic slave trade, African-heritage people outside the continent have embarked with God in mostly troubled times on an exilic journey into the unknown (Solomon 2021). A people in diaspora without a plan is like a ship loosed from its moorings sailing on an ocean without the navigational equipment to inform destination and route. The result is that it will be tossed to and fro by weather conditions and be in danger of getting lost, colliding with other ships, and it may even run aground.

Conclusion

I have been discussing four areas I believe are crucial to the construction of a philosophical-theological foundation upon which to build a flourishing diaspora life in Britain. First, that people of Black British heritage should unequivocally be reconciled with and embrace their status as a people in diaspora, having an ethnic identity that did not originate in Britain. This answers to the Jamaican colloquialism, 'me on here, but me no born here'. That historic ethnic cultural heritage therefore should be mined for material to create a flourishing life in diaspora in the ruins of the British empire and its colonies and their history in the transatlantic slave trade and chattel slavery. And yet Black British life extends beyond this sordid relationship and is rooted in the *imago Dei*. Second, I have been discussing Black British relationship with the idea of home, given a people's multiple displacement and current living in Britain as home. Until you have a home you cannot truly settle to become productive and build a present and a future. The concept of home is multifaceted, existing as a material and immaterial phenomenon. Third, I have been discussing ethnic identity and how such identity remains the same even as it changes over time. I believe that in a neo-colonial space where racialized difference plays a significant role, being assured of one's ethnic identity is not just desirable, it is crucial if you are not to be crushed by the weight of racialized difference rooted in inferiority and superiority differentiation. Key to identity in diaspora is rooting one's ultimate identity in being part of a humanity made in the image and likeness of God from whom identities flow. I conclude that Black (African-Caribbean) British is what best fits me. Fourth, I have been discussing the interplay between God and 'Nebuchadnezzar', divine and human colonizing forces and the expectation and experience of Black British people. Deep reflection is needed upon the nature of

God in diaspora as an accompanier and enabler, not a Father Christmas in the sky, but a God familiar with their troubles, aiding, discerning, emboldening, urging: 'Be brave, I am with you, always, even unto death.'

Which brings me to my final point in preparation for stepping into a plan for flourishing in diaspora (in Babylon, that is, Britain) that is, the faith concept of waiting on God. Here the thinking is that God wants us to learn to trust, rely and depend upon 'him' and will do whatever is necessary to teach us hard and necessary lessons, such as exile for the Jews. I argue that this is an unhelpful supposed coping strategy in diaspora. It suggests that God will come riding in like a knight in shining armour and slay our enemies and set us free, when, as I have been discussing, humans need to recognize God's existence as accompanier and empowerer who is ever present, or as my church mothers used to say, 'God no sleep!' So, to wait on God as though God is on a journey or distracted but can be trusted to return to your rescue, just in time as indicated by the refrain, 'God may not come when you call him but he's always right on time', is to misunderstand the nature of God and God's relationship to humanity. In diaspora, Black British people should reorientate our understanding of God, placing emphasis upon us to take control and act – not wait for God to act. This bears out my experience of an imminent God, and drives my pastoral passion to encourage my community to be more assertive, and assume more agency and self-determination in the context we find ourselves as a consequence of fate or faith, occasioned by the imperial activities of the Babylon we live in.

Questions for intergenerational discussions

- What difference is there between being in exile or diaspora?
- Can you be home and away at the same time?
- How helpful or unhelpful is it that Black British people are conscious of their African heritage?
- In what ways do Black British people's perspectives on God as liberator help or hinder?

3

Build and Settle

> Build houses and settle down; plant gardens and eat what they produce. Marry and have sons and daughters; find wives for your sons and give your daughters in marriage, so that they too may have sons and daughters. Increase in number there; do not decrease. (Jer. 29.5–6, NIV)

Introduction

The prophet Jeremiah's letter to Jewish exiles includes instructions concerning how to survive and thrive in Babylon; they are told to build houses, settle in them, plant and eat what they produce, build families and increase numerically. This represents a start to establishing them as a self-sustaining community of stakeholders in their enforced new homeland in Babylon, even though their status remained as prisoners or subjects of empire. This is not an isolationist methodology; rather, it is one that proffers a robust relationship based on empowerment and strength. My sense is that to enable them to challenge and free themselves from that status they needed to manoeuvre a shift in the power dynamics between empire and subjects of empire. This backdrop provides a rich context for possibilities for the Black British community in diaspora about how to conduct themselves. I explore ideas about some specific elements needed to help this community to flourish, that is to live optimally, in diaspora. As a prelude to discussing part of the Jeremiah plan, I want to highlight what I believe is an important theological and practical leitmotif that emerges from the letter to Jewish exiles – the imperative of agency. I have already discussed that empire's main interest is its own self-serving, and that God's providential love operates on God's timing that leaves us with divine accompaniment, and quest for liberation as a matter of human interpretation and action (Clay 2010, pp. 307–26). Finding oneself in diaspora, an adopted home from home, with a distinctive ethnicity from that of the majority, yet certain of a God-given place in the cosmos and aware for the most part nothing happens in your favour that you do not initiate and lead, the question of human agency therefore becomes of utmost importance. Flourishing does not just happen by accident or by osmosis or as an act of God, it is activated by human agency and inspired by God.

Agency

Agency is something of an interpretive insertion into these opening verses of Jeremiah 29, since the term is only implied in the letter. However, it is for me important since it seems clear that, particularly because subjects of empire are generally understood to either lack agency entirely or to be severely curtailed in their ability to direct their affairs, there is an imperative to be consciously aware of the power of their agency and to intentionally live in it. The alternative is to exist at the whim and will of empire's oppositional forces that do not have your best interest at heart. The meaning of agency can be elusive and mostly it is assumed we all know what we mean – from estate agent to human or divine agency (Weissman 2020, p. 4). Wolff refers to agency as to 'speak, act, narrate, be responsible, remember and promise' (Wolff 2021, p. 112). My main application of the word concerns the ability to act independently – although not necessarily alone – and self-determinedly, in matters concerning your best interest. The agency of Black British people in diaspora is my focus here, along with my assertion that, to flourish, this community has to do more than fit in meekly and deferentially – they must unequivocally assert their God-given agency to direct their lives and be part of the context as distinctively themselves. The exercise of agency, expressed as taking self-determining control of one's actions and outcomes in regard to opportunities and challenges, is key to establishing and retaining dignity and procuring flourishing.

I situate agency in the *imago Dei* and so regard it as integral to the makeup of human beings and recoverable if 'lost' or buried under the rubble of oppression, misinformation, or lack of self-awareness. Agency rooted in *imago Dei* endows humans with creativity and reasoning so that we initiate and create to effect change in self and surroundings. Indeed, the quest to flourish in an exilic context can only be accomplished by applying personal and group agency, never by reliance upon the malevolent other. Counterintuitively, the means for real change resides in the hands and will of those most harmed by or at risk of injustices, not in the determination of their oppressors (Miles-Tribble 2017). There is a nebulousness to agency that I seek to concretize in this book. It is mirrored well with reference to divine agency. Put simply, I take it as read that the cosmos, including humanity, is created by God as an act of divine agency which is not compromised by deliberations about whether God acts at all, within or outside the known laws of science, independent of or dependent upon use within material creation including humanity, or all or part of all of the above (Brennan 2015). For my purposes God acts in creation and imbues humanity with an image and likeness of divine agency in human agency, by which we act as individuals and have the ability to form critical mass for group well-being and as a bulwark against anti-agency forces. An effective expression of this transfer of divine agency to human agency is offered in Pentecostalism, the part of the Christian Church to which I belong, where the understanding is to exhibit confidence that God is an interventionist God through spirit-empowered human agency (Kay 2009, p. 15). The insight to look for divine agency expressed through human agency in the affairs of life is often missed when we look to the agency of the apparently powerful other, not God, or to notions of God in the clouds, not to God inside of us. For me, this has consequences beyond Pentecostalism since God blows where God wills (John 3.8).

It is possible for agency to be suppressed by a malevolent other, or neglected by the self, but never extinguished, and the ongoing awakening and fuelling of agency-consciousness is needed. The indistinguishability of agency means that irrespective of apparent human malign omnipotence, such as the power of the media, that is arrayed against a community, the 'masses' still have agency (Beckford 2014, p. 22). Were this not the case, at individual and group levels, as Wariboko warns, to be agencyless is to be zombified, to be a shell, a ghost, completely at the command of another (Wariboko 2014, p. 155). Any such possibility of zombification must be banished by Black British people. As stated above, it is possible for agency to become dormant and for docility to set in, indeed unless individuals and groups recognize the agency within and activate it, they will be at the mercy of an imperial system that is by nature oppressive and unrelenting. Black British people's flourishing is too often assumed to be in the gift of imperial forces with racism cited as the cause of ethnic disadvantage and with the reasoning that since racism is white people's doing, until they desist there is nothing Black British people can do. While agreeing that there is a universalizing impact of the idea of 'race' that contributes to inequality in the world, I fundamentally disagree with any depiction of a zombified Black British community dependent upon others to make progress (Yeboah 1997). Flourishing in diaspora does not occur by depending on 'moral suasion' by which you try to convince the oppressor of the unreasonableness and sinfulness of their racist ways in the hope and expectation that they will see the error of their ways and desist; instead, by deploying one's agency and dignified determination one can minimize oppositional forces, maximize opportunities and mobilize friends and allies (Cone 1992, p. 88). Key for Black individuals and community is how to extract what they want from 'Babylon'.

Self-determination is a necessary part of agency, not just in legal and theoretical terms in Western liberal traditions, but as a human right to exercise one's will and personal autonomy in the world in a manner that do not compromise another's human right (Foblets et al. 2018, p. ii). This makes slavery, colonialism and other forms of captivity contrary to the concept of agency. Any power that denies another human being their agency and the power to determine their will is an evil power contrary to the will of God in whose image all humanity is made. Jeffries, in studying the work of Nation of Islam Muslim African American women, found that education and the knowledge gained was the best expression of self-determination in the struggle against European hegemony (Jeffries 2014, p. 39). Without knowledge and self-awareness about one's autonomy, without the awakening that education brings, one can be sublimely unaware that one's self-determining privilege has been usurped and blissfully carry on in mental, spiritual even physical chains. The Bible teaches that those that are strong should help the weak, and this applies too to the weak from lack of insight and awareness whose chains may be invisible to them. The community therefore has a corporate responsibility for the enlightenment and freeing of all to become aware of their divinely-given privilege of determining the course of their lives. However, the poor, the weak, the oppressed should never leave their fate in the determination of the 'other' but should for their own good join with others to act for their own liberation. This principle of self-determination does not exclude God; instead without resorting to 'humanocentric theism' notions by hybridizing humanism and theism, a theology suitable for the Black British community has to emphasize human self-determination and avoid defaulting into a theodicy governed by divine determination (Walker 2004, p. 40).

Let the weak say 'I'm strong' (Joel 3), the sick should take up their bed and walk (John 5) and reject those that encourage them to become their vicarious liberators. There are occasions when by an act of self-determination some knowingly give up their right to self-determination to be part of a larger whole such as a club, a church, as part of a national democracy where if you are on the losing side the winning majority get what they determine. The volunteering of one's self-determining will by choice is quite different from having that will subordinated to some larger aim that leaves one zombified, which calls for the reassertion of one's will and self-determination by whatever means available (Getachew 2019, p. 71). These matters have import for Black British people at various levels starting at the personal autonomous to their part in national voting; at every level they should ask the question if their determination is being deployed and if not, what options do they have.

In a discourse about James Cone's construction of a Black Theological anthropology, Roberts makes some interesting observations. First, that the African American is engaged in a struggle for recognition as a human fully capable of carrying out self-determination politically, economically and intellectually. Second, that true humanity is affirmed only when people are free to be themselves – within the context of their own community – and exercise self-determination over the use of their creative energies. Third, that African American culture is an authentic expression of human flourishing and self-determination that stands against the dehumanizing effects of 'white' racism. African American folk culture – stories, song and other artistic forms – and spirituality are expressions of the Africanness constructed within Cone's theological anthropology which, I believe, capture the self-determination of the Black British community (Roberts 2014). Here I find African humanity is in the same breath denied and celebrated. Points one and two above intimate that the authenticity of African humanity is dependent upon European recognition and affirmation; yet the authenticity of African humanity is being affirmed. Both of these principles cannot exist together, and I argue that African humanity should never depend upon European affirmation for legitimacy. As previously stated, I reject the notion of *imago Dei* as an external contingency, and instead argue that it is rooted in creation and in the DNA of every human being. A theology committed to looking through the lens of experience leads us astray here if it suggests that the experience of European naming of African people is authoritative. European insistence that African is not sufficiently human should never be accepted by African heritage people who should engage with European human to human. Roberts' interpretation of Cone appears to assume that African people are fighting to persuade their European oppressor of their humanity, rather than that fighting European imperialism is conducted as humans engaged in an existential struggle of good versus evil, with righteous judgement on their side. The African struggle with European racist ideology is not to *become* someone, it is a struggle *as* someone. It is an African struggle grounded in African identity and rooted in the *imago Dei*, with agency and self-determination baked in, and out of which the fight is engaged with the usurper of African human rights. Indeed, it is not a liberation struggle on human level, as if one has imprisoned the other's humanity and it therefore needs to be freed, rather it is a human-to-human struggle against the one who seems intent on denying the other the reality and benefits of their humanity.

Again, utilizing the work of Cone, Joseph shows that his depiction of Jesus' identification with African people who have been unjustly attacked by European people provides an interpretative framework for African suffering at the hands of the unjust aggressor. This divinely assisted fight by African communities is not for recognition and acceptance of their humanity by the aggressor, but to live and to thrive, having found the ultimate ally to fight with them in Jesus who identifies in their suffering (Joseph 2019). I believe the term 'liberation' can usefully be replaced by 'flourishing' to indicate the situation we now have whereby Black British people are not held in bondage needing liberation, but within the limitations of a neo-colonial space engaged in a life struggle to flourish, but this from having realized their full humanity. To proceed theologically on the basis that African humanity is existentially determined by Europeans, betrays African humanity. Some may even be guilty of hypocrisy since I, for example, am entirely free to leave the UK to live in the Caribbean, Africa or anywhere else I choose and can gain residency access to, so can scarcely blame the UK for holding me against my will. Economic realities may be the real oppressor, and these are operated within a capitalist system which it may be argued is based on euro-American supremacy. However, that being so, the call should be for Africa and the Caribbean to set a self-determined course towards flourishing with Black British people working in support of that objective. Black British liberation begins with an understanding that Black humanity is already human and intent on living out that humanity in a self-determined way independent of the need for European saviour. To sum up, I have suggested that a precursor to applying the template for flourishing in

Babylon is clarity that a person's or group's agency, power to act in self-determining ways must be self-recognized as rooted in the *imago Dei*. Anything acquired other than through your own agency and self-determination is never truly owned and is never rent-free!

Build

Jeremiah's first instruction to the Jews in Babylon is to build! The prophet's call to build away from home in Judah, reorientates the exiles beyond enslavement status towards a more certain footing and hope in the future (Wittenberg 2002). Two basic human needs that building a house as dwelling provide are shelter and protection so that even the nomadic forest dwellers of Indonesia are known to prioritize shelter, using lean-tos, raised huts and bark houses (Schefold and Nas 2008, p. 8). Beckford highlights one of the functions of the Black church in Britain that was built by the Windrush Generation, as a place of shelter where radical transformation occurs driven by the Spirit (Beckford 2000, p. 5). The Judeans may have been involuntary migrants in Babylon, homeless and without security, but Jeremiah encourages establishing a sense of stability, permanence and independence in exile (Strine 2018). Jeremiah may have been well-connected with the Babylonian powers and his call to the Jews to build houses an attempt to demonstrate to the authorities that the new arrivals were not going to be a burden upon the state and its housing resources. Or using his influence, his may even have been a call to the Babylonian powers to provide land space for the new dwellers to build houses and live. This emphasis upon building, while not changing their designation as exiles in captivity to an imperial power, I interpret as a call to begin to exercise agency in exile. They were to replace homelessness and dependency with their own homes, replace displacement with placement, a lesson to displaced people everywhere, including in the modern world in which many are on the move whether voluntarily or by force, by political consequences or natural occurrences

(Davidson 2011, pp. 130–71). As people move, the need to build or acquire buildings becomes essential to their well-being as well as a prophetic act and statement in response to their situation.

In diaspora, a house of your own functions as an agent of life, progress and well-being. A house also provides a sense of pride and security for its occupants – even more so when you are the owner. How this house is to be secured in exile, however, is a matter of conjecture; and there may be a strong argument that the state should provide exiled people with houses. It is equally clear that hostile imperial power cannot be trusted to see to the housing needs of the exile, except for the basest of functional provisions, if any. In exile or in diaspora, Jeremiah's call is clear: build your house, and do not depend on a hostile power that builds only its interest and that of its empire. Black Theology rightly talks of working in solidarity with Black British people on the margins to transform unjust structures, of speaking truth to power (Reddie 2012, p. 60). To be of use the discipline has to embrace an understanding that because power is never given it is only ever taken, therefore the effective way to achieve 'liberation' from White oppression is less about speaking truth to power and more by demonstrating strength to power, so that power realizes it faces a force to be reckoned with. Jeremiah's instruction to build houses may lean towards capitalist thinking and self-help as opposed to a socialist-leaning Black theological fraternity that tends towards perpetual, and ultimately fruitless, negotiation with imperial power.

Jeremiah's message to build houses and occupy them did not provide the means, only the desired ends. The exiles needed to devise the means by which in a strange and alien land, among a hostile host community, they were to have a roof over their heads. I know from stories relayed to me from my parents' generation that Black people in Britain faced organized, racist and systemic obstacles to buying houses, with some estate agents willing to collaborate with some white sellers to keep prospective Black buyers out of certain areas. The challenge is how to acquire those resources including money, land, material and the goodwill of new neighbours worried that the alien community of 'empire slaves' will bring down their area and lessen the value of their properties. However they were to accomplish the task of this self-building project, the call was clear – build houses and occupy them. The home-owning enterprise in Babylon encouraged by Jeremiah was fecund with long-term prospects of a bumper harvest once they sold up to return to Judah. It is a pity the post-war Black British community arriving in Britain did not in much greater numbers take such advice as Jeremiah gave to Jewish exiles.

One of the pioneers of life in Britain after World War Two, the late Sam King, tells how it was the severe challenge, due to white racism, of Caribbean migrants finding accommodation to rent that compelled him and his friends to club together in 'pardna' – a community saving initiative, precursor to credit unions like the Pentecostal Credit Union – to raise sufficient funds for deposits to purchase their own houses in London in the 1960s (King 2004). The British Asian community have achieved a high level of home ownership, as reflected in the 2021 census. Among other initiatives, they deploy the 'Joint Family and/or community saving circle/system' called the 'committee' or in Indian/Hindi speaking, *kameti*, also known as 'gathering' in the Pakistani/Urdu speaking community, which are similar to the Jamaican pardna but significantly greater in scale, providing financial resources to acquire properties as well as being active agents pursuing their autonomous, culturally inspired economic goals (Werbner 2002, p. 15; Bowes 2023, pp. 20–22). Buying and building houses of any sort changes the dynamics between exiles and empire, not least because it provides both the solid foundation and the infrastructure that is needed for a sustained and substantive approach to flourishing, especially in diaspora with its anti-exile underbelly. Black British people need to do more than try to survive in diaspora, they need to make sure they flourish by becoming a property-owning people as a basis for building success in other areas of life such as education, business and politics. As Karl George writes about the need for robust systems of governance in the sphere of running a business, 'some only try, I make sure' (George 2003). According to a *Guardian* report, 16% of white people and 44% of Black Britons live in social housing (Mohdin and Garcia 2023). Housing is a challenge for most ethnic minority groups in the country, but the Black British cohort remains an outlier in all negative aspects of the housing sector including overcrowding, and based on the 2021 census statistics, while 61% of the overall population aged 35–49 owned their homes, comparatively, only 28% of Black British people were homeowners (https://www.financialreporter.co.uk/falling-homeownership-rates-among-ethnic-minorities-creating-two-tier-housing-system.html).

Whatever obstacles Black British people face in attempting to become home-owners, be they systemic racism in Western society, low socio-economic status or anything else, the community must apply self-determining resolutions and not rely upon help coming from elsewhere. In the past, anti-racism laws were needed, protests needed to be made, community savings schemes devised, however the community never can afford to throw their hands up and succumb to defeatism. Jeremiah yells at the Black British diaspora community, 'By whatever means necessary, build or buy houses!' This means that while acknowledging embedded racialized barriers across society, Black British people must never succumb to acceptance that these are immovable obstacles to home ownership, but commit to finding ways to overcome them and flourish. This may mean cooperating to identify and change prohibiting laws and practices and increase capital building to acquire properties.

Building extends beyond physical properties and implies establishing spiritual and philosophical accommodation for the community to inhabit. Jeremiah's concept of building to live in, points to organizations, societies and charities' metaphorical 'houses' being inhabited and operated by the diaspora themselves, not under the direct control of empire. Importantly, this includes such as building community through education and housing association provision (Kabongo 2020, pp. e1–e7). A significant achievement of the Black British community over the past century is the building of the Black church movement that has provided a space of nurture and affirmation for many including me. Far from being an 'illegitimate child of rejection' based on a common myth that the movement is built upon rejection by mainstream churches, this is part of the Church of Jesus Christ built by incoming migrants from the former colonies (Aldred 2005, p. 90). The experience of rejection in British churches in the post-World War Two era is well documented and occurred in the main within the so-called mainstream or historic churches (Barton 2005; Gordon-Carter 2003; Sealy-Skerritt 2018). Some belonging to British mainstream churches were told, 'Your people meet down the road', resulting in the new churches also rescuing those rejected (Smith 1989). These fledgling Pentecostal churches, Wood observes, 'attempted and succeeded in meeting the needs' of many new arrivals in Britain (Wood 1994, p. 8).

There are two distinct church traditions that affect Black British Christians, mainstream white and African Christian traditions, the latter with a strong overlay of Americanisms. Most Christians adopt their theological-doctrinal understandings and beliefs from the denominations and ecclesial streams they belong to. I would describe mainstream white churches as subscribing to liberal and more broadly based sources beyond *sola scriptura* whereas Black Pentecostalism for example subscribes to a kind of bibliology with significant conservative socio-cultural values. Much of Black Theology in Britain today linked to the academy is undertaken by Black theologians who belong to Western liberal churches, such as the work of Reddie. Those like me who have written theses accredited by mainstream academia also have to conform in the main to those Western values. Once no longer constrained by Western academia one is free to write yet is still tempered by Western publishers and the socio-cultural milieu in a liberal-leaning society. Black churches find themselves caught in this liberal/conservative vortex but increasingly with the skills to begin to grapple with theologizing in ways sensitive to their conservative theological values. One of the tasks of some who are part of the Black church is to engage as insiders in theological reflections and grapple with the theologies, teachings, doctrines and practices of their churches. This is an exercise in scrutinizing the 'holy grail' of those churches, some of which are headquartered in the United States and forbid tampering with established dogma. The likes of Brooks (c. 1985, c. 1970, 1982), Edwards (1992), Sturge (2005), Arnold (1992), Aldred (2005) and others have dared both to discuss and critique their traditions' doctrinal and theological positions. Sturge for example goes beyond traditional theological and doctrinal postures in dealing with the theology for and against 'prosperity gospel' while Trotman (1992) explored ecclesial identity of Black churches, and Aldred has raised questions about Black Pentecostal churches' teachings on pneumatology and other matters (Aldred 2010).

Another area that the instruction to 'build' is evident is that of theology. I regard theology as an oral or literary response by humans to lived experience in relation to God. This happens in the academy, churches and in everyday life. In academies there have been emerging theological reflections affirming the contextuality of theology, and in the case of Black Christians such theologizing happens in their worship, music, art, protest, healing, community development or social action in various forms (Gerloff 1992, p. 5). Gerloff notes that for Black churches the Bible provided the infrastructure within or upon which theology was done and that particularly in the context of Pentecostalism there was great difference between what was taught and what was done as people linked the Bible with their lived realities (p. 15), informed by a Christian experience bound up with political and economic forces across the Atlantic during the last four centuries (p. 44). Gerloff remains an example of a European academic who has sought to analyse the history, life and theological trajectories of Black British churches through the lens of African religiosity that crosses denominations and streams. Following on from Grant and Patel's call for an end to the colonial theological project of 'white interpreters of black faith' and their assertion that it is now a 'time to speak' (Grant and Patel 1990), a growing number of Black writers from within the academy have produced theological work interpreting Black British faith, with Beckford and Reddie foremost among them (e.g. Reddie 2006;

Beckford 2000). The emergence of a journal of *Black Theology in Britain* marked a turning point in academic studies of theological trajectories initially by Black British theologians (Lartey 1998; Jagessar and Reddie 2007a, b).

There are at least three distinct modes of theologizing. First there is denominational theologizing whereby Black Christians follow the beliefs and teachings of the churches they belong to. These vary along denominational lines and therefore vary widely, from liberal mainstream denominations to conservative Pentecostal churches, but what people have in common is that their beliefs run along their denominational didactic lines. A second strand of theologizing happens in the academy even as academies run along denominational lines too and can be described as liberal, centrist and conservative. A significant difference here however is that there is more critique of beliefs and difference. This has seen difference within difference as, say, in a conservative theological context the more critical engagement in a conservative academy, though attached to a church, may share divergent understandings, one by mostly uncritical acceptance of the denominational view, the other a more critical engagement with the same 'truths'. These two positions exist in parallel as the simple faith embraced in the pews rarely crosses over into the academy, and those who study in the academy leave their critical learning at the church door. Rarely, if ever do the two meet. Increasingly in this sector, liberal, centrist and conservative writers write and publish books that become available and, in some cases, clandestinely read by people – and the influence of such activity should not be underestimated. When, from the academy, Beckford wrote *Dread and Pentecostalism* (2000) and *God of the Rahtid* (2001), you would not find many Pentecostals openly reading these books. A third theological track probably influenced by both of the above is a popular practical theology in the lived experience of people attempting to follow Jesus or just trying to live independent of any denominational dictate. I quite recall my mother making Guinness punch for the family's Sunday lunch special drinks, sometimes straight after returning from church where the church rule was 'total abstinence from all liquor and strong drink'. She affirmed the teaching in the congregation and broke the rule as soon as she got home, and did this repeatedly. Another example of how these theological and doctrinal imperatives gave way to practical living based on common theological interpretations might be that most Pentecostal churches teach the tithe, yet reliable statistics say tithers amount to approximately 30% of members across the churches. And some are now refraining from attending traditional church at all and practising a non-churchgoing Christianity. This all adds up to what Hope Felder calls the 'hermeneutical dilemma' similar to that faced by Black British people as they attempt to embrace faithfulness to the God they have come to know in history and in their daily lived experiences, balanced against what their church tradition teaches, and what enlightened new insights bring (Felder 1991). Taking as instructive therefore Jeremiah's call to the exiled Jews in Babylon to build, Black British people could determine to become builders of homes to live in, education systems to enlighten, churches to spiritually nourish, and appropriate theologies to live by resulting in strength, stability and security, and to do so through their own agency.

Settle

Establishing a diasporic community as one which possesses its own 'building' is a first step in Jeremiah's plan for Jewish exiles in Babylon, a key to carving out their place in a foreign land while safeguarding their faith and identity. A second step is accepting the need to settle in diaspora since you cannot build or thrive in a swirling storm physically, mentally, spiritually or philosophically. What it means to settle can be discerned in Scripture from the use of 'to set', for example in Genesis 1.17 (cf 9.13; 18.8). The concept is to set or settle something that is unsettled, to bring stability, to organize, to prepare for next steps. To prepare the formless void of space for habitation, God set the cosmos in place (Strong 1990). Jeremiah's call to the newly arriving Jewish exiles in Babylon to settle down or inhabit the 'house' they had built, as is the case today for

Black British people, happens against 'an existential backdrop of life amid the hegemonic and oppressive power of Empire' (Miles-Tribble 2017). The adage 'rolling stones gather no moss' suggests the necessity of settling down before the creative act of building can occur. Hill and Hill observe that Jeremiah's instruction to Jewish exiles to 'settle down' is likely to have been made in the early years after their deportation from Judah to Babylon, at a time when they may have felt abandoned by God, full of grief, unsettled and with prophets among them circulating hopes of imminent return (Hill and Hill 2016, p. 26). Along with acknowledgement that their stay was going to be notionally 70, not two, years came Jeremiah's emphasis upon the need to settle into life in the land of their exile (Halvorson-Taylor 2010, p. 159).

The message to settle down was challenging not only because of the imperial context but because of prophetic disagreement within the Jewish community concerning the nature of their exilic circumstances. Some voices regarded by Jeremiah as false and oppositional, may have challenged the 'settle down' interpretation of what was needed for the exiles' well-being since they predicted this was to be only for a short duration; a controversy that would have destabilized the fragile community (Overholt 1970). Claiming prophetic authority, some were saying in effect, 'Do not bother to put down your bags because you will soon be on your way back home.' Jeremiah, on the other hand, offered the sole distant voice saying, 'This is going to be an intergenerational stay so settle down for the long haul.'

When I was young – in Jamaica and in England – a popular chorus sung in church said, 'Take a grip, my brother/sister take a grip', meaning 'Take a firm hold on your faith.' But it also reminds me of the 'grip' – the suitcase – that many travelled with when migrating to the UK. The 'grip' was small and came to symbolize the intended temporary nature of the odyssey – five years. This juxtaposition of 'grip' as holding firmly on the one hand and temporariness on the other is instructive. From my observation, many migrants were ill-prepared for a long stay in diaspora – settling down was not thought necessary for their short-stay plan that was rudely interrupted by their discovery that this is an intergenerational sojourn in Britain. Black British people have, in the Windrush era since the 1940s, been overtaken by exilic reality and may be yet to fully accept that they are part of a people in diaspora and need to face up to the unprepared-for consequences of living in 'Babylon' for the long term. Even in the third and fourth generation, settling can be problematic in terms of identity and belonging, an expression of which can be self-blame and inner uncertainties.

Cartledge shows how some African theologians rationalize the economically disadvantageous place of Black people in Africa and around the world, locating the challenges not in international, historic, scientific and economic developments rooted in capitalism and colonialism, but rather in detrimental character and cultural flaws in Black people (Cartledge and Cheetham 2012, p. 156). They believe Africa's social, economic and political ills are cultural in origin and due to persistent idolatry, witchcraft, superstition, distorted family values, tribalism, poor governance and an inferiority complex. Their remedy tends towards repentance which suggests that wealthy advanced Western countries are so because of their righteousness and peace with God in ways African people are not. This for me is a wrong and contradictory diagnosis – as is evidenced in the growth of reverse mission by which missionaries from Africa and the Caribbean believe their mission now is to preach the Christian gospel to a backslid Britain and Europe (Kwiyani 2014; Olofinjana 2017; Adedibu 2012). The power of empire to hold its subjects in its grasp should never be underestimated. For a people to flourish in diaspora therefore requires a high level of intention to settle down and resist the forces of empire and forced transplantation, and to accomplish their own aims and ambitions, rather than those of empire. Those who have borne the burden of recent racialized atrocities and as a consequence struggle to settle and be productive endure the pain migrants feel in a strange land, a pain made worse when there is hostility. For those faced with settling down in exile or diaspora Masango identifies traits like emotional and mental pain, unpleasant feeling, abuses, suffering, hurt, shock, sadness, unexpressed anger, anxiety, suicidal thoughts and shame (Masango 2019). Perplexity about whether to prepare to stay or leave, brought on by competing voices, is a natural occurrence in the exilic context, and renders settling difficult.

The challenges faced by Black economic migrants in the Windrush era – whether to go to Britain in the first place to seek a better life for themselves and their family, and once there whether to settle down or aim for a speedy return, or whether intentionally to move permanently elsewhere – can be discerned in the writings of some who lived at the time. There was active encouragement to go to Britain and make enough money to return home to make themselves and their families economically secure, at home. Echoing the thoughts of many migrants, Smith says, 'I had no intention of staying in Britain for more than five years' (Smith 1989, p. 35). This popular 'five-year syndrome' proved illusory, and soon the call to a longer stay in Britain was accompanied by the call of God to the twin task of providing shelter or pasture for wandering pilgrims buffeted by racial discrimination, allied to various absurdities of inequality and disadvantage as well as preaching the gospel to the natives. As a founding pioneer in the Black Pentecostal churches in Britain put it, 'I along with many of my compatriots came to Great Britain in search of work ... I learned about advertisements that England was in need of workers to help rebuild the bombed-out cities, towns and factories. A few opted to go. As they communicated with us in the homeland, they assured us that it was worthwhile taking the chance' (Lyseight 1995, p. 25). Arnold confirms that Britain was also understood as a 'divinely led mission field' (Arnold 1992, p. 24). As mentioned elsewhere, missiologists refer to this as reverse mission by Black British Christians to whose parents Western missionaries came to Africa and the Caribbean but who have come to Britain with their mission to evangelize the 'backslidden' country (Olofinjana 2010). This call to preach the gospel in Britain was a factor in helping some settle down; it gave them a sense of purpose beyond their own needs.

Black churches in Britain helped the settling down process by establishing regular meeting spaces, everywhere from bedrooms to church vestries, from school halls to church buildings, on Sundays and weekdays, conventions, camps, prayer meetings – meeting spiritual, physical, intellectual and social needs. Personally, arriving in the UK as a teenager and being enveloped in a Black church community then and still, has been a great source of nurturing in this racialized space. This has contributed to my development as a person, affirmed by seeing Black examples of coaches, advisers and companions on the way. In an environment which otherwise was anywhere between hostile and indifferent, many who might have run away back to their homelands stayed because there was respite from the storms of life in Britain. Like the prophets in Jeremiah's day, preachers competed with each other to provide better cultural, more theologically and ecclesially wholesome spaces. Adherents are able to identify schools of prophets akin to those in Jeremiah's day among pastors and bishops who lead a disparate loose alliance of churches and ministries in Britain. It is the case too that in the eyes of some, others have been false prophets, disagreeing about the nature of God and how the Christian life should be ordered.

We get some sense of the nature of the denominational contestations even while acknowledging that for their members their pastors and bishops are true prophets helping them to settle down in this challenging social and spiritual space into the lived experiences of their congregations, week in, week out (Aldred 1999; Tomlin 2019; Edwards 1992). In my view, no one is comparable to the status of a sixth-century Jeremiah, but there have been voices from home to the 'exiles' in diaspora. Pemberton cites a story from D. A. Samson concerning how God spoke to him in his native Antigua, instructing him to go to England to rescue 'pilgrims', that is members of the then Pilgrim Holiness Church who had travelled to Britain to seek employment, found jobs but had not found their denomination there, and were wandering in a proverbial wilderness as sheep having no shepherd. Samson duly migrated to Britain where he became founder and national leader of the Wesleyan Holiness

Church in Britain (Pemberton, Pemberton and Maxwell-Hughes 1983, cited in Aldred 2005, p. 97). And so over decades preachers have gathered in Britain under various denominations all contributing to helping Black people, especially Christians, settle down optimistically for the long haul in this foreign land. Settling down, then, is situating oneself and one's community in the exilic space in such ways that past and present realities are reckoned with and the future is seen through possibilities created by one's sense of the *imago Dei*, agency and ethnic religious identity in diaspora, and not primarily through what empire determines.

I note with surprise the manner in which during the Windrush era, colonial subjects, earlier generations of subjects and their descendants seem to take pride in referring to Britain as the 'motherland'. I am struck by the apparent lack of political awareness, lack of critique of the imperial system that was at work (Smith 1992). While this sense of going to the 'motherland' must have helped some feel less vulnerable, to settle down with dignity it is necessary to be aware of the historical and contemporary context. Instead, there appears a certain naivety that accompanied embracing Britain as 'mother', given the level of murderous abuse endured by Africans for centuries up until the present time. Absent is the political awareness concerning empire and its misuse of power to drive conformity of behaviour to its will, including the use of the church and its instruments of influence in bringing about compliance and conversion. This is particularly true of church leaders who seem to show signs of political awareness only retrospectively, subsequent to experiencing racism and the unfulfilled promise of work supposedly available to all. What history might have taught people about life in Britain based on European/African encounters in Africa and the Caribbean seemed only to become apparent in light of actual lived experience in Britain, though the historical evidence stares us in the face from generation to generation (Miles 2006, p. 34; Burrell 2011, p. 14). The failure to predict, based on the historic evidence of the transatlantic slave trade, colonialism and racism, what lay ahead in the 'motherland' left political power in the hands of empire operatives, deceiving Africans into believing either that there was no history or that what there may be was benign. The lack of a Jeremiah figure to orchestrate group awareness and response to empire has left the Black British people in diaspora wanting. Successful settling down requires knowledge and understanding of the nature of the space being occupied since in so doing the exile cannot afford to be ignorant of the devices of imperial operatives.

It would be wrong to suppose that only diaspora Africans experience unsettledness as a result of centuries of racialized and economic antagonisms; we know that the Africans who remained on the continent and were not deported, unlike their parents or ancestors, underwent disruption of their homelands by, for example, the re-drawing of Africa according to the European will (Aldrich and Stucki 2023, p. 346). Prior to that time, the African continent, like other areas, endured turbulent social, economic and political instability. It is clear that the historical roots of present stubborn African underdevelopment is linked to deep-rooted systemic international trade in people and goods initiated by Arabs in the fifteenth century, followed by the Portuguese and other Western countries, including Britain, since the nineteenth century (Alpers 1975). I live in Britain now, but when I was born in Jamaica the island was a British colony, and even after its independence the British monarch remained as head of state with all the subjection implications of that arrangement. What did it matter whether I lived in Jamaica or in England? I was separated from family and friends who migrated out of necessity while I lived in Jamaica, and once in England I was separated from those I left behind in Jamaica and who lived in other parts of the world. Citizens in a British colony are subjects of the colonizer, irrespective of where in the empire they live, and settling down to flourish is a challenge everywhere in the shadow of empire. Mdingi shows how in 1960s USA, arms of state like the Federal Bureau of Investigation (FBI) allegedly operated in ways that sought to oppress and repress African American subversive militant groups, intent on destabilizing and antagonizing them to prevent the emergence of messianic figures that might unify and electrify them, thereby leveraging effective resistance (Mdingi 2022). A people under imperial surveillance therefore should beware that their need to settle down is in order to work out their liberative aims, carving out an alternative ontological existence, and not to appease empire.

In settling down, diasporic people often face paradoxes, the equivalent of squaring circles, or in religious thinking making the impossible possible; what van Wyk refers to as denoting categories that supposedly cannot co-exist, the apparently contradictory yet interrelated (van Wyk 2019). The antidote concerns getting rid of binary thinking, away from either/or to both/and, since binary thinking can lead to unnecessary and unhelpful polarization. Settling down in exile can seem an oxymoron yet need not be so. Settling down in exile need not imply falling in, compliance, submission or assimilation. Here, settling down points to situating oneself in a manner that prepares for a challenging present and future even in a hostile context made possible by inner attributes implicit in the *imago Dei* with moral reasoning, creativity, dignity and self-determination. As Caribbean people in the Windrush post-World War Two era had a plan to spend five years in Britain, making as much money as possible, and return to the Caribbean, so some people from Africa came to Britain to get a Western education before returning home to situate themselves well back at home, Western education being highly valued there. However, because these intended achievements take much longer than many think, settling down for longer periods than intended often becomes necessary to achieving the intended outcome.

Settling down in exile, though necessary to accomplish one's mission, can also pose a threat to one's judgement of when or whether to leave; and we note that when '70 years' were complete, many Jews were so settled in exile they did not return to Judah, preferring to remain Jews in diaspora. They lost the will to protect themselves from Babylonian culture, intermarrying with the people of the land to which they had now come (Hinson 1990, p. 150). Over time, some of the exiles lapsed in the practice of their religion, adopted Babylonian religious-cultural practices, and, we might assume, passed theirs to the

Babylonian people (Ackroyd 1968, p. 41). Settling down therefore is a complex call, but as a sense of stabilizing the self and community, putting down roots sufficient to bear fruit, it is a necessary act while maintaining self-awareness of who and where you are and assessing what tools you have to accomplish your mission.

As Hall reminds us, it is important from a pastoral theological point of view to recognize that Black Britons are complex and multiple communities with different experiences (Hall 2017, p. 164). This means that settling down may mean different things and situating the self and the community requires getting involved, contributing to and bringing their particular qualities to all aspects of life in Britain. Even so, the Black British person or community being settled should never lose sight of and links with their corporate history, never allowing themselves to forget that living in Britain is tantamount to living in 'Babylon', in exile, in diaspora with an imperial influence particularly over those and their descendants whom were previously ruled by them. And if the Black British are to impose their identity and presence with integrity it is important to know and be at peace with their complex multifaceted persona. Settling down will include being in solidarity with others of the group in order to represent a self-supporting block in the spheres of social, economic, political and environmental affairs. Settling down means a focused dedication not so much to integrate (certainly not assimilate) as contribute from within British society even as they consider how and what they may contribute to those people, areas and countries from which they hail. 'Settle down' implies physical, philosophical and spiritual single-minded acts of solidarity towards self and other. I agree with Niemandt who, from the contested land of Southern Africa, reminds us that identity and destiny are core facets in a theology of the land (Niemandt 2019). 'Settle down' means not waiting to be invited into society but assumptively taking a seat around the table of life considering all conceivable levels and spaces of society approachable, accessible and habitable. Such a single-minded approach to life is the opposite to some Black British people saying, 'They don't accept me as British, so I am not.' I say, if they lock you out of their circle, create your own, or if they won't allow you around their table, get your own; as humanity we live in a shared space. This assumptive approach is not based merely on responding, but on proactively creating, doing and being, never conceding that any space or any table belongs to any one person or group, and that the occupants have right of veto. Instead, the assumption is that as a child of God made in the divine image with agency and self-determination, nowhere is off limits and nowhere inaccessible based on race, colour or creed. Settling down assumes this right. It says 'here is the Promised Land and I am taking it, sharing it. I am not asking for acceptance or permission.' Until a people build and settle, physically and spiritually, they will not be in their best state to advance the cause of their own flourishing and to make their contributions to wider society.

Plant and eat what you plant

As 'build' and 'settle' encourage the exiles to deal well with their stake-holding self-assertion, so 'plant and eat' encourages them towards provision and nourishment. Wirzba emphasizes the significance of eating by reminding us that it is the daily confirmation that we are always already in relation with others (Wirzba 2019). It is also significant that the source of your food is secure and reliable. Jesus' teaching in prayer, 'give us this day our daily bread', may be seen as a passive expectation of delivery parcels from on high, but I prefer to see this as a divine invocation to us to roll up our sleeves, gather material and tools and with the help of the Almighty who gives life and increase to what we plant and tend, engage in food production activities with each other (Matt. 6.11). In a critique of the parables of Jesus, Van Eck and Mashinini highlight that food security carries broader social implications, including personal dignity, the ability to openly associate with others and a loss of self-identity (Van Eck and Mashinini 2015). Because eating is such an emotive issue, with stigma attached for the have-nots, it is little wonder the Bible prioritizes the vulnerable and there is the example of the first-century Church moving to swiftly resolve a situation of inequality in their communal food administration (Acts 6).

Green says that for the exiles, simply being in Babylon was not all, since unless they found ways to resist imperial forces, they would likely be trodden upon further by it (Green 2013, p. 113). The prophet's call to become self-supporting in their food supply strengthens further their status on foreign soil, having already been told to build and settle. Having found territory on which to build and settle, the foreign 'slaves' needed the same ingenuity to acquire farmland, which may have been the same place if we assume present-day kibbutz in Israel. Nebuchadnezzar may have reckoned that by making land available to the exiles for living and agriculture he would have a self-sustaining band of workers in his empire; the exiles in return got the freedom they needed to exercise their agency in ways that provided a bulwark oppositional to empire. Even in exile under exploitative captors, the captives need room to negotiate, impose themselves upon their captors, however submerged under self-interest and indifference to them they may have been. While the ultimate aim of the exiles was freedom, Jeremiah's letter shows how to live in freedom now even as they moved towards a return 'home'. Babylon would not have to be laden with finding them shelter or food from government reserves because they would have enabled a self-sustaining exilic community. Later in their stay in Babylon, Daniel and his peers demonstrated an example of the sanctity of food when they refused to eat that prepared by the royal kitchen, preferring vegetables (Dan. 1), no doubt aware of their high nutritional value (Shemesh 2018). The exiles are affirmed in their humanity and dignity in that they are self-supporting and do not have to beg or depend upon state handouts from the very enemy forces responsible for their plight. And to the exiles the message again is clear: don't go into depression and resentment, distress or helplessness mode in your 'captivity'. No time for a 'poor me' pity party since oppressors do not attend them, rather the exile must use their righteous anger to plan towards flourishing now and in the ages to come.

Jeremiah's letter addressed an agrarian society, while the Black British's context is a more industrial, urban-centred one and so the Black British community will need to translate 'plant gardens' into finding the means by which it can be self-sustaining in terms of food, clothing, shelter and the creature comforts a people need. But we shouldn't just read 'plant' figuratively. I was born and raised on a half-acre of rural land which produced much of the food the family ate all year round. I have vivid memories of our mother planting seeds that would soon produce food, and caring for trees that produced their fruits seasonally. My family lived off the land to a great extent where I grew up, which taught me lessons in how to be self-sufficient. Now in retirement, my wife and I cultivate the verges of our back garden and two small greenhouses to grow healthy organic foods such as runner beans, dwarf peas, cauliflower, cabbage, spinach, peppers, tomatoes, white and red potatoes, figs, pak choi, french thyme, beetroot and health-enhancing plants like bay and eucalyptus. (I hasten to add that in this farming endeavour I am the labouring assistant.) When I was a local church pastor, there were many occasions when after the Sunday morning service, a brother would say, 'Pastor, please give me your car key.' I learned soon to just hand over the key, and sure enough, once home, I would find in the car boot groceries grown on their allotment. The Anglo-Saxon/ medieval Europe-wide practice of cultivating slabs of land has been taken up by many Black British men and women who have continued this practice of small-holding organic farming from the agrarian communities many originated from (Nilsen 2014). And of course, the Black farmer Wilfred Emmanuel-Jones, with a national profile, has encouraged others into farming (www.theblackfarmer.com). So even in a developed, industrialized and scientific context, 'plant and eat' is not necessarily a thing of the past. The communities I have been part of in Britain understand a link between the earth God created and its potential to sustain humanity, when we are prepared to work it. There is evidence that 'peasant societies' in the Caribbean and elsewhere have long embraced resilience and self-sufficiency, and although spatially circumscribed, they seek to create their own world within but beyond hegemonic contexts (Carnegie 1987). To make demands effective on the imperial system the Black British community should possess the means by self-help to exert irresistible pressure, or they will scream louder and louder and get less and less in return. Of course, localized self-help initiatives do not replace the need for structural macro, social, economic and political engagement with 'empire'; rather, the same spirit of agency and self-determination must be applied at all levels.

Growing your garden to eat from it applies conceptually and metaphorically too. Materiality and spirituality have a clear relational existence and I want to borrow from African and Pentecostal spirituality the notion advanced by Adamo that pursuing abundance is answering to the will of God for human flourishing (Adamo 2021). For example, 'education feeds the mind' and 'you are what you read' are commonly known assumptions. We now know that during the 1970s Black British children were intentionally or unintentionally typecast as educationally subnormal by the British educational system, fed a diet of no or low expectation, and received culturally inappropriate education particularly concerning the treatment of African history. Wallace argues this may still be the case decades later in spite of many public policy reports purporting to address longstanding discriminatory dynamics that shaped educational experiences of the Black British pupils. Yet it appears 'the principal challenge of providing equitable opportunities for Black pupils remains largely under-addressed in schooling' (Wallace and Joseph-Salisbury 2022). Growing intellectual spaces to feed self and community are part of the call to grow and eat in diaspora as at home. There has been, it can be argued, too much dependence upon the food of empire, so that the diaspora community do not have intellectual security in terms of an appropriate education system that feeds the mind of Black British people concerning their past history, their humanity, their infinite ability as human made in the image of God with agency endowed by God (see for example the daily history reading of 'The Black presence in history' by Hudson 2021).

There is an ongoing conversation about teaching Black History in British schools in terms of scope, where it is taught at all. In part there is a reasonable expectation that a national school system will develop a curriculum for everyone in a diverse society. This has clearly not been the case in Britain – unsurprisingly since the dominant culture tailors its education programme for its majority needs and perspectives. Andrews' work shows that from racist inequality that affected the education achievements of Black British children, a supplementary school movement emerged, delivering what these children were missing due to the inadequacies in the education system as it related to them, and also providing what was missing such as a focus on African centredness (Andrews 2013). In my view, minority groups will never have their niche needs met sufficiently, and should always provide supplementary education within their group, in the same way as education about the family has to be taught at home. The Black population does not need to feign surprise that this is the case but can do at least two creative things while leveraging pressure on the national system to deliver better for Black children and young people. First the Black British community should recognize that education of their children is first and foremost their responsibility and create their own supplementary education for the areas that mainstream education lack; teach it at home and in supplementary schools in the same way as other 'minority' communities such as the Jewish and Muslim communities. Second, the Black British community should use their organized weight of presence socially, economically and politically to put consistent pressure on the British education system to evolve the national curriculum to become more inclusive, drawing where necessary on lessons from the priorities and methodologies of the Black British supplementary education programme. Writers already have indicated how this can be done: Sewell (2009) looks beyond the realistic claim and experience that racism is responsible for low Black British pupil attainment at school, and explores the complexities surrounding masculinities; Byfield (2008) explores how social and spiritual capital can contribute to Black British boys succeeding in education;

and Channer (1995) focuses on Black British children's success rather than failure, achievement rather that underachievement as well as highlighting how the Black British churches act as fertile ground in the education process. The issue here is clear that in diaspora discrete communities assume prime responsibility for feeding the body and the mind of their community assured that the imperial mainstream will never be adequate, even as they apply pressure on the mainstream to do better. Education that feeds the mind and character is too important to leave it either to chance or in the hands of others.

In 1996, I was appointed director of the Centre for Black and White Christian Partnership, a small intercultural ecumenical organization that ran a Certificate in Theology course, for which I as director was administratively and academically responsible. The University of Birmingham accredited the course. The majority of the students on the course were Black British with a sprinkling of white British. It soon dawned on me that the Black British students had next to no literary resources in the form of textbooks by writers of their ethnic origin. There were ample European and American resources. This was a classic example of not eating what you plant, but instead eating what other people planted for other people. This deficit led to the Centre developing initiatives under my leadership to encourage home-grown writers. Significantly, in 1998 there was the launch of *Black Theology: A Journal of Contextual Praxis*, which was eventually relaunched as *Black Theology: An International Journal*. I edited three multi-authored books, *Preaching with Power* (1999), *Sisters with Power* (2000) and *Praying with Power* (2000). These were part of a campaign to encourage Black British Christians to write, which along with the encouragement and activities by others led to a proliferation of publications from within the Black community – real cases of 'plant to eat'.

The maxim 'we are what we eat' is an excellent way of highlighting the significance of healthy eating. Who controls your food chain controls the health and well-being of those who eat from the source. This is the case literally and metaphorically. Allow me to share two anecdotes. First, during the Covid-19 pandemic we learned that Black British people were among the most susceptible communities to fall ill and die from the virus. This had little or nothing to do with the myelinated pigmentation of African people; rather, they disproportionately live and work in ways that increase the risk of catching Covid-19, and they disproportionately suffer from comorbidities including diabetes. In the United States, the UK and around the world inequalities in health outcomes during the Covid-19 pandemic were observed, but everyone had to make it a priority to protect themselves (Hass 2021). This health risk linked to diet played a significant part in the Black British community suffering disproportionately from Covid-19. However, rather than taking responsibility for their plight, some campaigners resorted to highlighting racism as the reason for this disproportionality. Indeed, racism existing as it does institutionally in the fabric of Western society means there is almost always an element of it behind statistics affecting this community. But the community is not without agency and should never be portrayed as helpless or hapless. The Black British community might take eating healthier very seriously, which does not necessarily imply spending more. Recent data from the government's ethnicity facts and figures website says while the overall obesity is 63%, among Black British it is 72% (https://www.ethnicity-facts-figures.service.gov.uk/). Eating healthily and exercising more are two simple habits promoted by Tony Kelly, a diabetes control champion, as a significant way to control Type 2 diabetes and for general well-being. Controlling what the community eat is well within the power of Black British people (see Jones 2020).

On a personal note, I was having difficulties with stomach cramps and was referred for several tests, all negative. At length I discovered quite by accident that my problems were being caused by lactose intolerance – my system was not digesting dairy products such as milk and butter. Since going dairy free my stomach health has been transformed. My consultant was surprised and signed me off, while my GP practice remained reluctant to spend NHS money for me to get an allergy test. Yet my self-discovery has saved the NHS lots of money by stopping the tests and saved me much stomach discomfort. We are indeed what we eat, and the Black British community should take responsibility for what they eat and how much they exercise as a way of exercising agency, and refusing to be manipulated by those who want to detract from personal and community responsibility because their primary aim is to point a finger at the racist state, to which some look also for funding to run their not-for-profit community initiatives. Saying that the West is institutionally racist is to state the blindingly obvious, and moves Black British people nowhere forwards towards flourishing unless such pronouncements are accompanied by agency-driven action. As a minister I have been saying to congregations in Pentecostal churches to temper the practice of inviting worshippers to come forward for prayer for healing, knowing many of the illnesses being prayed over stem from poor diet and sedentary lifestyles. To eat wantonly and not exercise and then come to God to ask for healing for resultant ill-health is irresponsible and an affront to the Creator in whose image Black British people are made.

Pentecostalism's embrace of the availability of 'healing in the atonement' is rooted in their heritage from a Western holiness church movement, evident in the United States with its 'eager expectation of the miraculous'. It is mostly unhelpful, and here I am less interested in the premise for such healings and more interested in the negative attitudes it breeds towards healthy lifestyles (Hejzlar 2010, p. 4). As mentioned elsewhere, the Black British community can do much more to eat healthier self-grown organic vegetables; and need to be more self-determined in their provision and consumption based upon what the community plant literally and metaphorically. This can be done while still seeking timely medical help, and while also having a wholesome attitude towards God's healing powers that are simultaneously preventative and miraculous. Churches that serve the Black British community and do not promote a healthy lifestyle through diet and physical exercise are a major part of the problem of the disproportionate ill-health suffered by this community. This emphasis on 'healing provided in the atonement', mentioned above, is problematic given that the esteem in which spiritual leaders are held means followers tend to pattern their lifestyles on the practices of their church.

While Pentecostal churches in the Black British community have cases to answer for under-emphasizing healthy eating and over-emphasizing divine healing, one church in particular that promotes health and well-being is the Seventh Day Adventists, based on the consumption laws of the Christian Old Testament (Lestar 2022; Sánchez et al. 2016). Often this comes with a leaning towards vegetarianism or veganism which may be fine for some but not for others, including me. Eating healthily and exercising is not synonymous with becoming a vegan or vegetarian. Choice should still be highly regarded – for example, I follow a dairy-free diet but I am neither vegan nor vegetarian. Those churches however that prioritize divine healing over preventative health practice are doing a disservice to their members. This emphasis on healing gets more problematic given the tendency by some preachers to associate financial giving with healing. And it is noticeable that the same individuals return time after time for laying on of hands and anointing with oil because they do not receive the healing they seek and are promised is available through the atoning death and resurrection of Jesus. I have called this the sin of simony (Aldred 2013, p. 179). Here also lies a religious philosophy of 'prosperity gospel' based on sowing and reaping (the more you sow, the more you reap). The more acute the illness the bigger the offering seed needed. Some have been known to discourage taking up the service of the NHS, in favour of just depending on God (with the preacher as a proxy for God's healing power). By de-emphasizing healthy lifestyle through diet and physical exercise and regular check-ups the way is cleared for dependence solely upon the preacher with the healing ministry and churches that deploy similar practice. Jeremiah's call to 'plant and eat' is a call to consider healthy eating which reduces the need for reliance on often bogus 'name it and claim it' preachers or churches with usually unfulfilled promise of healing, but with an inescapable financial bill, seed that rarely bears the fruit promised (Sturge 2019, pp. 179–96).

To practise the self-sufficiency implied in 'plant and eat', is not to neglect macro socio-political action by engaging with the state and other powers. It is not either/or, it is both/and.

Cummings and Beard (2021) remind us that even though democracy ought to deliver fairness and equity for all, to get your share requires a strong support system and fiery self-discipline. Since the structures in an imperial situation like Britain were established with the interests of the majority population in mind, the Black British community should aim to care for itself, especially those within the community who are needy and less fortunate, while strategizing how to get a bigger slice of the public cake by political action and spiritual resolve. Getting their share of public services is a form of 'plant and eat' philosophy since they have contributed through taxes to the public purse that make such provision. Access to mainstream resources coupled with self-provision leads to the exilic community prospering in a manner unlikely to succeed by looking to external forces alone or even primarily. Self-sufficiency is a model for those made in the divine image and likeness. In multiple ways, therefore, the call to plant and eat what you plant needs to be taken seriously and implemented by Black British people leading to a healthier community in mind and body, clearer about maximizing take-up of national resources and the interface between that and discreet provision. Success in life depends, as I have mentioned elsewhere in this book, on strength, not weakness, so to get what we want requires strength and sometimes cunning and resilience.

Increase, do not decrease

Finally in this chapter, I briefly explore Jeremiah's call to increase and not decrease. The prophet's purpose is the 'flourishing' of the exiles in Babylon, and I read his urgent call for growth through those lenses. Imperial forces had deported a relatively small cohort of the Judean leadership and they were an ethnic minority in a foreign land. Growing made the Jewish exiles less likely to be ignored and blown away by the ill-wind of adversity in Babylon occasioned by a paperweight community, socially, economically and politically. Jeremiah instructs, advises, encourages, 'increase, do not decrease'. I acknowledge elsewhere the way the Jeremiah text emerges from an imperial and patriarchal epoch when women were legally the property of their father or husband, therefore twice property, of empire and of their father or husband. In borrowing the instruction to increase by having children and giving them in marriage, I am cognizant that this had very different implications for girls and women than for boys and men. It was women that were given in marriage in a transaction between parents for the transfer of ownership of the girl or woman to sons. The areas of feminist and womanist studies have successfully highlighted women's experience in light of scriptural and theological praxis (Grant 1989; hooks 1993; Hayes 1996). In this book, increasing family and community is what is at stake, by non-oppressive and ethical relationships that provide justice for all. The call to today's small Black British community is to grow in numbers to the optimal possible by biological and/or migration means.

Currently the Black British community stands at approximately 4%, or two million, with African British outnumbering Caribbean British almost two to one, which is not surprising given the population size of Africa compared to the English-speaking Caribbean and South America. These two main blocks are also not a cohesive whole in Britain or elsewhere but are represented by significant diversity, some of that oppositional. In the Caribbean British community there is inherited inter-island rivalry, and among African British there are east–west as well as north–south African dynamics at work, all of which have their roots in the divisiveness of the imperial powers of European colonizers, including Britain. There is African British versus Caribbean British rivalry, some of it based on a tendency among African British to be better educated than Caribbean British, and some Caribbean British people hold the African British community responsible, as descendants of the Africans who betrayed their ancestors, for selling them to European slave traders. Were Black British people to work together cohesively in spite of their challenges they would represent a critical mass of two million that could not be ignored in any sector, religious, cultural, social, economic, environmental or political. Were the Black British community to take seriously

Jeremiah's call to increase and not decrease numerically as well as in property ownership, in income generation and other sectors of life in Britain, Babylon would soon feel the weight of that presence, realize that this community is clear about its identity, its values, its history and culture that is lived out in its midst in ways that contribute to, not put a drain on, the state. For example, were the thriving African British and Caribbean British churches to join forces rather than operate along continental, nationalistic and denominational contours, their impact upon the British Christian landscape could be significant (Olofinjana 2010, p. 53). The Bible helps us understand increased presence in some key ways. This does not always concern numerical superiority – indeed, at times it might mean the opposite – but it does mean a sense of cooperation, and presence of the divine. So, one chases 1,000, and two put 10,000 to flight (Deut. 32.30); and around the throne of God in heaven there is an innumerable crowd of all peoples (Rev. 7.9).

To settle, build and grow requires a focus on self, community and other. Ironically, by building strength in the place of adversity, empire realizes that it has to do business even with those it has exiled. Empire is based on power, recognizes competing power, and will always bargain where it appears an opposing power threatens its dominance, in the interest of empire. I have witnessed how in the face of the growth of Black churches in Britain, a group initially looked down upon and called cults have become sought-after partners by the mainstream churches (Aldred 2005; Sturge 2005). The exiles have to exercise the same instincts of self-preservation and the Black British community will do well to address issues of bulking up in all aspects of its life in this UK diaspora. 'Increase, do not decrease' is a political statement, since politics is about numbers utilizing their weight to negotiate their interests to the fore. The warning not to decrease doubly emphasizes the danger of remaining small, insignificant, not taken seriously as a partner, or threat. The organization Operation Black Vote (https://www.obv.org.uk/) emphasizes the importance of Black British people exercising their franchise to turn out to vote en masse in elections, as well as participating in all other facets of Britain's civic and political system. At times OBV has highlighted that were the community to vote en bloc it could hold the balance of power that could determine which candidates win or lose (Woolley 2022). There is urgent need for the Black British community to take seriously the power of numerical, political, spiritual and every other weight of presence by seeking to increase and not decrease.

Finally, a dimension to increasing not yet fully realized by the Black British community is networking with African heritage people across the diaspora and utilizing the synergy of Pan-Africanism, something long advocated by the likes of DuBois, Blyden (Lynch 1967) and Garvey (Jacques-Garvey 1977). By 2023 the population of the African continent was about 1.4 trillion people, the Caribbean about 50 million, and Black British people would do well to consider themselves an extension of these populations. Similarly, were Black churches to develop non-colonial forms of partnerships with churches in Africa and the Caribbean across denominations and denominationally-aligned this would increase their strength of presence economically, theologically and politically. Currently, some of the alliances that exist are neo-colonial with power of determinations usually within European-USA headquarters. With or without these anomalies, partnerships could rally international support for mutual benefit and to influence the wider contexts in which both secular and religious communities exist. For example, liaison between Black British people and, say, Nigerians and Jamaicans in secular or religious endeavours could create synergy greater than the sum of their parts. African, Caribbean and British people with heritages from those regions could lobby together to put pressure on whichever authorities they needed to force issues with. Religious leaders abroad could solicit support from religious leaders in Britain, and vice versa. In these and myriad other ways numerical increases could lead to weight of presence that ensure attention. And as has been mentioned, corporate political action in Britain could impact those who desire the votes or following available in the Black British community. 'Increase, do not decrease' is an economic statement and suggests the Black

British community should find ways to increase exponentially its economic base. 'Increase, do not decrease' is an environmental statement that pushes the Black British community to consider that the earth which scripture says is the Lord's and humanity its caretakers, its stewards, is under threat from what is called generally manmade climate change. Jeremiah's call to increase and not decrease reminds the Black British community that solidarity with one another matters, that division is unhelpful, even sinful, that numbers matter and especially when a community starts from a small base it should do all in its power to grow to exert social, spiritual, political and economic weight of presence in elections and in representations across society.

Conclusion

I have discussed in this chapter the importance of agency, build, settle, plant and eat, and 'increase and do not decrease', all contributing to Black British people deploying their agency and self-determining presence. This marks a significant section of Jeremiah's letter to Jewish exiles which today's Black British people can use as a template for responding to their diasporic life and intent to flourish. Black British people are being prompted to pursue self-sufficiency as stakeholders at the centre of the historic and contemporary empire that Britain is.

Questions for intergenerational discussions

- What do you understand by 'agency' and how might it work in exilic society?
- What might greater property ownership mean for the Black British people as stakeholders in society?
- In what ways might the Black British community work at being more self-reliant as well as securing what mainstream services have to offer?
- In what ways might the Black British community exert more influence in Britain, the Caribbean and Africa?

4

Peace and Prosperity

> Also, seek the peace and prosperity of the city to which I have carried you into exile. Pray to the LORD for it, because if it prospers, you too will prosper (Jer. 29.7, NIV).

Introduction

Jeremiah's letter to Jewish exiles continues in what appears to me a counterintuitive and controversial manner. The idea that the exiles should seek the peace and prosperity of the oppressive Babylonian power holding them captives against their will, seems frankly absurd. And for Jeremiah to suggest it, seems outrageously sympathetic to hostile enemy forces, tying the fate of the oppressed and oppressor together. The prophet goes even further, telling the exiles to put Babylon on their prayer list since this now is their home too. For this same reason the exiles are to seek the welfare of Babylon into which God has brought them as part punishment and part redemption. If the city where they are prospers, they prosper, and conversely, if it fails, they fail. It seems that even in this tough oppositional situation with differences polarized and seemingly irreconcilable, God's desire for humanity is *shalom*, meaning peace and prosperity (Barber 2016, p. 21).

This interesting dialectical, espoused by Jeremiah from the relative safety of Jerusalem, which was itself under imperial rule, can speak to Black British people today. It challenges the conceptual reasoning of a diaspora community to take to heart the place they find themselves though neither to the abandoning of ancestral belongings, or uncritically given the historic exploitation and oppression orchestrated from Britain upon African-descended people in Africa, the Americas, the Caribbean and in Britain. Black British people are being called upon to respond in our racially, socially, politically and economically hostile shared space into which fate has brought us, by acting out of our sense of human integrity and ingenuity to find common ground with descendants of our ancestors' captors, in our own interest rather than lashing out in uncontrolled anger. This now becomes a space to shape a future together and to contribute towards mutual prosperity, or share in mutual suffering. Vicariously, the prophetic voices of their ancestors and the God inside of them call upon Black British people to take a lead in a foreign land under racialized duress because interwoven welfares call for interwoven praxis.

I am interested in the use of liberative tools such as the awareness of God-created humanity, agency and self-determinative intention to deal wisely with oppositional forces for the common good. Ways forward have to be found to do so without compromising their humanity in the midst of those who already take their superiority for granted. To create a better world, we sometimes have to work with powers and people, some of whom we consider or who consider themselves our enemies (Kahane 2017). The Jeremiah text calling on exiles to seek peace and prosperity, praying for the hostile place and pointing out the interwovenness of all in the space, offers some useful hooks that inform the basis of the discussion that follows, taking further practical and prophetic steps to secure Black British flourishing.

Seek peace and prosperity

From its Greek origin, the theological/biblical meaning of peace is much more than the absence of war and speaks of a state of well-being as implied in the term '*shalom*'. Prosperity means to thrive, to flourish, to succeed. This is a much more ambitious term than is supposed in the so-called prosperity gospel that presumptively assumes financial abundance and perpetual good health (Attanasi and Yong 2012). Shalom signifies wholeness of life that all of us desire for ourselves and for those we love

– which should be all humanity. In a study that uses shalom as an interpretative lens through which to examine the outcome of Pentecostal conversion as a state of being that God originally intended for humanity, Grace Milton links shalom to peace as restoration to wholeness (Milton 2015, p. 198). Peace and prosperity is what we wish one another in greetings and is what is implied by 'Dear friend, I pray that you may enjoy good health and that all may go well with you, even as your soul is getting along well' (3 John 12). Peace and prosperity are interwoven in shalom and as Jeremiah told exiled Jews to seek it in their new hostile home, so Black British people are encouraged here to seek it in Britain.

I believe the basis upon which Black British people seek peace and prosperity begins with an understanding of a shared destiny for all humanity whereby the self-sustaining image of God in humanity expresses itself at individual and corporate levels. It is important too to acknowledge that Christian teaching emphasizes peace not as an inevitability in God's time, but as something desired by God to be sought after and made by human goodwill and effort. This sentiment is echoed in the words of Jesus, 'blessed are the peacemakers' (Matt. 5.9), as in our Jeremiah text, 'seek peace and prosperity'. Much more than wishing is required to seek or make peace accompanied by prosperity, however, and the pronouncement of blessing – happiness – upon the peacemaker highlights the value placed upon peace itself, achievable through ingenuity and dedicated work. This can be taken as encouragement to engage in the act of peacemaking and a pointer to the state of happiness when it is achieved. The concept of making anything strongly suggests innovation, identifying and accompanied by marshalling resources, applying oneself to the hard work required to make it. Seeking peace, as Jeremiah instructs Jewish exiles, has to be accompanied by making peace in order to usher in prosperity. To achieve the just and peaceful world we seek, the momentum of unjust and unpeaceful oppositional forces must be met with equal and opposite forces through policies, structures and the courageous acts and voices of many (Castillo et al. 2022). Self-evidently, peace does not just happen; even when we say 'peace has broken out' between warring factions, a process can be identified that led to that outbreak. Attaining peace is a challenge that takes humanity beyond the cessation of war, important as that is, to a place of human well-being and flourishing.

In an article that highlights a poetic tribute, 'an elegy for Martin Luther King', by former president of Senegal, Leopold Sedar Senghor, Spleth correlates the African statesman and the American civil rights leader and their pronouncements about the search for justice, reconciliation and harmony for people in oppressive conditions. For me this contextualizes King's assertion that 'the arc of the moral universe bends towards justice' and his 'I have a dream' speech, pointing away from some kind of divine inevitability and towards tacit acknowledgement that in all situations the desire for justice and peace is fulfilled by conscious and determined engagement in actions that bring it about. And this is so for colonized peoples everywhere, including in the Caribbean and on the African continent in their struggles for independence and the African American's quest for civil rights (Spleth 2017). To pursue peace and prosperity in a place of adversity for sixth-century Jewish exiles, as for Black British people today living in the historic land of the descendants of those who enslaved, racialized and inferiorized their ancestors and them, can seem a particularly tough ask. However, peace is such a quintessential element to making progress towards flourishing and to doing well in life that it should be sought by any means necessary, in every and any situation. And as Loba-Mkole suggests, peace-building and mutual edification are closely interrelated (Loba-Mkole 2019). To be starved of peace is akin to being starved of oxygen, it renders existence intolerable, maybe impossible.

Even in circumstances that appear steeped in structural power imbalances, it remains important for individuals and groups to remember they have agency to effect change particularly through learning processes and knowledge mobilization that allows us to understand our own power, how to strategize for influencing and changing external constructions, by understanding the power operating in and around our everyday lives

(Baillie Abidi 2018, p. 65). Human beings are rarely powerless to effect change, the question is how to consciously mobilize and utilize our power as people made in the image and likeness of God to deconstruct and reconstruct the environment we find ourselves in. Peace requires effort in all instances because it is not a naturally occurring element of human existence, it has to be made, pursued, enacted even when this appears counter-intuitive. For some Black British people it can be challenging to commit to peace and prosperity, that is, the well-being of British society, given the history of trials and tribulations of African people and their ancestors over the past half a millennium. Yet the Jeremiah plan calls for peace to be sought in order for flourishing to occur.

In the teachings of Jesus, we find much to be encouraged about concerning a form of realized eschatology as peace in the here and now being worked out in the rough and tumble of life under colonial occupation or post-colonial realities (John 14). It calls upon us to transcend adverse realities and find peace in God through practical and active faith by which God enables us to overcome in the struggle against evil powers. Some may regard this as a placebo, like an ostrich burying its head in the sand, since experience teaches us that faith in God does not guarantee expelling colonial power, or liberation from oppressive powers, requiring a certain suspension of realities. In my Pentecostal tradition there is much mention of being saved, which carries the implication of escaping the wrath of God against sin after death in the judgement. Being saved can also imply escaping the troubles of life. However, apart from the occasional reported miracle, for much of the time those who are saved do not escape trials and tribulations but are taught to rest spiritually in faith in God even in the midst of hellish experience. In addition to laying blame at the doors of exploitation, poor governance, corruption and greed – present in even more prosperous societies in the West – it is also possible to question whether a largely God-believing people need to embrace God-given independence and self-reliance that recontextualizes the fallacy of looking to former colonizers and exploiters, towards an understanding that power lies in us to make the change necessary for prosperity (Burrell and Malits 1997). God's immanence is an enabling source in humanity made in the divine image and likeness that allows us to survive and thrive in adversity. For me, this kind of faith emboldens rather than immobilizes us to work for peace and prosperity in the here and now.

I locate the start of black contributions to the peace and prosperity of Britain in the transatlantic slave trade that fed the system of chattel and plantation slavery. This contribution to the development and well-being of the West, Britain in particular, was not with consent, in spite of efforts by vested European interests to portray the image of the happy African slave (Hampton 2013). As Marley reminds us, there was a constant state of war. They were 'fighting on arrival, fighting for survival' – it was war! (Marley 2002). Maintaining the semblance of peace when war is really what is going on is perverse and a travesty of truth and justice since it camouflages reality. That the prosperity of the Britain of today has its roots in the barbarism of slavery provides a reflexion point for the Black British community pointing towards the need for a more intentional contribution to the well-being of the current setting. As we learn from and become wiser by the past, we do well to seek after shalom, a state in which all work together to create the atmosphere in which all can prosper and flourish. And if this feels like the 'victim' making the running, as I am sometimes told when I talk about self-agency, I merely point out that not to take responsibility and control over your life and its trajectory is to bequeath that control and determination to a nebulous 'society' and/or the malignant or disinterested other over whom you have no control. As a pastor who is interested in the welfare and flourishing of all, I say, especially to my Black British 'parishioners', wear that 'victim' label lightly as an externally imposed and circumstantial status, and instead embrace the status of your humanity made in the *imago Dei* with inherent dignity, agency and self-determination.

To make and maintain peace requires clear thinking and strength to match and challenge the strength of the opposing forces that seek to deny and destroy the peace and well-being of vulnerable people. The colonial tendency is to create and preserve flourishing for itself, and the call to seek peace is not to heap more privilege upon the privileged, but to seek to ensure that all share in the justice that makes for peace. Kabongo states that for peace to thrive the social fabric of a society has to subscribe to certain key principles, based on Micah 6: Act justly, love mercy, and walk humbly with God (Kabongo 2021). I have no argument with this except that for the socio-economic and political situation of minorities to change towards peace and prosperity cannot, in light of history and based upon known human tendencies, leave it to the operators of a colonial system to deliver. Not without the active insistent input of the minorities themselves. New communities have to develop strategies to impose themselves upon the context and by weight of numerical, social, economic and political presence upon the diasporic home so that all share in a new peace for all. When this does not happen minority communities suffer wrath at the hands of the oppressor and may even grow to believe that is just how things are and are meant to be. But the migrant assured of their humanity and agency refuse to be sidelined, instead preferring to seek peace, shalom, the well-being of people old and young, black and white, rich and poor by refusing to consider themselves objects of pity or as dependencies upon the powerful other.

To seek the prosperity of Britain can appear anachronistic since Britain is one of the richest countries in the world, a so-called 'First World' country. The countries from which Black British people hail are by comparison poor 'Third World', 'developing'. Yet without making grandiose claims, Black British people have contributed to Britain's development before and since the Windrush era from 1948, aided by the fact that the main reason many including me are still here, is because of the economic benefits available which are scarce in our countries of origin. This is undoubtedly linked to Britain's plundering and exploitation of the countries that fell under its colonial empire, leaving most in so-called independence but shorn of national social, economic and political infrastructure, rendering them chaotic and unprosperous (Beckles 2013).

What, though, does peace and prosperity as well-being and flourishing look like? Is this state even possible or is it a mere utopian dream? A perspective can be discerned from Scripture when it shows glimpses of the eschaton in the life of Israel when disputes will be settled between nations as the tools of war would be transformed into lifegiving tools, swords into ploughshares, spears into pruninghooks, when nations cease from preparing for and conducting wars (Isa. 2.4). Isaiah further envisages not only humans at peace but animals too with wolf and lamb, leopard and kid, calf, lion, fatling together being led by a child, cow and bear with their young grazing and lying down, and in this interactivity hostilities are replaced by peace and prosperity; a key in this text is the prevalence of knowledge of God (Isa. 11.6–9). Then Revelation 21.1–4 envisages a new heaven and new earth with God in the midst of the people wiping away tears, abolishing death, mourning, crying and pain. Such utopia seems beyond this life and to the extent we experience aspects of this vision of a hoped-for utopian eschatology, deployment of the resources God places in the Church and the world need to be engaged in for social, political and economic structural transformation (Yong 2010).

Black British people like me are only too aware of the difference between the UK economy including its social security and, though much derided, the National Health Service that provides a level of creature comforts that far exceeds my country of origin – a factor that encourages us to remain in the UK in old age in spite of the sentimental desire to return to the nations of our ethno-cultural historic roots. Even in the shadows of the British empire many nationalists have been so concerned about protecting British sovereignty that it led to the almost incomprehensible departure from the European Union, the country's closest trading bloc, to go it alone (Baimbridge, Whyman and Brian 2011; Reddie 2019). The Bible conjures up an image in the Psalms of the one who is like a tree planted by a river; Jesus speaks of the person born again and in whom water springs up into everlasting life. This concept of being connected to a lifegiving source gets to the root of what is meant by prospering. Such a proverbial tree however is not without susceptibility to storms, rain and heat. It suggests a situation in which those not so connected to the source of energy are deficient and lack in a way that those who are connected don't. When we talk about seeking the prosperity of Britain, therefore, we have this in mind. What is envisaged is a country that prospers to its full potential and plays its part in the world, not as an exploitative empire but as a magnanimous nation, like the tree in Jesus' parable with branches to which birds fly for a place of refuge and refreshing in their journeying across the globe. Black British people are encouraged actively to seek the peace and prosperity of Britain, notwithstanding current challenges and the provisos of history, the transatlantic slave trade, chattel and plantation slavery, colonialism, racism, and conversely exploiting to the full the opportunities that present themselves and are created as they journey on the long road started by their ancestors and continued by us and our children. It's a tough ask, but less so when we understand that what is being called for is not fattening the already fat society but asking how a diasporic community can enjoy prosperity and wellness. This is a prompt to join in and share in the wealth of the city or country to which you have come in spite of the shortcomings and challenges of the space.

Seeking peace and prosperity in the place of the Black exile/diaspora, we can draw lessons from Black churches in Britain that have often sought to improve the area they worship in by being a place of incubation for the talent and skills inherent in its members, especially young people who utilize leadership and public speaking as well as scientific skills within the Church before broadening their involvement in society. I have seen churches develop their areas by acquiring derelict land and buildings and bringing them into use. My local church in Winson Green, Birmingham, erected a new building that became a hub for worship and community outreach offering various services to the local community without discrimination. Such facilities therefore offer dual use for the discreet use of the Black British secular and religious community and use by the mainly white local people. These approaches, common around the country, mainly in inner cities, are consistent with the biblical model of loving neighbour as self, and of loving those who hate you and spitefully use you, even in a generational and historic sense. By improving an area, the well-being or peace of everyone in the area is enhanced. It is possible to picture the national contribution too to church life as well as the contribution of the Black British community to British life. Seeking the peace and prosperity of this society then indicates the use of agency to assist in making this diaspora space one in which flourishing happens because everyone is empowered to both contribute and take their share of the communal pot.

Pray

Jeremiah's letter to Jewish exiles tells them to pray for the welfare of Babylon as part of their continuing interest in the affairs of the place of their exile and captivity. To pray carries the basic idea of petitioning, beseeching or imploring, intreating and supplicating God for matters that concern you. Wright tells how the Psalms can help us connect and commune with God, a concept I prefer (Wright 2014). This broader understanding opens opportunities, for those who believe in God, for engagement in conversation with God in a relational way that understands God as more than the supplier of needs and wants and more as personal God who a believing community and individuals can 'walk and talk' with as the old song says. In my Pentecostal tradition it is common practice to refer to God in the person of Jesus as saviour and friend who accompanies you on life's journey. This becomes poignant when you find yourself in a strange or foreign land with few or no friends and at times hostile enemies; in those times you can pray, that is, talk or commune with God in worship, giving thanks for favour and petitioning for needs. What prayer should not be is an excuse or delaying tactic for human action in word or deed.

Jewish people have been familiar with prayer since antiquity, whether individual or communal, for varying reasons and occasions, adopting different physical postures, at home, in the open or in the temple, by officers such as kings, prophets, rabbis and lay people. Reif confirms that prayer was practised widely among the Jews before the rise of Christianity and Rabbinic Judaism, as is evident throughout the Jewish Bible which Christians regard as our Old Testament (Reif 2015). With reference to the centrality of prayer in the Hebrew tradition, Widmer says human beings 'have praised, thanked, and petitioned God through prayer and sacrifice from the beginning of public worship' (Widmer 2015, p. 1). The Jews prayed for themselves, families, friends and allies and against their enemies, something Jesus was to reverse with his teaching to love, pray for and bless your enemies. Further, Widmer portrays Jeremiah as someone acquainted with intercessory praying directed to solicit God's wrath to destroy and overthrow enemies and to find grace and mercy for Israel/Judah (Widmer 2015, p. 330). Yet, indications are that God did none of these things; they were done by people who attribute them to God.

Furthermore, we get a sense of what Jeremiah may mean by prayer from the attitude to prayers in the book that bears his name (O'Connor 2012, pp. 269–70). Jeremiah's laments arise from the unique difficulties of his prophetic mission, in the midst of which he raises an angry fist to God, accuses God of treachery and deceit, and even tries to escape his mission. Yet despite his outbursts of anger and disappointments, the relationship between God and Jeremiah remains intact. Indeed, Jeremiah's expressions of anger serve as a vehicle of his fidelity. The confessions end by praising God, who 'has delivered the life of the needy from the hands of evil doers' (20.13). Balentine depicts Jeremiah as a 'confessing, complaining pray-er', on one hand confessing God's presence in his life, on the other hand complaining or lamenting God's absence, or that the divine presence is so disguised that Jeremiah cannot discern it (Balentine 1981). Jeremiah's unambiguous call to the exiles to pray for the well-being of Babylon that held them captive and colonized back home may be understood as an invitation to engage in a complex decoding of the relationship between the exiles, the Babylonians and God, with all the power dynamics implied. To pray for Babylon is to bring to the fore the complexities of these relationships and to lay them bare before divine and mortal eyes, remembering that God and Nebuchadnezzar were co-belligerents in their deportation. The exiles were to pray for the place that held them captive, the enemy, because matters were not straightforward any more, if ever they were; and as Wilson puts it, based on the reality that 'their welfare [is] now bound up with that of their conquerors' (Wilson 1990).

In my ecumenical work, I have seen how prayer can have as a purpose bringing people together who might otherwise not meet and share fellowship, but what of the actual content and of prayer itself? Prayer as a means of bringing people together in person or virtually online has a ring of relating to the performing arts or therapeutic industry rather than an encounter between the divine Creator and the humanity made in the divine image. Jeremiah's call to pray for the place of your captivity has to indicate more than a mass counselling and therapeutic session between Jews and Babylonians. When I pray for the UK, I am not asking God to simply bless everyone, rather I take all that has gone before me, all that is still here, and all that can be into my dialogue with the Almighty as we reason how the exercise of my humanity, agency and self-determination can impact where I live for good, maybe even contributing to the conversion of some sin-sick soul who may believe their humanity superior to mine. And how I might meet well-meaning 'natives' with whom I can do business human to human for the betterment of our mutual home. Indeed, 'pray for' becomes 'pray with' yet doing so in profound self-interested ways about the matters that count towards human flourishing, mutuality and shalom all in the presence of God in whose image all are made. In praying for and with the place to which God has brought them, Black British people could benefit from a more nuanced understanding of prayer than merely a means of petitioning God for the basics of life and to include social, economic and political influences upon their lives; all the while knowing they must be prepared to action what they pray about, because this is what our experience teaches us.

At the start of the twenty-first century, I published an edited book on prayer with 14 contributors. For my sins, only four were women, two of whom collaborated – which is a significant discrepancy since by general consensus women are in a majority in the Black British church in Britain (Aldred (ed.) 2000). Also, the three people I credited for their support in making the publication possible were women. Notwithstanding this *mea culpa*, the compilation is helpful in understanding how the Black British Christian community perceives prayer in this Babylon experience. I summarize the three main perspectives on prayer as conversation, power and authority. Prayer therefore is a means of intimacy and empathy as the pray-er engages regularly maybe even continuously with God; a means of power to confront principalities and powers of evil; and a means of living in divine authority akin to earthly ambassadors abroad living in the authority of the One in whose name they act. One chapter in particular speaks to the current discussion in this book, as Nathan explores prayer as a tool of liberation, while noting this was not always the case (Nathan 2000). This politicizing of prayer is not to everyone's liking, but Nathan poses a significant argument that to live in a racialized society with so many oppositional forces to the existence and flourishing of Black British people demands that what believers talk to God about include insights into spiritual warfare against principalities and powers and the rulers of darkness.

Black British people might listen in on the way their ancestors prayed under the pressures of the transatlantic slave trade, chattel and plantation slavery and colonialism as we reflect upon how they might pray in their context, which in many respects is not of the same magnitude in terms of levels of oppression. Having scanned several slave narratives, I conclude that enslaved people do not appear to have spent much time praying for deliverance, if references to prayer are any guide to their prayer lives, unlike much of Black Pentecostalists that seem to revel in all-night prayer meetings, waiting for their miracle (Gates 1987; Douglass 1995; Washington 1901). Enslaved Africans seemed to be aware that praying to God did not offer a quick solution to their situation. Gates' work contains four narratives of Olaudah Equiano, Mary

Prince, Frederick Douglass and Linda Brent (also known as 'a slave girl'), with a sense throughout that all acknowledged the divine, and yet on the theme of prayer there appears a realism and profundity that in their longsuffering, and even their greatest hour of need, allowed for a mere 'Lord, help; Lord, save me!' uttered more as a sigh than in hope of being saved (Stowe 1995, p. 47).

People in difficult settings ought always to be on the lookout for ways in which hegemonic forces can use teaching prayers to the oppressed as a way of indoctrination into compliance in the name of God, distracting them from using their agency towards genuine liberation, lulled into being satisfied with using the adopted prayers of their oppressors to claim social space still on the 'plantation'. Downs articulates well the recommended posture of the Black listener to the preachers who encouraged them not merely to ask God for favours, but to approach the task with thanksgiving for what has been received and understand the interchange as human weakness casting itself upon divine strength, prostrating the creature before the Creator who knows best what the children need (Downs 2011, p. 153). Bellagamba, et al., in their work highlight African voices in prayer during the era of slavery and the slave trade in Africa, expressing fear, anger and defiance along with the sorrow felt about the loss of family and friends, and explicitly about slave raiders and the desire to wreak vengeance upon their attackers (Bellagamba et al. 2013, p. 117). Communion in prayer with the Creator of the cosmos will always include praise, reverence and worship for who and what we understand God to be. Praying specifically about the place of my exile/diaspora will call to mind the disturbing history between us, discerning God's perspective on that history, and seeking a clear way forward for flourishing in difficult situations.

An example from the slave narratives, however, recognizing the divine as ever present, but knowing instinctively that prayer that does not fight back because 'the will of God be done', is mere opiate in the face of terror that suggests weakness, and is in fact submission to an evil fate. In the black experience God does not act salvifically in this manner to 'deliver us from evil', and the only beneficiary of this meek submission to terror is the terrorizer. Prayer for Babylon asks God to strengthen us as we fight opposing foes to deliver ourselves in the power and authority of God. In a poem, 'Plantation Prayer', an unknown author opines 'Of primal sorrow and bane of birth' and references the ambiguous figure of Jesus Christ in relation to generational crying and suffering (Parks 1937, p. 301). The example of Jesus hanging on a cross refusing to help himself was meant to be a once-for-all sacrifice, with no requirement for Black British people to submit meekly to the lynching tree awaiting miraculous deliverance (Cone 2022). Prayer as liturgy and ritual has to be more than an opiate as we pray for Babylon, since what is happening is not an exercise in hope that God will change the hearts of the operators of the Babylon system; rather it is a strengthening of the hand of the exile to find ways of contributing to and extracting from the resources of Babylon towards their flourishing (Isasi-Díaz 1996). Even the act of remembering Zion by the rivers of Babylon (Psalm 137) cannot afford to be an act of dismay and desperation but a must be a strengthening of resolve to connect with home and draw strength to move closer to the liberation and flourishing sought. In my experience disciplines such as petitionary prayers examples of which are widespread in Black British Pentecostal churches in daily, weekly, monthly, quarterly, even annual prayer sessions serve mainly to keep the undiscerning in their becalmed place. Lack of progress towards flourishing is often facilitated by well-to-do leaders for whom it matters little that the petitions of the masses go largely, if not entirely, unanswered since they have need of little, and their unanswered prayers have little to no effect on leaders' personal situation (Adams 2021).

The way to engage prayerfully in the struggle with an oppositional force is to stand up to it, never to surrender and submit. In the same way that it is the resurrection, not the cross, which has the final say, so too the lynching tree, racism and inequality cannot be allowed to have final say either. But maybe prophetic prayer can. As the resurrection of Jesus fulfilled the divine plan of redemption so prophetic prayer can take before God the plans of Black British people to burst out of the entombment of racist structures and locate them victoriously at the right hand of God. Praying for the UK therefore includes prayerfully developing and outlining Black British strategy for flourishing and contributing to the country, in faith that God is with them as they deploy that plan. Finally, in my experience the prayers of the diaspora people differ from those of the majority culture, and because of their different circumstances the 'natives' appear to go through the motions of engaging a higher power, while the prayers of the exiled minority is a call to arms to discover how to flourish. For them prayer as an action word, not rooted in passivity of contentment, really does matter. Prayer therefore in the context of diaspora is not a request list, it's a to-do list for flourishing that is worked out between us and God in conversation.

Shared interest

In pointing out the shared interests of the Jews in exile and their Babylonian captors, Jeremiah is continuing his mission of laying out how and why to position themselves in their new situation. Wessels argues that in a chaotic world with many prophetic voices, Jeremiah's voice represented pragmatic realism for the exiles who may have been tempted to rebel destructively against their captors and the place of their captivity, an unwise strategy since the upkeep and prosperity of the place was in their interest too (Wessels 2016). The prophet was aware that in their alienation and distress, the exiles may easily have overlooked the common destiny of captive and captor. Similarly, Black British people face a challenge in Britain, a place and people historically hostile towards them, who having remained well beyond their notional intended five years, find that their destiny is wrapped up with that of the majority culture. It may seem logical to say if the place where you are prospers, you prosper. Yet we know that the way resources are shared in any country or city favours those who are privileged by class, and in the West people of colour tend to be outdone by the wealthy and connected who get a disproportionate share of the available resource (Bullard 2008). This is true of a city or country in normal times for citizens; it is even more so for exiles, asylum seekers, refugees and immigrants in general who in almost all cases find themselves at the bottom of the social, economic and political system. Black British people know this only too well, having started at the bottom of British society doing menial jobs to get by and pursue their vision towards economic betterment for themselves and their families.

Jeremiah's task then, in seeking to influence the Jewish exiles, was similar to addressing the Black British diaspora, proposing that we do not view Britain disproportionately through the lens of diaspora oppression but also as a place of opportunity. It is not either/or, it is both/and; and we should intentionally view it as such. When I came to England in the late 1960s, I recall being told by members of my church that my father, who was a lay preacher, had preached a sermon titled, 'the door of opportunity swings on the hinges of opposition'. As well as being profound, this hinted at the singularity of opportunity versus the plurality of opposition. In our approach to life in diaspora that truism can be easily forgotten as attention is naturally drawn to the pluriform nature of the opposition we face being viewed in negative isolation. Escaping this dilemma is tricky and Kgatla offers an interesting insight through the prism of the work of Pentecostal theologian Anderson, who the writer depicts as 'one of the few white South Africans who succeeded in getting out of the entrapment of racial prejudices when it came to the written history of African-initiated churches.' Anderson, Kgatla says, recognized that to assess African Independent Churches authentically and theologically, examination had to be conducted within their context on the margins of the dominant European hegemony, not based on the assumptions made by his European contemporaries (Kgatla 2023). This is to say, particularly in contested situations, attempts must be made to engage in interdisciplinary and multidisciplinary analysis so as not to be drawn into lopsided, unfocused and unhelpful conclusions. This is a real danger for a people in exile/diaspora, where the negative impacts faced tend to exacerbate positive energy, spiritual and temporal. Jamaican people often speak of having mixed feelings towards their exilic home, with their original home viewed romantically as all good, while the adopted foreign home is viewed as a place of racialized hostage-taking. What is insightful here, however, is that in spite of this unfavourable perspective of the adopted home they do not abandon it and return, because deep down they know this is the goose that lays the golden egg. Theirs is a love/hate relationship. The challenge is to move from this spiritual and psychological false binary, towards a balanced perspective that better articulates opposition and opportunity. The challenge of black enforced or adopted home is one of wisely, cunningly differentiating between good and ill in the interest of flourishing – a challenge to everyone within a contested but shared context.

So, how might Black British people both contribute and receive their fair share of the available prosperity? Should Black British people lay aside their hesitancy rooted in their experiences, historic and contemporary, of not getting their fair share due to a combination of race, class and more? I believe the answer is a resounding yes! Away with hesitancy and non-involvement and waiting to be invited to the table. As Sowell helpfully shows, the roots of and differences between discrimination, and disparities are never as apparent as they seem, misdiagnosing them produces more than difference in words but policies and activities less likely to achieve hoped-for goals (Sowell 2019, p. 34).

In the face of multiple indices indicating negative disparities for Black British people, this book does not call upon them to exercise faith in 'better will come'; rather, it calls for Black British people to change their attitude from one of expecting things that look like theirs by right, or that they are told are faits accomplis, or being promised someone else is fighting for your rights. Instead, take charge of making things happen through your own belief in the *imago Dei* in you, through God-given agency and self-determination. What I suggest here ideologically is less an essentialist African nationalism or a form of 'nation within a nation' and more a Black British pragmatism that understands the self as first and foremost an ethnic group, integrally part of the human race and British society, that responds situationally to ensure they underwrite their flourishing (Jeffries 2020). By building upon the foundation laid above, the Black British person is ready and able to take their share of the growing economic realities they contribute to. It will not happen by accident, only as, individually and together, they take what is theirs thereby fulfilling the notion that 'if it prospers, they prosper'. It may be problematic were we to take Jeremiah's word at face value and assume that when Black British throw their lot into building the peace and prosperity of the country they can be certain that they will share the spoils.

This sharing in the spoils is never a *fait accompli*; the diaspora community will still have to contend determinedly to get their fair share of resources, will still have to wrestle variable levels of multiple isms: racism and classism in the main. However, as the levels of peace and prosperity rise, the share they fight for and get increases too. There will never be a level playing field, but everybody's share increases as resources increase, and Black British people must position themselves to get their fair and just share. This still leaves issues of justice and equity as a battleground to be fought over. In my experience those who suggest they can make demands upon the system, and the system will deliver justice, mislead us, deliberately or not, since all know the Babylon system is self-serving and only 'gives' what is 'taken', a lesson Jesus taught 2,000 years ago (Mark 3). Jeremiah makes no promise of voluntarily ceded equity, since even when a justice system exists justice has to be pursued. Every gain has to be fought for, at home and in diaspora; it will never be handed to anyone on a platter. And importantly, hesitancy, or leaving matters in the hands of others, results in further waiting for better to come, but it never does. Better never (or, optimistically, rarely) comes unless and until you take it.

The Bible gives examples of the uneven nature of life, from Jesus' parable of the distribution of talents (Matt. 25), to rich churches being encouraged to look after poorer ones (2 Cor. 8). We must beware any who tell us to wait until they have created a better world before we participate in and extricate from in society. Problematic as Britain is, it is the Britain we have and there is no guarantee any other context poses a lesser challenge. A healthy dose of honesty, truth, realism and pragmatism, but not cynicism, is needed concerning the frailties of human existence and the challenges that accompany the promise that if Black British people contribute to the building up of the nation's well-being, they will benefit. It is conditional on several factors in diaspora, without which equity and justice will not happen. The wisdom of Jeremiah's words can be seen in the unfolding story of the Jewish exiles; however, the prophet in this letter highlights a difference between public theology and prophetic theology (Laubscher 2022). Jeremiah's contemporaries lacked imagination and a plan, while the prophetic theology of Jeremiah articulated a radically different solution to the dilemma faced. Among Black British people a public theology voices fighting and protesting inequalities, however a prophetic theological voice points towards a philosophical 'all in this together' and an agency-focused plan to take matters into their hands and impose the solution upon the context by the strength of your thoughts and actions. The examples of Daniel in Babylon and, before him, Joseph in Egypt shine through as possibilities of accessing the very top echelons of a foreign society by display of wisdom and hope, instead of fear and despair (Osborne et al. 2015).

Together, Black British people, their ancestors and parents, have a deep resource of memories of inequalities since the transatlantic slave trade, chattel slavery, plantation free labour and colonialism all to the benefit of the West and the destruction of African souls. The Africans did the work, suffered and died, the European benefitted. Now in Britain as a direct consequence of that unequal history, they know that the racist attitudes that facilitated the past 500 years and racial prejudice have deep roots. Based on this history no one should assume that Britain, a motherland of that vile and inhumane history towards their fellow humans, is a place of fairness and equity and justice for African-heritage people. When therefore Black British people aim for shared existence and shared resources they have to assume that this has to be wrought without undue dependence on the generosity or pity of those who are the inheritors of such historical atrocities. Having come to Britain in search of economic betterment, Black British people need to find ways of moving psychologically, spiritually, economically and in myriad other ways beyond the determinative traumatic vestiges of the future we live in that was created by slavery (Brooten and Hazelton (eds) 2010, p. 1). While focusing on the impact upon women and girls, Brooten's work highlights the need for transcendent strategies by all descendants of trans-atlantic chattel slavery wherever in the world they happen to live. For Black British people, based on the model of Jeremiah's letter to Jewish exiles, we can identify three facets that act as insurance to getting a fair share of corporate resources. First, belief in and exercise of agency; second, building up your presence and worth; and third, allegiance with allies on your terms.

Black British people's own agency and self-determination to achieve their fair share of the resources available in society should never be underestimated or undermined, including not by themselves. Especially against a background of the worst kinds of adversity and injustice, past and present, Black British people must stand fearlessly in their God-given humanity at home or in an estranged place among people who may be hostile. It is a challenge to meet others on the level of mutual humanity especially when there is history and experience between enslaved, slave owners and the descendants of both. The common tendency is to meet those who are different from us with suspicion, even hate and resentment; this book however calls for engagement in knowledge of history, individual strength and community solidarity, expecting little from others while making abundant provision. Black British people should cease expecting benevolent responses from sources that black experience tells us have not been forthcoming for half a millennium. Low expectation of Western benevolence towards dark-skinned people can become a modus operandi for the African diaspora even while coexisting in the same space by pragmatically positioning themselves to exploit the available resources. Bowers Du Toit helpfully explores through the prisms of Black Consciousness and Black Theology how faith-based organizations can play a role in social development through decolonizing praxis and recognizing the importance of identity and self-reliance towards attaining justice and liberation (Bowers Du Toit (eds) 2018). Such an approach, I believe, has currency in other walks of African-heritage people's life too. In sum, if Black British people are to guarantee getting their share of the wealth and resources they contribute to, they are going to have to look to themselves to take responsibility for extracting from public resources whether social, economic or political.

By positioning themselves in all sectors of British society, not waiting to be invited but as fellow human beings considering themselves the equal of all others, Black British people can identify what resources there are and access them as is useful to them. Some of what prevents Black British people from accessing resources is self-inflicted. Sometimes we limit ourselves in terms of what places we visit, what careers we pursue, which political persuasion to adopt, what religion to follow and even whether to consider ourselves British. I have heard people say, 'They don't accept me as British anyway, so I don't consider myself to be British'. Or, 'The teacher told me I am not academic enough to go to university and I should think of a vocational career, so I did not pursue academic qualifications.' Such self-restrictions based on what a European person says about an African person's options ought never to be instructive or restrictive to our access to services in health, education and other choices. Nor should Black British people consider it permissible to cite racism when because we allow over-emphasis of the views of others on our paths, we then say our limitations are due to racism. This would be racial scapegoating, and indicative of the Black British community being lulled into passivity instead of being agency-led. In an institutionally racist West there are sufficient actual instances of racism to not blame racism when in fact we have held ourselves back.

Historically, Black people have had to stay in their assigned place in white-controlled societies under racialised enslavement,

Jim Crow, colonialism and apartheid, obeying legal and social norms under threat of punishments including beatings, imprisonment and death by lynching. A clear danger of living in the shadows of that history are abstentions whereby we live by codes of self-imposed domestication (Zimmerman 2008). Even during times of the imposition of the severest punishment, Sharpe, a Baptist deacon and anti-slavery resistance movement leader, was willing to say, 'I would rather die upon yonder gallows than live in slavery' (Morrison 2014, pp. 127, 149). How much more should Black British people in a post-imperial context remove all semblance of physical and mental chains and live in our full God-given humanity? Given all we know about how life is conducted it seems to be living below our agency, overvaluing the status of others or impersonal systems for non-action and reluctance to engage. The principle of God-given agency means that while we cannot control what others say or do, we can and should control our actions or non-actions and take responsibility for them, not merely blame other people and things. However culpable they may be, experience teaches us that laying blame at the door of the guilty does not tend to result in their repentance and restitution thereby securing what is yours. Adult franchise calls for adult responsibilities in a way that blaming others and crying wolf is unlikely to bear fruit. To get fair share of resources in the public space the Black British community should move beyond self-imposed inaction based on fear, suspicion and adverse experience.

Unfortunately, some in society benefit from labelling the Black British community 'hard to reach' because with that label comes funding to raise awareness and increase participation. Gul's work mentions how it seems that in attempts to work for the betterment of society, often the focus is on government and public agencies, with little or no mention of the potential and contributions of communities and citizens, thought to exist outside the professional practice of statutory agencies (Gul 2012). Little thought seems to be given to the so-called 'hard to reach' other than as passive people to be done to, rather than active partners within reach and who are capable of reaching in. Black British people must refuse to be classified as 'hard to reach' and endeavour to have done our reconnaissance and be first in line as active partners. I have known instances when funding has been returned to the funder because the successful funding application sponsor were no more successful at reaching the 'hard to reach' than mainstream attempts. The obvious reason is that the Black British community are *not* hard to reach. They are sometimes disengaged and will remain out of range until they come forward to take up services available to all. Black British people should, like other persons in society, take responsibility for their health and take preventative measures to eat and exercise and go to their GP when a health issue presents. To not do so and blame something or somebody else and then to be supported in this irresponsible and infantilizing way is not in the interest of the person or community. After several years as a pastor and living in community I know the majority of the Black British community are adept at accessing resources, with a minority needing assistance to make good choices. However, for their own reasons and benefit it suits some to portray the entire community as hard to reach and in need of special treatment and provision. There can therefore be obstacles to Black British people accessing their share of community resources but in the spirit of Jeremiah's statement that if the place where the exiles or diaspora live prospers, they prosper. Applying individual and group agency is a first step in securing their share of resources, not depending upon the benevolence or permission of others.

A second way Black British people can advance the cause of getting their fair share of the national resource is by impressing upon the context their presence and worth. When a group is less than 5% of the overall population their presence is necessarily sparse apart from specific inner-city demographic areas where, for cultural and work availability causes, they form clusters (Phillips and Phillips 1998). This is evident in formerly industrialized areas such as London having the greatest concentration of minority ethnic population according to the latest national census, followed by Birmingham, Manchester, Sheffield, Bristol and historically Liverpool. Even before the Windrush era, observers have highlighted the visible presence of people of colour from Africa and the Caribbean with Fryer reporting that in the eighteenth century there was evidence of cohesion, solidarity and mutual help among African people in Britain (Fryer 1984, p. 67). Over the years this Black British community has become more visibly evident in the press and media as well as in literature for various reasons, both good and not so good. Since 2017 there has been a significant increase in national visibility of Black British people under the guise of the 'Windrush Generation'. Unfortunately, this visible presence has not necessarily brought recognition of the value or worth of the people concerned. The Windrush scandal relates to an episode that led to some, who were British but unable to prove their status under 'hostile environment' legislations introduced by the British Government since 2014, losing jobs, being denied access to public services and deported (Gentleman 2019, p. 15).

Presence and value are important to the people themselves as well as to the majority and other minority ethnic communities since it creates self-awareness and awareness among other people groups of the extent and nature of the Black British people. In significant ways the Windrush scandal was the antithesis of creating presence and weight as it fuelled false narratives that infantilized Black British people by suggesting they were unaware of their citizenship rights, or status, and unable to act in light of the inhospitable legislation brought in by government, which although it was not aimed at them, affected them (Williams 2020). While those found to be unable to prove their right to live and work in Britain, though entitled to it, were greatly disadvantaged, the overwhelming majority of the Windrush Generation having had their citizenship status in good order were unaffected, but assumed in the narrative to be equally affected along with those who were. There are sound reasons to adopt a view that much immigration legislation since the 1940s was designed with a two-pronged rationale to keep overall numbers down and to keep 'coloured' immigration even lower on the basis that they 'are not from here' (Goodfellow 2019, p. 161). Black British people facing up to this historic and contemporary reality know they cannot change it but should also consider how to overcome it to flourish in Babylon, in spite of its past and current behaviour and attitudes. To be an effective tool in getting their fair share, however, this presence has to be accompanied by the self-assuredness of a people who know of their worth rooted in the *imago Dei* in them, that legitimizes their sense of agency and power of self-determination. This awareness lends weight to a prophetic and transcendent presence.

One of the objectives that Black British people should challenge themselves with is to occupy every conceivable facet of life with a plan, not for domination, but for presence proportionate to their representation in society. I am keen, in this book and particularly when discussing fair share, to distance my work from the idea of domination, particularly as historically domination has been patriarchal and racial across secular and religious contexts, leaving women and Black British people as victims of a tiny European male elite (Cornelius 2022). In a post-exilic situation a person or a minority ethnic group almost certainly will need to be assertive to ensure they are not sidelined or excluded but this in no way implies replacing European racial oppression and exclusion with an African one, even were their number to permit such. Black British proportionate presence in sectors such as social, economic, political, and religious will suffice for fair share. In Britain, the social sphere might include education, health, housing, the arts, music and such like and Black British people living here should prayerfully, strategically, intentionally and determinedly set about a strategy for accessing all areas. This could begin with educational choices at school, college, vocational and university courses and hobbies; assisted by group consciousness and awareness of these areas that should be considered when thinking about career and vocational choices. With such consciousness Black British pupils and students can spread across the education and entrepreneurial spheres from medicine to space studies, banking to politics, science, technology, engineering and mathematics (STEM) subjects. It should be normal for them to access redbrick university politics, philosophy and economics (PPE) courses that often lead to a career in politics. Entry into the various strata of the social context from educational and other perspectives as users and career professionals must also be considered normal, and we cannot wait because we think 'you can't be what you can't see'. Particularly from a faith perspective, we must be about bringing into being those things that are not as though they were, and make them so (Rom. 4). Applying Black British humanity to the economic and political spheres requires similar approaches to the social area from an educational perspective.

Having settled down, become property, land and business owners, entrepreneurs and prayer partners, Black British people can increase their leverage, punch their weight better even in diaspora or exile by ensuring we are present in all spaces, to the extent our numbers allow. For example, in politics, where there are 650 Members of Parliament, Black British people should set their sights on having around 5%, 33 Members of Parliament from their ethnic group. This principle can be applied to all other areas of British life, such as teachers, heads, lecturers, Justices of the Peace, architects, accountants, scientists, medical doctors, theologians, authors, police, statisticians, judges, councillors etc. Black British people should not content themselves with speaking and writing about areas of under-representation as though this somehow makes things different. They should tell themselves that they must see to it that these things happen by casting a vision, encouraging, holding to account, being accountable, and never franchising out their humanity to bringing into being those things that are not. By so doing, Black British people receive a bigger piece of the public resources cake in the British economy at all levels.

An area that is an example of potential for getting a fair share by taking it is in the religious sector of British society, through the rise of the Black British church movement (Gerloff 1992). This Christian presence in Britain was birthed in the Windrush era from migrants belonging to churches back home whose parent bodies such as Catholic, Anglican, Baptist and Methodist were in Britain but offered little to no reception to newly arriving fellow denominational members. Then there were those who belonged to independent and denominational

Pentecostal churches back home, some with parent bodies in the USA, and which had little to no presence in Britain, so initiated fellowships from bedrooms, front rooms, church and school halls (Sturge 2005). These two streams soon converged in the Black British-led churches, but as the years have passed there has been a resurgence of Black British presence in the British 'mainstream' churches. In my doctoral studies the matter of 'prophetic presence' is cited as a pillar of the Black British church movement (Aldred 2005, p. 200). Prophetic presence says, 'we are here and will not be denied', a presence that has been evident across the churches in Britain as Black British people take their places in the face of unwelcome and sometimes hostility. Black British Christians are spiritual and denominational siblings whether they are in European British-led mainstream churches or those peopled by minority ethnic groups. Together this prophetic presence is similar to the resolve called for by Jeremiah to Jewish exiles to take their flourishing in a hostile and unfriendly Babylon into their own hands. This was necessary because whatever they may think of each other, descendants of colonized and colonizer were bound together in one fate by virtue of circumstance, and the exiles could not depend upon their captors to do right by them. Black British people belonging to mainstream European British-led churches continue to contest lingering racialized treatment that limit potential for service within those churches. At the same time Black British-led churches exist as self-governed partners in Christian mission.

A third means by which the Black British community can ensure shared interest in Britain, as Jeremiah suggests in Babylon, is by collaborating with white people and those of other ethnicities. The national census identified five main and 17 sub ethnic groupings in England and Wales with the Black British category utilized in this book referring to one main and three sub ethnic groups, constituting circa four per cent of the overall population (https://census.gov.uk/). This means that in the British context there are many potential partners and allies even allowing for the existence of some who may be hostile and a historically hostile culture. As a Christian I believe everyone is made in the image and likeness of God, as we share in human fallenness that makes us fallible, and that therefore we have more in common with other humans than what separates us. When we look for allies, therefore, we are not expecting to find perfect human specimens as partners; rather they will be similar to us, imperfect as we are, but willing to explore ways to contribute to mutual development, well-being and flourishing. By working with Black British people, white people help to further their own sense of development, well-being and flourishing. I have also experienced in some people the gift of altruism that the Bible introduces us to in giving as a gift of the Spirit (Rom. 12.8). Just because a devilish spirit of oppression and other evils have pervaded European relationships with Africans over past centuries does not mean the gift of generosity and reciprocity is dead or that people are beyond redemption and doing good. Through the prism of Pentecostal theology Vondey reminds us that human beings are considered a composite tri-partite being of soul and spirit or mind and body, and that the mind with its capacity for reasoning enables stability and consistency of purpose (Vondey 2020, p. 81). This commonality makes possible human to human relationships that hold out possibilities of transformation and change.

An ally is an 'associate, a helper, an assistant, a supporter in an ongoing effort, activity or struggle' (Merriam-Webster.com). For people in diaspora or exile determining prospective allies there is both need for this kind of support as well as for circumspection, a trying of the spirit for authenticity (1 John 4). An ally in the Black British context is one who is positioned to help or support in their effort to get a fair share of the available resources and discover ways of making an effective contribution. This presupposes that the Black British person already has an intention to access and contribute to those resources and is unable to do so fully or partially due to factors that are beyond their reach. What is termed 'white allyship' presupposes active Black British engagement based upon self-awareness and self-determination concerning what is needed to get to a desired destination. Without this prerequisite, Black British people disarm their power of agency and are in danger of accepting that the white person alone has agency and that they are powerless and redundant without Euro-saviourism. This is the basis of the saviourism of Jesus, that humanity was dead in their sin, incapable of helping themselves, until God comes in Jesus to breathe new life into the spiritually dead (Rom. 6). The idea of a Saviour who rescues us from a sinful, futile and aimless past is not one best suited to the allyship needed in the British context by which the Black British becomes indebted to the white British for saving them (Williams 2011, p. 81). Allyship that denies, supplants or replaces Black British agency is to be rejected in favour only of allies who recognize and honour the absolute humanity and agency of the Black British person or group concerned.

In my view much of the debate about 'white allyship' simply replaces one form of denial of Black humanity in the form of racism with another form of denial, namely patronizing Euro-saviourism, with little to no role for Black British agency (DiAngelo 2018; Bhopal 2018; Lindsay 2019). Eddo-Lodge begins her celebrated work by pointing a finger at those Europeans who refuse to accept the legitimacy of structural racism, its symptoms and effects. Her final chapter, probably out of resignation, gives a nod towards Black British agency playing a significant role towards their flourishing by titling her final chapter 'There's no justice, there's just us' (Eddo-Lodge 2018, pp. 213–24). The error may be to assume white British sympathy for the cause of Black flourishing, given the history of the past half millennium. The Black British community cannot afford to be the needy recipient of white saviourism as a step towards becoming their advocate or source of atonement. Even the Europeanizing of the person of Jesus runs a risk of bringing atonement into disrepute when it intimates that the white person takes the Black British person's place and transposes between oppressor, ally and saviour (Kotsko 2010, p. 27).

I want here to highlight briefly a few examples of good and not so good white allyship that do or do not observe the theological principle of a common humanity, none superior or inferior, none with divine right to be ruler over or subject to the other. Given the history of the past centuries where European superiority over African people has become standard, if European allyship is to be helpful its order must be supporting alongside African leadership, never assuming hegemony. When the British finally accepted that slavery should end from 1834, a four-year apprenticeship was imposed in the British Empire from 1834 to 1838, during which the African would work most of the time for their master or mistress owner and a tiny part of the time for themselves. According to Lovejoy, slavery was conceived as a kind of religious apprenticeship for pagans (p. 16) that could lead to assimilation and social mobility (p. 181), provided the enslaved satisfied their masters and owners that they had learned enough to be considered by them as human (Lovejoy 2011, p. 221). This had the double aim of weaning the white slave owner off ownership of their property and the impending loss of free service; and for the enslaved it was preparation for adult autonomy for which it is apparent the system thought they were not quite ready. It appears that the work of allies in support of enslaved people resulted in the kind of amelioration that continued to undermine African humanity. Arguably, it was rebellion by enslaved Africans who understood themselves as made in the *imago Dei* that brought about the state of affairs towards liberation, yet those who apparently meant the enslaved well saw them only through the lens of pity. For the enslaved, as soon as opportunity became available, driven by their sense of agency and self-determination they responded to these inherent human traits; bona fide allyship needed to understand this (Dick 2002; Reid-Salmon 2012).

In a similar vein, I have heard severally how among the Black British, demand for greater diversity in the workplace in various fields is often met with a response that suggests or offers more training for Black British workers (Aldred 2021). This response comes with implicit intentions to be supportive of the call, but carries the undermining sentiment that the Black British person is not good enough yet. Some in these situations testify that they have witnessed the introduction of white colleagues with less skills and experience than Black British colleagues and that at times they are called upon to 'teach' their white colleague advancing up the ladder, leaving the Black British worker languishing, immovable, not good enough, yet. The implications are clear: irrespective of how well or badly the white British person does a job they are seen as OK, but the Black British person does not enjoy the privilege of being allowed to do well or badly. On this basis the Black British person in a white setting is routinely seen through the lens of inadequacy for which the starting point is more training, a period of white tutelage, apprenticeship, to get them on a level of humanity on a par with their white British colleagues, maybe. Pursuing this way, the Black British person may never achieve fair share, and they must avoid the trap of accepting this as normal and instead deal robustly with it, take charge, and refuse to be cowed! The Black British person should rise up in their full God-given humanity and call it out, demanding change, with the threat that if not addressed they will rely on equalities law, community support and ultimately, if fair share cannot be found here, they will seek opportunities elsewhere and let the world know why. The kind of ally needed in such situations are not those whose first instinct is to assume that a period of apprenticeship is needed to bring a Black British person up to an acceptable level on par with white colleagues. Allyship that perpetuates the sub-humanity of and further infantilizing Black British people must always attract the righteous indignation of those who are threatened to be affected by it.

I have been the recipient and beneficiary of instances of legitimate white allyship that was initiated, determined and led by me that abides by my theological and social principles of agency and self-determination implicit in *imago Dei*. An example is that at the close of the 1990s while director of the Centre for Black and White Christian Partnership, termed the 'Black School' by missiologist Hollenweger (1997, p. 106), directors decided to make available published material by Black British writers, as mentioned earlier, so that the centre's majority-Black students could have greater access to religious and theological material by people like them. It was decided that I would edit a book of sermons by Black British pastors; this came with warning that I was embarking upon a near-impossible task as these preachers are oral not literary, and none was known to have been published before. Although this was an untrodden road, I had no doubt about the abilities of these preachers I had heard preach eloquently, like preachers and thinkers elsewhere in Britain and around the globe, had the ability to produce literary work, some better than others, based upon their gifts and training. The project was challenging but probably the greatest test was finding a publisher for my first publication. I had no connections in the publishing industry, nor did anyone else around me at that time. I asked many people as I went about my business around the country in multiple contexts who I hoped might have connections in the publishing industry. I persisted and eventually a sympathetic white person gave me an introduction to a publisher for my first edited book, *Preaching with Power* (1999). One of its contributors went on to win that year's national preacher's award, sponsored by the College of Preachers and *The Times* newspaper. Several books followed, building towards a corpus of self-written religious and theological material for students and wider readership. We knew what we wanted to do and finding allies who assisted us along the way made our self-determined plans come to fruition. Publishing is not new to African peoples, but in my local context within Britain we needed to gain access, and allyship was helpful. With hindsight, I should also have reached out beyond my local Black circle, beyond my national work circle and into Africa and the Caribbean in search of allies to help source a publisher. An ongoing challenge is the awareness to avoid myopia and a preoccupation with European-centredness when exploring areas such as publishing. The objective of finding allies to enable publishing was achieved, but I was guilty of not broadening my horizon in where to look.

A second example is that having been brought up in a Pentecostal church tradition that did not value academic and ministry training, after years of ministry but still young, I began to develop a deeper desire for further training (2 Tim. 2). As I looked for a suitable institution to study theology and ministry, it was a white person who suggested I try St John's Theological

College that did distance learning. Although an Anglican theological training college (and me a Pentecostal), and although it was Eurocentric in its theological and ministry orientation, I soon realized that in order to develop intellectually I needed to navigate Eurocentrism, take what is helpful and learn the art of cultural hybridity. In navigating the contours of Christian faith and praxis, despite the habit of some churches to project some kind of denominational faith essentialism, the real world is much more syncretized and hybrid, from understandings of the identity and nature of Jesus to the complexity of ministry (Bantum 2010). One of the lessons I learned in initiating studies beyond the boundaries of my denomination is that my use of white allies is best if it supplemented by Black ones. To advance my self-determined goals and retain control of my destiny, allowing for healthy cross-fertilization, I found Black luminaries essential even when they were not trained in traditional academia. Theological training colleges are plentiful in Britain, and the Black British contribution to and benefit from them only adds to the richness and complexity of the teaching and learning experience, enriching the texture of the religious and secular space we share. White allies continued to be useful as I deepened my theological and ministry development, including invitations to speak and participate in British mainstream spaces. A white academic became my supervisor as later I studied for my Master's and PhD in theology and ministry, and remained with me for over a decade as I underwent a life-transforming period of study development. Getting one's share of the resources available in a post-colonial, post-empire, racialized Britain by utilizing white allies while retaining your integrity (presence and value) and agency I believe is a key towards flourishing in exile/diaspora for the Black British community.

Many years ago, when I struggled to reconcile coexisting in Britain with racism as a past and present reality, a wise head told me that even in a shark-infested sea there are dolphins too! As I have explained, accessing resources in this exilic space means harnessing your own abilities and working with others, both similar to and different from you. Some of the jobs I got in my career were based largely on my forwardness and my refusal to acknowledge that any position was beyond me because of my ethnicity – like the white sales manager in the 1970s who greeted me with a racial slur the first time we met but half an hour later wrote me a cheque for £300 as an incentive to join his company. Indeed, there have scarcely been any key moments in my professional life when there was not a white person playing a key role for my benefit. Added to these, in my experience good neighbourliness between Black British and white British has been overwhelmingly the norm. However, the relatively fewer examples of poor neighbourliness get into the press and overwhelms the good since, as the BBC taught me as a presenter, 'Dog bites man is not news, man bites dog, this is news.' None of this is particularly surprising since the Black British community is tiny as compared with the white British majority ethnic group. However, knowing human nature convinces me that to predicate my flourishing upon the expectation of a white society where everyone loves and treats me right is to consign my flourishing to oblivion.

Conclusion

In this chapter I have sought to explore how the shared interest of Black British and white British may contribute to building a peaceful and prosperous society. The word of the prophet Jeremiah to the Jews in exile that they should throw their lot in with the place of their captivity counselled them to make it their home, take it to their hearts, contribute and flourish. Black British people are being encouraged here to do the same, yet extend their reach towards their people beyond the British context. Through the autonomy of agency and self-determination, Black British people might go on to become confident and strong in diaspora, actively seeking the peace and prosperity of Britain by involvement in all strata. Though strewn with challenges and never perfect, I argue that Black British people can find a way to flourish in the now while working towards a better shared future, even keeping open possibilities of return in strength to their historic homelands in due course. The alternative is a life of constantly begging, pleading, demanding, depending upon the sympathy, generosity or exploitation of fellow humans exploiting the vulnerable nature of Black British humanity living without agency and self-determination.

Questions for intergenerational discussions

- How can Black British people work best towards the peace and prosperity of Britain?
- What are some of the consequences of uncertainty about whether this is home or not?
- What do Black British people pray concerning the country that once exploited them?
- There can be little or no interest in building a country if you do not feel assured you and your children and grandchildren will benefit from the spoils. True or false?

5

False Prophets

Yes, this is what the LORD Almighty, the God of Israel, says: 'Do not let the prophets and diviners among you deceive you. Do not listen to the dreams you encourage them to have. They are prophesying lies to you in my name. I have not sent them,' declares the LORD ...

You may say, 'The LORD has raised up prophets for us in Babylon,' but this is what the LORD says about the king who sits on David's throne and all the people who remain in this city, your fellow citizens who did not go with you into exile – yes, this is what the LORD Almighty says: 'I will send the sword, famine and plague against them and I will make them like figs that are so bad they cannot be eaten. I will pursue them with the sword, famine and plague and will make them abhorrent to all the kingdoms of the earth, a curse and an object of horror, of scorn and reproach, among all the nations where I drive them. For they have not listened to my words,' declares the LORD, 'words that I sent to them again and again by my servants the prophets. And you exiles have not listened either,' declares the LORD.

Therefore, hear the word of the LORD, all you exiles whom I have sent away from Jerusalem to Babylon. This is what the LORD Almighty, the God of Israel, says about Ahab son of Kolaiah and Zedekiah son of Maaseiah, who are prophesying lies to you in my name: 'I will deliver them into the hands of Nebuchadnezzar king of Babylon, and he will put them to death before your very eyes. Because of them, all the exiles from Judah who are in Babylon will use this curse: 'May the LORD treat you like Zedekiah and Ahab, whom the king of Babylon burned in the fire.' For

> they have done outrageous things in Israel; they have committed adultery with their neighbours' wives, and in my name they have uttered lies – which I did not authorize. I know it and am a witness to it,' declares the LORD. (Jer. 29.8–9, 15–23, NIV)

Jeremiah's contentions with false prophets and their prophecies provide an opportunity to discover similarities between then and now. The dangers posed to sixth-century Jewish exiles by false prophets telling them their odyssey was going to be short-lived, are similar to some narratives among today's Black British people. What individuals or groups believe informs their mindset and actions as they pursue flourishing. By the time of Jeremiah's letter to the exiles, prophets were an established phenomenon in the Jewish community – they had been around for centuries and were present in Judah and Jerusalem, and in Babylon, forming part of the exiled community and continuing the established role as the voice of the only one God, Yahweh (Petersen 1981, p. 99). Particularly in exile with its upheaval and uncertainties, the prophet's role of 'mediating the divine word' between the Jews and God consistent with their covenant relationship was crucial (Shepherd 2013). However, for this communicative bridge between God and the people to be authentic and effective, they had to be connected to both. On the one hand the prophet lived among the people, and on the other they 'stood in the counsel of the LORD' (Jer. 23.18). The Old Testament prophets' authenticity through such interconnectedness enabled them to understand the will and purpose of God concerning the present and the future of the Jewish people (Oosthuizen 1992, p. 4). However, this ideal can be easily compromised, requiring discernment among recipients of the prophetic in religious and wider settings, as to whether they are dealing with schools of prophets in the Old Testament, disciples of Jesus in the New Testament, or narratives within the Black British community today.

We find some clues in the Jeremiah text as to why the false prophets of that time are said to have incurred such wrath of

God as conveyed in the words of the prophet's letter. A central issue seems to be God's declared determination, first that some Jews would be taken to Babylon and second, that their length of stay would be 70 years, meaning intergenerational. Jeremiah understands that Yahweh has revealed both matters to him, but faces stern counter prophetic narrative in Jerusalem, represented by the prophet Hananiah and among the exiles in Babylon, represented by Ahab and Zedekiah. Prophets opposing Jeremiah use the same mode of address as him, all purporting to speak on behalf of 'the Lord Almighty, the God of Israel' (Adeyemo 2006, p. 913). Although these prophets purport to speak with the authority of God, Jeremiah indicates that their moral and spiritual lifestyles bring them under divine judgement (Adeyemo 2006, p. 905). Their inconsistency of life and ministry renders them unreliable and untrustworthy, and therefore Jeremiah's warning to the exiles is 'do not let them deceive you', just because they say they speak in God's name. A cacophony of prophetic voices opposing Jeremiah in Judah and Jerusalem, and in Babylon, understood first that there would be no deportation to Babylon, and then, when that prophecy proved misguided, that the captives would return home in two years. This was a misreading of the religious-historical times since the momentum of divine judgement allied with Babylon's imperial intentions and actions informed Jeremiah's pronouncement and ought to have done the same for other insightful, true 'seers'.

The arrival of Jeremiah's letter in Babylon would have further polarized the situation in which false prophets had raised the exiles' hope of an imminent return home (Adeyemo 2006, p. 914). Jeremiah's seemingly pessimistic and unpopular prophecy of a long multigenerational exile was the divine word and necessitated a change of mindset from one ready to leave as soon as possible to one of settling down, acquiring land, building houses and marrying and growing families (McGrath 1988, p. 184). In their vulnerable exilic state, presented as they were with two opposing prophecies, the Jews in exile had the task of discerning which to believe, and following the wrong prophetic counsel as though from the Lord could be dangerous and life-defining. Jeremiah's response was to condemn all those he believed were prophesying wrongly (Adeyemo 2006, p. 916). Ultimately, true prophecy is not what is convenient or popular, but what is in the best immediate and long-term interest of the people, which calls for, on the part of the prophet, deep rootedness in the experiential realities and aspirations of the people, helping to nurture good choices. And the prophet was willing to call out those prophets whose prophecies he believed were not from God and therefore not in the exiles' best interest.

Extrapolating further from Jeremiah's encounter with prophets he deemed as false, the prophet seems to question their calling, motive and lack of spiritual depth. They were self-appointed, did not listen to God, willing to tell the people what they wanted to hear, and managed to establish themselves in Judah and Jerusalem, and in Babylon. Jeremiah's severe critique of them branded them selfish and dangerous liars and their recompense would be dire. However, Tarrer, in an examination of true and false prophecies in the book of Jeremiah, suggests the difference may be more complex than indicated so far; showing, for example, that Hananiah and Jeremiah agreed about much – such as that a true prophet must stand in the counsel of God, and the importance of repentance and justice. Concerning the crucial points of whether the Jews would be exiled and for how long, Jeremiah seemed willing to bide time to discover what God's will was; maybe allowing for the possibility of a divine change of mind. At issue was whether he or Hananiah read the mind of God correctly (Tarrer 2013, p. 156).

Black British people, unlike the sixth-century Jewish exiles, are not a religious community bound by covenanted relationship with God; they are a transplanted community needing to adapt and flourish in Britain. This community, identifying as a group through ethnicity, colour and historic geography, are influenced by narratives that play a role similar to that of the prophetic as they attempt to navigate the UK diasporic space over generations. Like social, economic, political, even theological commentators, transnational, regional and localized idioms, proverbs and sayings contribute implicitly and explicitly to philosophical and cultural mores that inform the lives of Black British people in Britain (McKenzie 2002; McMillan 2005). It is by these and other media that the equivalent to oracles by Old Testament prophets are communicated; and their validity, helpfulness or otherwise have much to do with whether the narratives and their sources are rooted in the Black British community and have their best interests at heart. I do not claim that all who speak or write what I may refer to as unhelpful or untrue words, do so deliberately to mislead or harm, but rather that they express what they sincerely believe are solutions to the challenges encountered. Nor, indeed, am I claiming to be the sole righteous one; I merely speak as seems best to me. All truth claims should be examined not just in the immediate but also over the course of time, without regard to who speaks or writes. Clearly though, Black British recipients of 'prophecies' have a task of discernment of who and what to believe concerning how to conduct themselves to flourish.

Given the common African heritage (in part or whole) of Black British people, the prophet in traditional African settings, including indigenous Christian churches, is of interest. While playing a role as a go-between for God and people, the African prophet also acted as healer and exorcist challenging prevailing contextual forces (Oosthuizen 1992, p. 15). Black British people exist at that intersection where Africa meets Europe, the latter secularized and given more to metaphysical rather than to phenomenological encounters. This leaves Black British people needing to reconcile historic and contemporary understandings of the role of spirituality and materiality in the world in which they find themselves. The kind of 'seer' that could help may be typified by a description of Jeremiah as a prophet who had the ability to receive and transmit oracles or messages, and images that spoke into the Jewish situation; a prophet who knew and loved them too much to lie to them (Adeyemo 2006). Jeremiah postulates an image of two baskets of figs, one very bad and the other very good, where counterintuitively the good figs represented the fate of those Jews who were taken into exile in Babylon, while the bad figs represented those Jews that remained in Judah. This is an example of how the prophetic ministry is not simply a matter of repeating words, but involves all the prophet's emotional and spiritual faculties, deliberately looking in order to see, to understand, to grasp with intelligence in order to communicate to others what has been divinely or intuitively communicated to them (Adeyemo 2006, p. 907). Even in its looser sense, a true prophet identifies with challenging circumstances pointing to the appropriate choices, while the false prophet espouses the popular ones. Flourishing in spite of historic, prevailing socio-economic, spiritual and political conditions is what diaspora people endeavour to do, and any 'prophet' who does not understand this can rightly be called 'false'. From my experience in Britain, I want to mention some, what I call, 'contextual false prophetic oracles' that I believe, though well-intentioned, risk hindering Black British people's attempts to flourish. As elsewhere in this book I explore these issues with the twin optics of the Black British church community and the broader Black British community in mind.

First, I begin with a 'contextual false prophetic oracle' that 'the reason Black British people are in Britain is because we were invited to come'. Usually linked to the Windrush scandal, and how the monarchy or the British government had invited Black people to come then once here turned the table on them by creating a hostile environment (Gentleman 2019; Goodfellow 2019). This 'here by invitation' theory is an unhelpful misrepresentation of reality, an insecure and insincere basis upon which to build an existence in diaspora. The relationship between Britain, Africa and Caribbean had been for centuries enslaver/enslaved, colonizer/colonized and empire/subject – scarcely the basis of cordial mutuality that facilitates an invitation worthy of the name. The 'invitation' is usually invoked to introduce the absurdity of bad treatment by a host to a guest, typified by the Windrush scandal, as suggested in the 'betrayal' title of Gentleman's book. This supposed invitation usually refers to the period since World War Two when colonial subjects were needed to join the country's war efforts, and the Windrush era that followed when workers were needed in the post-war rebuilding efforts. The failure of Britain to honour their invitation supposedly accepted in good faith now prevents Black British people from flourishing, or so the rationale goes.

As is widely accepted, people of African heritage came to Britain by force during the slave trade era, voluntarily during the Windrush era, and for various reasons since, but few if any have come because of a cordial invitation from the British monarchy or government. As Usongo says, 'Many West Indians who emigrated to Europe did so mainly because of economic hardship, and they all seemed to nurse a desire of returning home in case of better economic opportunities' (Usongo 2018). Former slave colonies like Jamaica, part of the British Empire and operated for the benefit of Britain, struggled to provide the basic requirements for the subsistence of their growing populations (Davies and Witter 1989). Williams reminds us that the Caribbean region was at one time regarded by some in Britain as the slum of the Empire, a land of flattering statistics and distressing realities (Williams 1993, p. 443). Drawn to the centre of empire in search of economic betterment, Black British people must know where they are, how and why they came to be here, know what they want, and relentlessly set about strategizing to achieve it knowing the odds are historically stacked against them. As John states, focusing on education, Black communities across Britain should commit to action, organize themselves independently of national systems and embrace their responsibility for the future of their children; determined to fix what needs fixing in their own houses and communities (John 2006, p. 117).

The idea that Britain called and Black British people obediently and docilely came to do its bidding unhelpfully contrasts with the previous half a millennium of enslavement and colonial exploitation. The reality is that Black people have come to Britain historically under duress socially, economically and politically but specifically since the Windrush era with an intention and a plan for self-betterment. This expression of agency and self-determination should never be forgotten by succeeding generations but embraced knowing that whether the environment is hostile or friendly they are in Britain for and with a purpose. Indeed, this is not a space of invitation and acceptance, it is the site of centuries old struggle to live true to Black humanity and to flourish in the presence of some of whom can be described as enemies (Psalm 100). This struggle for flourishing exists cheek by jowl with the myth of the *Windrush* which, though a real ship that docked at Tilbury in June 1948, has now come to symbolize post-war immigration, multicultural Britain, the Windrush Generation and the urban myth of their being invited to Britain by the British government (Phillips and Phillips 1998, p. 2). Paradoxically, there was no need for an invite since imperial subjects travelled to Britain as citizens of the British Empire with freedom of movement throughout – a feature that was to change in later years in response to just how many empire citizens of colour were travelling to Britain for better economic prospects that were unavailable in the former slave colonies.

In view of the past half a millennium, were the people of the Caribbean and Africa to have received and accepted an invitation by the British sovereign or government to travel thousands of miles to the capital of the British Empire that had wreaked genocidal havoc on their parents, fore parents and ancestors, that would not be an act of which to be proud, since it would be an indication of sublime naivety, lack of self and historical awareness, and infantilization; unbecoming for a people made in the *imago Dei.* A few years ago, I was invited to speak at a British university on the topic of the resilience and achievements of the Windrush Generation, and was introduced by a professor who confidently stated that when we think of the Windrush Generation, we must always remember that we were invited to come to Britain. I felt compelled to preface my talk by dissociating myself from the assertion. In a poignant poem by Professor Laura Serrant (https://www.youtube.com/watch?v=3XMZhbcBl4M), eulogizing the Windrush Generation coming to the 'motherland', each stanza is punctuated by the refrain, 'you called and we came'. Poetic licence being taken, probably, but in view of the history between the people of the Caribbean and Britain, any such call ought to have been met with utmost cynicism and, if accepted, done so with much circumspection when viewed through the lens of a murderous past. This history is in no way captured by 'you called, and we came'. It has been shown repeatedly that the majority of workers from the Caribbean, taking what jobs they could find, were concentrated mainly, though not exclusively, in marginal, low-paid industries, in transport and textiles (Werbner 2002, p. 6).

An example of the challenges posed by the choices made is illustrated well by Ali who points to one of the classic signs of migration, particularly economic migration, where women tend to be the ones caught in the liminal space between those who leave and those who are left behind (Ali 2019). In my family it was my father who travelled first in search of economic betterment. As soon as he could afford to, he brought over two elder sons, then returned to Jamaica before travelling again to England long before mother and other children joined him. The women and children were the ones left behind in a manner that suggests that, were my family the recipients of an invitation, my parents might have struck a deal better aligned with our domestic needs. Such was the economic plight of our deeply rural family that with faith in God to keep him and his family left safely behind, my father ventured ahead into the unknown. This was an exercise of his agency and self-determination towards the future of his growing family. It is to this specific action that I owe my presence in England.

Phillips and Phillips make reference to Caribbean servicemen who joined the British armed forces in World War Two, mainly as pilots and ground crew in the RAF as Britain recruited from across its empire and commonwealth. They describe how the subjects of empire and commonwealth had ambitions of their own in their desire for adventure, to escape economic hardship, and to further their education (Phillips and Phillips 1998, pp. 26–46). Although some were reasonably off, all saw and exploited opportunities to improve their lot as subjects of the British Empire. Fryer describes how the situation in Asia and the Caribbean was so economically desperate that it is surprising not that so many citizens of the United Kingdom and

Colonies with rights to settle left to find better prospects in Britain, but that so many stayed (Fryer 1984, p. 373).

Yet, this urban myth of an invitation from the British government has taken root, undermining Black British agency. An amplification mechanism has been found in the Windrush scandal, and the public outcry that these lovely people were invited and were now being deported. In reality this was more about a British government's determination to create a hostile environment for illegal immigrants by 'stitching immigration checks into every element of people's lives ... through measures brought in by the 2014 and 2016 Immigration Acts' (Goodfellow 2019, p. 2). This hostile environment sucked in non-illegal immigrants (legal citizens) who when asked or challenged were unable to provide documentary evidence, such as a passport, for their legitimate status and right to live and work in Britain. Although technically applying indiscriminately, effectively the people challenged or asked to show documentary evidence of their right of abode were likely to have been 'non-white', which meant a racist element woven into the hostile environment affecting disproportionately 'people of colour'.

Olusoga has helpfully shown that during the 1960s, well after the *Windrush* docking in June 1948, a junior government minister by the name of Enoch Powell did encourage recruitment of nurses from the Caribbean to come and find work in the newly formed National Health Service (Goodfellow 2019, p. 79; https://www.youtube.com/watch?v=f_rzJTNZSLM). This, however, could scarcely be backdated to the Windrush or generalized to the entire migrating population that travelled from the Caribbean to Britain. In fact, Olusoga points out that historical records show that while the *Windrush* was en route to Tilbury, efforts in government were being made to either turn it back to Jamaica or divert it; along with intense political activities aimed at working out how to handle so many 'coloured' members of the British Commonwealth who were entitled to come, were certainly not invited, and were definitely not welcomed.

There are good reasons why the narrative concerning Black British people being here is important. First, because the 'you called, and we came' narrative is not true. Second, because it denies the agency of the adventurous émigrés who decided to go to Britain in search of better prospects for themselves and their families. Third, because it feeds into an age-old European stereotype of African docility, lack of original thought and imagination, and are always reactive to European action, never proactive. And fourth, because if the basis on which Black British people are in Britain is wrongly understood to be located in anything other than their own agency, that suggests a continuation of the servant/master, slave/owner, empire/subjects basis that locates Black British people permanently indebted and responsive to their historic rulers. I find this reflected too in the popular narrative about Black British churches that they came into existence because white churches rejected Black people from their churches and in response Black British people resorted to starting churches of their own. This attitude of 'if only we had treated you better you wouldn't have needed to start your own churches' deals in a similar patronizing currency that suggests Black British people are responders to European action. As mentioned elsewhere, while there was white rejection of Black members of mainstream churches from abroad, those mostly joined the churches Black British people started out of a missional intent, in the interest of establishing denominations that did not already exist in Britain (Aldred 2005; Sturge 2005). Urban myths which become widely accepted national narrative constitute an attack on the agency and self-determination of Black British people by attributing their initiative to others. It implies a simplistic childlike forgetfulness in which a child does not initiate and respond to parental authority. It is clear to me that a mindset conducive to flourishing must liberate itself from the notion that Black British people are here because the old empire called and the descendants of enslaved and colonized people obediently came.

Theologically, undermining one's humanity made in the image and likeness of the Creator does a disservice to God and to the self. In all humanity there are implicitly the attributes that flow from being in God's image and likeness, made explicit as they are lived out among other humans without feeling or projecting inferiority or superiority. Domeris reminds us of the place of honour and shame among Jewish people in antiquity, often linked to proximity to high status rather than to righteousness. He notes how Jesus challenged this by reversing the order of things, making the weak strong, the last first, and raising up the lowly (Domeris 1993). This disruption is necessary too in the case of Black British people and the racialized way of discounting their humanity and actions in favour of attributing them to those thought more worthy of credit. However, in the spirit of this book, Black British people cannot assume divine intervention in their affairs that does not involve them in the acts of their own defence and flourishing, therefore when their credit is given to another they should ensure they put the record straight. They should never meekly surrender their honour or permit the erroneous labelling of African peoples as lacking creativity and underachievement. For Black pioneers to have their initiative-taking stolen and credited to a false notion that the only reason they are here is because Babylon invited them, or the reason they have churches is because they were turned out of white ones, is a wrong that must be corrected; and with it the attribution of glory and praise where it is due (Isa. 42.8). Such credit is due to the brave pioneers who travelled with their 'grips' into the unknown following their adventurous spirit to Canada, the USA, the UK and elsewhere. Their voyages were not due to a benevolent British government suddenly warmly inviting a people it had oppressed for hundreds of years, and the God-image in Black British people must not be discredited by misallocating and plagiarizing their actions. Worse, and probably even more sinful, is for the people themselves to give away their due credit to some other because of a historic deficit of self-appreciation and conversely an over appreciation of the European other due to an imbibed assumptive superiority located in a miseducation about European God-likeness and African God-unlikeness. The Windrush Generation came, not because they were called, but because they saw opportunities for economic betterment and bravely travelled into already proven hostile terrain, convinced the deployment of their God-given agency could sustain them.

A second 'contextual false prophetic oracle' is that Black British people are identified as 'oppressed', or as Rastas might say, 'downpressed'. I hasten to say the veracity of historic realities of the transatlantic slave trade, chattel-cum-plantation slavery, colonialism and racism perpetrated by Europeans upon Africans over centuries are not in question here – those events genuinely occurred, and have lasting consequences. What I would question is the use of 'oppressed' as a characterization, an identifier, and 'liberation' as their corresponding aspiration that because of the nature of things is always out of reach. The permanence of this oppression/liberation dialectic may have spawned a self-sustaining race industry, that has, in the view of this pastor-writer, consigned Black British flourishing to entrapment in the dialectic's orbit. Jesus' manifesto statement in Luke 4 speaks of the poor, the prisoners, the blind and setting the oppressed, or 'bruised', free (v. 18 KJV). This is such a catch-all list that scarcely anyone can fail to identify with some aspects or other. Jesus' idea of the bruised interests me when attempting to define oppressed in relation to Black British people, but racialized bruising is not restricted to Britain.

Cone makes reference to his early upbringing in a racialized America and the people he grew up among in their daily struggle to survive, the ups and downs of black existence, and their 'attempt to seize a measure of freedom in an extreme situation of oppression' under Jim Crow laws (Cone 1975, p. 4). Cone refers to a time when racism in America, that is the inferiorization of Africans by Europeans, not merely existed but was legal, and African people were perpetually challenged to stay alive and maintain human dignity in a situation of racialized oppression – physical, psychological and spiritual bruising. In the same book, *God of the Oppressed*, Cone shines a light on a major problem with this discourse when he asks rhetorically, why does not God destroy the powers of evil oppressing Black people? And why does God permit white people to oppress helpless Black people? (Cone 1975, p. 163). While Cone sought theological answers to the dilemma posed by theodicy, that God is either unwilling or unable to deliver the oppressed from injustice, I baulk at the assumed divine determinism, the assumed European ownership and hegemony over African, the assumed African docility, lack of agency and lack of ability to change their situation. The acceptance of the European/African dialectical fixedness is alarming and distressing. I do not believe this label 'oppressed' or 'downpressed' is liberative, and ask, why would a people choose to understand themselves through a negative identity imposed by their oppressors rather than through their true humanity and its indominable spirit to rise above principalities and powers? Indeed, I argue that our ancestors managed to resist oppression, whether successfully or not, maintaining their human identity as primordial, while also retaining an understanding to expect divine intervention only through their own God-given agency.

A lesson from biblical history is that the liberation of the bruised such as occurs in the story of the Jews in Egypt and later in Babylon often occurs after centuries of suffering during which the people cry out to God for freedom and at length God is said to answer in the affirmative. It is possible to observe also that during the long periods of oppression liberation theorists emerge, but there are few actual liberation activists like Moses in Egypt and Ezra in Babylon/Persia. By the time they do, many of the oppressed have discovered coping mechanisms and resist liberation or prefering to remain where they are in diaspora. Correspondingly, those who remained in the homeland resist returning expatriates as meddlers. Professional liberation theorists however continue to utilize the language of oppression/liberation way past the sell-by date of these terminologies. Hence I argue that Black British people need to reflect deeply upon the meanings and consequences of being labelled 'oppressed' and in need of liberation, and ask what theorists mean by them. Are they a help or hindrance to the flourishing of Black British people who must deploy their agency and self-determination as individuals and as a people if they are to make progress towards flourishing? What is the destination here, how will the people know when they arrive, or is arrival not intended?

I first came across the theological language of oppression/liberation among Latin American Catholic clergy writing in solidarity with the poor masses. African American theologians and subsequently others especially in the global south have adopted this approach without much, if any, evidence that the liberation of the oppressed is advanced by the theology. Surely the understanding that 'Christian theology is a site of struggle' should be accompanied by an assessment of success in the liberative strategy before accepting and advancing an ideology (Rowland and Vincent 1995, p. 11). Proof of a pudding is in the eating, as a saying goes, and the liberation envisaged in the main is socio-economic and political power that has rested in the northern hemisphere while poorer people in the south remain poor and left to depend upon the rich north 'taking an option for the poor' to alleviate the plight of 'the oppressed and deprived in personal, community and social terms' (Rowland and Vincent 1995, p. 12). Saying and wishing it does not make it so, however. Vincent, my former supervisor, rightly identifies a crucial gap in the process as he bemoans the lack of poor and oppressed people themselves being engaged in the theologizing about liberation of the oppressed as well as acknowledging that readers of his and other theological books are likely to be mainly (white) middle class (Rowland and Vincent 1995, pp. 13 and 15). There is tacit recognition that the people likely to be 'acting, thinking and working for change' are not the 'oppressed' themselves, although they may belong to a group so labelled (Rowland and Vincent 1995, p. 21). Alas, if there is one person I know who understands the fallacy of depending on (a) middle-class Christians marked by 'enlightenment, education, moderation, responsibility, personal compassion and a very deep commitment to particular self-interest', and (b) a wrong-headed hermeneutics about God as Liberator, it is Vincent (Rowland and Vincent 1995, p. 17).

Gibellini tells that the earliest tenets of Liberation Theology emerged at the time of European conquest of South America among the missionaries against the colonialist exploiters (Gibellini 1986, p. 1). In effect, the European colonialists have had it both ways from the beginning, as commercial and religious interlocutors tend to look alike and come from similar backgrounds, usually with privilege and in search of more.

Wrongly premised and owned from the start (even if well-intentioned), Liberation Theology has grown over the years, driven by indignation at the poverty and marginalization of the masses and so has been termed by those with relative power as a theology from the underside of history (p. 4). The type-casting of a people or group as a means of supposedly helping them tends to further enhance the reputation of those doing the naming while objectifying the named without necessarily changing their circumstances. It is my conviction that in spite of the recognition that two-thirds of humanity are dominated by one-third, resulting in millions of deaths from hunger and malnutrition, and that this ought to become a starting point for theological praxis, the poor will not be saved from their plight by those with vested interests. Change may come only when those who experience oppression decide to throw off their oppressive yoke in diaspora or in their historic home-lands and lead the discussion about categorization, identity and epistemology. Poverty and oppression survive because the self-serving intentional social, economic and political structures that perpetuate Western hegemony remain dependent upon the middle and upper classes purporting to want to change it (Gibellini 1986, p. 94). Re-reading some of my old textbooks on Liberation Theology I am reminded that good intentions are good, but they are not good enough to transform life unless in the hands of transformative people with vested interest in trans-formation of the status quo, as opposed to those who mean well but have an instinct to protect that from which they benefit.

Gutiérrez's insightful 'we drink from our own wells' recog-nizes the stark reality of poverty's link to premature death and raise hopes of the arrival of a Kairos moment in the world, but I doubt there are many today who believe that Liberation Theology has bequeathed us a new world (Gutiérrez 1984). The same can be said of other luminaries like the Boff brothers, who cite Liberation Theology as a prophetic and comradely commitment to the life cause and struggle of millions of debased and marginalized human beings and express a com-mitment to ending this historical social iniquity (Boff and Boff 1987, p. 3). As is the case with those mentioned above, Cone and subsequent practitioners of Liberation Theology and a Black Theology of liberation, those doing the theologizing are invariably situated among the privileged middle class. Even when the liberation theologian is of the same phenotype as those they designate 'oppressed', the meaning of identifying their ethnic peers with the suffering Jesus is usually by proxy for them, and what seems like an accompaniment is an exercise in affirming Jesus' words that 'the poor you will always have with you' (Matt. 26.11).

During the 1990s, Black British theologians and practitioners (including me) established *Black Theology: A Journal of Contextual Praxis* (Lartey 1998) with an initial aim to critically reflect upon our Christian faith in light of our experience of life as Black British people. My memory informs me that weight of opinion then was not heavily dependent upon an oppression/liberation dialectic, but on asking what, as a people whose ancestors were oppressed under the transatlantic slave trade, chattel/plantation slavery, colonialism and who currently experience racism, was our experience of attempting to flourish in Britain as a diaspora community. It was clear that while much of the oppression Black British people suffered in past centuries was now largely being viewed in our rear mirror, racism in new forms was still with us. However, once that journal gave way to *Black Theology: An International Journal* (A. Reddie (ed.) 2012, pp. 2–3), a critical shift occurred that used the lens of a 'Black experience of oppression' as the journal's focus. I bemoan a central aspect of this and its (re-)appropriation of the oppression/liberation that locks the Black British in that place of liberal fatalism. While paying due attention to an analysis of past oppression, and present racialized oppression or bruising experienced today, I would welcome a wider embrace of Black British experience in terms of how Black British agency, self-determination and *imago Dei* pursue flourishing in diaspora in Britain. I would also welcome a more balanced liberal/conservative approach reflecting Africentric/Eurocentric theological epistemologies. This might be achieved by ensuring a better balance of articles between theological liberal thinkers and conservative – ones mainly to be found in Pentecostal churches and academies. Unlike Black British people in mainstream European churches who tend to emphasize oppression/liberation, Pentecostal thinkers reflect much upon pneumatology, living a victorious life even in the face of adversity.

Writing plays an important part in maintaining the 'oppressed' narrative as a permanent feature of Black British life, even as liberation is continuously mentioned. If we assume there has been a developmental phase where the available religious literature about Black British people has been written by Europeans and a second phase where the narrative is further developed by Black British people in mainstream churches; then a third phase has to be one led by Black British people from *bona fide* Black British-led churches. The predominance of Black British theologians from mainstream churches is self-evident and I argue that that expression of Black Theology is heavily imbued with Western liberal sympathies rather than African, usually conservative, sympathies. In this regard there may be little philosophical difference between Black British and white British theologians where both theologize from rootedness in Western ecclesiological bases. Black British people should together ponder if they have allowed themselves to be seduced in a voluntary humility (Col. 2.18) into accepting labelling such as a people from the 'underside of history' (Wilkinson 1993, p. 3) by asking, whose underside and whose history? Or that we should embrace and therefore solidify 'black' meaning oppressed. Or that we meet at the cross of Jesus as 'victim and oppressor' (Wilkinson 1993, p. 171); whereas the more wholesome meeting roster is as in Revelation 7.9: 'every nation, tribe, people and language'. At the foot of the cross of Jesus or around the throne of God in heaven we gather as who we really are, a diverse humanity, not victims and victors, oppressed and oppressors, not 'nobodies' trying to be somebodies (Reddie 2003). The time to do righteousness is now or not at all and it is only a theology out of sync with black realities that defers a day of reckoning till the hereafter.

The labelling of Black British people as 'oppressed', maliciously or with good intention, is usually done by the materially more privileged, who therefore constitute part of the oppressive system though never admitting to it, and always pointing away accusingly to others. I find poignant Freire's assertion that education is freedom, but can be undermined when traditional teaching styles keep the poor powerless by treating them as passive, silent recipients of knowledge instead of practising education by co-operation, dialogue and critical thinking through which there come development of the sense of self and fulfil their right to be heard (Freire 2017). This example has broader implications beyond education, and I detect a philosophy by the better-off that encourages or even induces the 'oppressed' to find comfort in collective misery, as they help them see just how oppressed they are and how much the oppressor is to blame, yet without a scintilla of how the power within can alleviate their situation apart from the benevolence of their oppressor. Passivity of the so-called poor, powerless, oppressed colludes with the power of the oppressor and serve their purposes. In a similar fashion to the recognition that there were not 'African slaves' but 'enslaved Africans', a situational descriptor, so too I argue the term oppressed should be used situationally, not superimposed upon a people by those who take the power to so name them, from inside or outside the community. Boal reminds us that

> words designate sets, but ignore unicities. Blacks and whites, men and women, proletarian and peasant are imagined as sets, but do not exist as concretion ... what exists, corporeally, is this particular black person and that particular white person, this woman and that man, this peasant and that worker – and even then, all of these are in transit, in the state of becoming, of coming to be and ceasing to be. None of them is the same as it was, from one moment to the next, in this permanent state of becoming. (Boal 2006, p. 13)

Unicities include epochs too, and building upon the trauma of the past I believe Black British people should regard the current era as one of post oppression/liberation dialectic; a time to assert African humanity rooted in the *imago Dei* working through the contours of diaspora towards flourishing. Their ancestors and parents have managed to liberate themselves from the slave trade, chattel/plantation slavery and colonialism and conveyed to them that the way to combat racism is to become and remain strong, combative and transcendent. When a people think of themselves, when they dream of the future, do they self-conceive as an oppressed subset of British society, or of society in general, or do they self-understand as a people made in the image and likeness of God who have known oppression, been bruised by it in its various guises, but remain resilient and not dehumanized by it, belonging to an identity that extends beyond the shores of their diasporic adopted home? Black British people should reject the voices and narratives labelling them 'oppressed', and instead contextualize oppression as part of their historic human experience. Black British people are no more to be identified as 'oppressed' than as 'kings and queens' which is also true in their experience as people of African heritage.

My summary of this 'oppressed' condition applying to Black British people is that while they will have experienced British colonialism and ongoing racism, Black British ancestors alone encountered chattel and plantation slavery and the transatlantic slave trade, which some argue has morphed into 'post traumatic slave syndrome' (Hicks 2015). Drawing upon various studies, centred on the USA but with application for the enslavement of Africans everywhere, Hicks argues that the African Holocaust or Maafa perpetrated by Europeans upon Africans for half a millennium has had immediate and sequential impacts of the traumatization on enslaved and liberated Africans and their descendants. The effects of historical traumas, unresolved grief, multigenerational trauma transmission, has left a psychological and behavioural legacy behind that continues to oppress, including discrimination and marginalization in Western societies. Black British people need to take note of this while assuming total responsibility for exercise of their agency and self-determination as they look to a future in Britain (Hicks 2015, p. 42). The historical and contemporary trauma that Black British people and their ancestors suffered is unquestionable, the question is whether to collapse African experience into its desperate subjectivity or to remove the African self completely off the 'plantation' by creating a psychological and spiritual alternative reality rooted in Black *imago Dei*, agency and self-determination even without changing geography. Black British people are not oppressed as an identity, they have suffered oppression, but they live liberated in the humanity made in the image of God; and refuse to depend upon liberation coming from some other source beyond themselves and over whom they have no control. Black British people have to see themselves through their own lens as human, first of all, never equating the self with the negativities of the bruising encountered through the oppression at the ill-will of evil others.

A third 'contextual false prophetic oracle' I summarize as, 'racism must be dismantled and eradicated from society'. This has now come to be popularly regarded as a given, with reams written on the subject, but I believe it is an unhelpful albatross around the necks of Black British people. Let me be clear that I too wish racism was never created. I despise racism and condemn it as a sin against *imago Dei* in black humanity, but that does not uninvent it, nor can it be wished away. Therefore, responses to it must be appropriate. Further, I understand this dismantling and ridding society of racism as an emotional response since there is no known historic or contemporary examples of eradication from any society of racism or similar prejudice-induced '-isms'. To make Black British flourishing conditional upon something outside their control is foolhardy and Black British people should prioritize what they must do in response to the racism they face. Black British people cannot afford to be beholden to racism for another half a millennium! Responses must retain integrity, pride, agency, self-determination and honour the image of God in African humanity. From a perspective of counselling and psychology on disrupting anti-African systemic racism, come calls for re-envisioning of approaches (Pieterse, Lewis and Miller 2023, pp. 235–43). I suggest re-envisioning should include an awareness that dismantling and eradicating racism from Western societies is an unworthy challenge for Black British people.

From my experience, Black British people's preoccupation ought to concern constructing a philosophical, spiritual and physical 'empire' that is strong and profound enough to offer an alternative to the Western form that enslaved them for centuries and now threatens to preoccupy them eternally in their desire to dismantle and eradicate racism. We have witnessed how as Black British people have established their presence and identity, British anti-racism laws have come into being with protection against racism. Justice is God's will and command but it is never achieved without exertion and the persistent exercise of one's agency bearing down upon resistant interests and institutions, beating them into submission. This bears a similarity to when enslaved African people on plantations from sunup to sundown picking cotton, cutting and gathering sugar cane, strengthened their presence and identity and caused or contributed to the end of chattel slavery. The alternative kingdom to which they belonged, built upon love, righteousness, justice and peace found the oppression of enslavement an intolerable sin, refusing to live any longer under it as enslaved people. Slavery did not end but Africans freed themselves from its yoke. Discernment is needed for this time in Britain, learning from the past that it is establishing a people's presence and identity that changes the dynamics in the opposing empires that exist and want to dominate and exploit for their gain. Black British emotional, intellectual, conscious and subconscious awareness is foundational for flourishing in diaspora. Instead of forlorn attempts to 'mash down Babylon', that is, to break down someone else's kingdom, responses should be informed by an awareness that systemic, institutional and endemic racism is woven into the fabric of Britain and other white Western societies after centuries of racialized practices against people of colour. The acceptance of this reality is necessary for Black British society, and should not be ignored or be something upon which Black flourishing is conditional; dependency should be upon the people's own agency and self-determination.

Over the past few years and particularly since the death of the African American George Floyd in 2020, there has been a surge of writings by Black British authors addressing issues of liberation relating to the Black British community. Their demand, though expressed differently, is for racial justice and equality, sometimes including reparations for the damage done through the slave trade, chattel slavery, colonialism and racism. Enabled by articulate, educated and well-placed Black British people, the community now has libraries of books and lots of writers in the press and plenty of appearances on TV demanding justice. White people's willingness to engage comes now in the wake of George Floyd's death which some see as a Kairos moment, the most receptive in living memory. White people are listening and are interested in conversing and acting for the better. However, while the tragic death of Floyd has opened doors to greater conversations, the pillars of white dominance do not go away as easily or quickly. In several conversations I have been in, what has become clear is that what is being asked for by some, wittingly or unwittingly, is absorption into white normativity. 'White normativity' is not exceptional in and of itself since all majority cultures become the dominant force, with equality and justice hard to find for disadvantaged minorities. In the field of ethnographic theology or qualitative research, Csinos refers to white normativity as an epistemology shaped by dominant approaches and values. Wisely, the writer, while aiming to dismantle white normativity, accepts that the study does not offer a definitive solution to ending white normativity as the aim implies (Csinos 2020).

Black British people would do well to admit that inequalities and injustices exist everywhere in the world including where their ancestors come from. What is needed is human coexistence based on being true to one's compound self, while contributing to an enriched new reality in which African history, culture and philosophy is present in an incarnational manner adjoining other peoples'. There is no desire for a colourless or colour blind society, rather one constitutive of the sum of its distinctive parts. Having been brought up in a Black Pentecostal church I have seen how minorities or sometimes a single convert from a different church tradition have to navigate the contours of denominational or local church normativity if they are to settle down, make a contribution and flourish in the space. The majority culture rarely understands the need to make accommodation for minorities, and it is not unusual to find white minorities in Black majority churches becoming used to eating Caribbean cuisine and speaking Caribbean dialects – to fit in! For Black British people to flourish, they will need to do other than be shocked at white normativity including the West's attempts at normalising Black subjugation and inferiorization. They must be prepared for it and armed with a response. From my observation, a majority of the commentators on the challenge of Black British flourishing, expressed usually in terms of level playing field, diversity, equality, inclusion and justice, seem to have bought into the alluring ideology that the key to Black success is to dismantle and eradicate racism in all its forms from British society; since only then can Black British people flourish. This represents a significant groupthink from which there is scarcely any deviation. I disagree with them and argue that the way to deal with racism is to confront it through Black British empowerment, through the exercise of their agency, and self-determination, while maintaining their dignity rooted in the *imago Dei.*

Some examples of books by Black British authors linking dismantling and eradicating racism with Black flourishing may be helpful here. An arrowhead concern of this argument is that white people do not take Black British people's claim to British identity seriously. Worse still, that they consider 'black' and 'British' to be incongruous, an oxymoron. Hirsh, in her book *Brit(ish)*, makes a statement in the title, that African people in Britain have their Britishness questioned every day, and that 'Britain has still not made itself a place where we can unreservedly belong' (Hirsh 2018, p. 281). A weakness of this position is how it hands the initiative to a nebulous 'Britain' to validate Black belonging, apparently unrelated to one's actual status of belonging or one's confidence to assert one's identity and belonging independently of 'Britain's' view of oneself. When you are in exile or the descendants of exiles, you cannot afford the luxury of depending upon Babylonian natives to unanimously welcome or vouch for you. Presumption has of necessity to be that some never will. Eddo-Lodge's *Why I'm No Longer Talking to White People About Race*, a *Sunday Times* best-seller, is a rage against white people's 'refusal to see racism as structural in order to see its insidiousness' (Eddo-Lodge 2018, p. 222). Calling time on explaining to those white people who are either incapable or who refuse to grasp how terrible racism is upon the lives of Black people, Eddo-Lodge concludes that African people in Britain and other ethnic minorities need to take their prospects in their own hands to create a better country. I agree! The irony is that the book created such a stir that the author appears to spend even more time talking to white people about why she's no longer talking to white people about race. What Eddo-Lodge has in common with Hirsh is an over-emphasis upon white behaviour as determinative of Black flourishing, a resort to Black agency only coming a poor second option, whereas I argue this must be *a priori*.

Lindsay's *We Need To Talk About Race*, represents an example of a Christian retort extolling the virtues of, indeed the necessity for, tolerant communication as an inadvertent or deliberate riposte to Eddo-Lodge's loss of patience with 'hard ears' white people, as Jamaicans might infer. Taking aim at the Church, Lindsay is clear about the imperative of conversation about race and that the racism that flows from the theory of race is a sin against God and the cause by which 'Black British people have been unmerited by the Church' that has a responsibility to be an example to the world (Lindsay 2019, p. 62). Like Eddo-Lodge and Hirsh, Lindsay understands the key to African people's progress in Britain lies in what white people, in his case white Christians, should do about the plight of Black British people. As I write, the most recent of these books, another Christian text, by Roach and Birdsall, takes a similar trajectory to Lindsay's by appealing to the conscience of especially white people who are Christians to play their part in getting their knees of oppression off the African neck (Roach and Birdsall 2022). This is tantamount to an appeal – 'surely you can see that you are hurting me ... please in God's name, stop' – in the interest of apparently pitiful objects unable to save themselves. Jeremiah's letter to Jewish exiles envisages a much more agency-led and robust relationship in Babylon. Similar is needed in Britain today.

Mukwashi's *But Where Are You Really From?*, published while the author was Chief Executive of the significant church-led Christian Aid agency, rails against a British society that insists on asking her and others like her who are apparently 'not from here', 'Where are you from?' As in a prior discussion above, almost irrespective of what the answer to that question is comes a follow up, 'But where are you really from?' For Mukwashi this is 'microaggression' of a high order and points to a white determination to 'other' those they do not regard as British, or suspect may not qualify. Dark skin colour and a foreign accent mark them out as not from 'here'. However, what becomes evident reading Mukwashi's book is that similar 'othering' occurs in the context from which she hails, Zambia (formerly Northern Rhodesia) and Zimbabwe (formerly Southeern Rhodesia). In a discourse about the plight of migrants from south to north during past liberation struggles she says,

> As the children of those immigrants grew up and started their own families, they inter-married with the indigenous population of Northern Rhodesia, or Zambia as it was called by this time. They seemingly integrated very well, but the reality was different. I remember we were called derogatory names as children, referred to as vana vanaBwidi, meaning children of foreigners, but it also used to imply a primitive people. (Mukwashi 2020, p. 38)

I am struck by the similarities of 'othering' in an African context between Africans in Africa and othering in Britain between Black and white people. Consideration about dealing with othering in Britain may draw also from the citation of othering in Africa and conclude that this is a human trait, wrong in every setting, but not peculiar to one particular ethnic group. Othering is unhelpful in western Europe and in northern Africa. There is risk of a charge of hypocrisy if Black people are uncritically non-condemnatory of the practice in African lands by Black towards Blacks while critical when it occurs in Britain by whites towards Blacks. Such narrative risks feeding into an unfortunate blind spot on race and racism within the context of Britain and elsewhere. In Africa among Black people, a phenomenon may be observable and viewed as a fact of fallen human life with which we have to deal and wrestle, while similar things in Britain perpetrated by white people must be eradicated from society in order for Black British people to flourish. Care should be taken not to inadvertently authenticate white people as a superior species from whom more is expected than of Black people.

I view this apparent need for racism eradication in Britain as due to Black British identity being perceived as 'a problem', imbibing a white view, actual or perceived. This is evident in the work of counsellor and psychotherapist Hall in *Redemption Song* (2021). Here, Black British people do not see themselves through their own eyes, but through the eyes of the white system and people, particularly those with a malevolent intent that denies the legitimacy of Black identity. A culmination of thought seems to be that white people's view of Black so inferiorizes them that only by ridding the context of that view can the victims of this negativity find freedom. Hall, while providing psychotherapeutic ideas for a battered and bruised African people living in Britain appears to do so from a perspective of Black victimhood where the best they can hope for are coping strategies for survival. Hall does hold out hope of a more assertive 'transatlantic dialogue', in which Africans from the Caribbean, USA and Britain engage, since united Black British people are strong, but divided they place themselves on the path of failure in such changing and unpredictable times (Hall 2021, p. 160). Again, the desperate state of blackness seems beyond redemption given their apparent inability to help themselves and the accepted truism that power will never be given away. Hall's pastoral advice lacks focus upon Black agency, belief in Black power for self-liberation, and a bloated assumptiveness of white pervading power against which Black transcendence cannot hope to prevail in the struggle within a multiethnic community. This writer says: 'away with this counsel of despair' and let us recall the words of Marcus Mosiah

Garvey, 'no justice, but strength' (Jacques-Garvey 1977, Vol. 2, p. 13), and as the Bible says, 'we are more than conquerors' (Rom. 8.37). The best pastoral advice is that which empowers the weak to be strong, not that which assumes inherent weakness and dependency on external forces, sometimes malevolent, to rescue them.

Some writers offer glimpses of deviating away from generally fatalistic, even nihilistic approaches. Mos-Shogbamimu in some senses represents a case of Black British agency belligerently asserting itself against white racism. Regrettably, this occurs still within the gambit of appealing to white people and systems to desist from racism in Britain, while offering little if anything at all towards the imperative of Black British people becoming powerful socially, spiritually, economically and politically enough to take justice. In this template of belligerent Black agency unless oppositional forces cease to be, Black British people are doomed. So important is white cessation of racism that they must be browbeaten and shamed where necessary into demonstrating their compliance not only by ceasing to be racist themselves, but by becoming 'actively anti-racist' (Mos-Shogbamimu 2021, p. 242; Kendi 2019). Yet again however, in the absence of Black agency of self-redemption, white change is the only hope for Black British people. White people who have created the problem of race and racism should desist or their life will be made a misery until they do.

Campbell-Stephens (2021) offers an insightful approach to tackling racism in Britain and indeed the West, while still subscribing to the notion that it must be dismantled and eradicated for Black British people to flourish in the world. The writer's solution to the problem of overcoming racism is rooted in the concept of mobilizing a Global Majority of people who are 'not White'. Global Majority calls for the 85% of the world who are not labelled White to be in solidarity with one another in contradistinction from the 15% White minority who invariably identify as majority in richer countries where they are an ethnic majority. While I continue to question the worthiness of spending time, energy and genius attempting to dismantle and eradicate racism from the planet, Campbell-Stephens raises the utilization of agency, that is, something Black British people can actually do to effect change in the war on racism. A central aim is for Black British people to get rid of a minority mindset inelegantly propagated in the term 'BAME' (Black, Asian, Minority Ethnic). In this upside-down world, the Global Majority are inversely labelled 'minority' in the few spaces where white is a majority ethnic identity, yet whites are rarely labelled 'minority' in spaces where black is a majority. We can but imagine the effect of a Global Majority consolidated to transform the world not by pleading with the minority to desist, but by building a new social, economic, political infrastructure apart from and/or around it! Those in Britain who belong ethnically to the Global Majority ought to view themselves through that global majority identity, instead of through the minority status in vogue in Britain. Campbell-Stephens argues that in Britain a minority labelling leads inexorably to a psychological minority mindset in the people so labelled and in the attitudes of the majority culture. Liberation from a minority mindset is important as that can also lead to genuine embrace of the identity of the African self as a person of worth and agency at home and in diaspora. A downside of Global Majority, however, might be that no such consolidated identity exists in reality, or looks likely, and fundamentally replacing BAME with GM represents another version of 'white and the rest'.

Akala's *Natives: Race and Class in the Ruins of Empire* (2018) situates what I am calling Black flourishing within the context of empire. At stake therefore is not racism as a standalone entity, but as a component of empire that is time sensitive and built upon capitalism and whiteness, which may be coming to the end of its life. Pointing to the ending of South African apartheid 'due to black South African resistance, international pressure and material assistance from Cuba', Akala at least envisages African agency contributing to the 'shape of the world children born now will inhabit' (Akala 2018, p. 308). Akala's end of story is double edged, one of hope that resides in the interconnectedness of humanity into which all, including past victors and victims now have opportunity to contribute to, but also one of despair that things can or will actually change for better. Akala's contrasts with the singularity of Andrews' envisaged end, about which he says, 'As we leave the house we should bring it crashing down in order to truly liberate not only the black nation, but all oppressed peoples' (Andrews 2018, p. 298).

In order to deliver the Black self from the intractable deployment of expunging racism from the world in order to flourish, it is necessary to embrace black values and ethos and situate for coexistences (Mukwashi 2020, p. 37). Rather than seeking to overthrow empire, the smart way forward might be co-existence with empire as Jeremiah suggests to the exiled Jews in Babylon, bringing their whole humanity to bear upon the context, undesirable as it was to be there. Focusing upon the creative possibilities of the Black self rather than the limitations posed by the white other, Black British people might embrace their British identity enshrined in hard-fought-for laws, British passport in hand and disregard those who wish to be in denial over Black Britishness. When Black British people arrive at a place of self-certainty, cease seeking for white validation as justice, they might conclude, 'there's no justice, there's just us' (Eddo-Lodge 2018, p. 213). In a final analysis, Black British people cannot afford the luxury of others being the determinants of their identity, and while holding on to their African and Caribbean identities can legitimately co-embrace their identities as British, English, Scottish, Welsh or Irish in a rich compound identity and belonging (Ramsey 2021).

There seems little need for Black British preoccupation with eradication of racism unless you believe its powers are so superior that Black humanity cannot meet its force with its own and win. I live also in the belief, knowledge even, that my parents, predecessors, ancestors have bequeathed to me a cultural heritage that includes pre-slavery, slavery and post-slavery resistance and flourishing. Although the politics of dehumanizing the African by the European has included attempts to obliterate all positivity of that heritage, stealing and destroying whatever was possible of African culture, iconography, art and religion, it was there and with some effort is being uncovered for all to see, repent, restore and increase in knowledge and pride. Years ago, as a young pastor, I travelled from Sheffield with a minibus load of young people to a lecture in Manchester to hear an African American lecturer speak on 'The black presence in the Bible'. The lecturer started by saying, 'The question is not "Where is the black presence in the Bible?", the question is "Where is the *White* presence in the Bible?"' It took until I was well into my thirties before I became conscious of the people and places staring me in the face every time I read the Bible. Attempts to identify me with being enslaved, and so to categorize a people as therefore innately of inferior intellect, should be resisted.

False narratives that, like false prophecies, do not benefit the poor, and those seeking justice can serve the interests of the Black bourgeoisie that exploit African American and Black British as much as white Americans and white British (Cone 1992, p. 95). Instead of contributing to Black empowerment through God-imaged Black humanity, agency and self-determination, a cadre of Black saviours may be guilty of de-skilling, zombifying and infantilizing the Black British community into a spirit of victimhood and believers in false promises of 'better will come' by means other than through their own self-belief and actions. My community needs to be delivered from the bewitchment of these false prophesies and revert to the freedom they have already got through the example written in blood, sweat, tears and death of their formerly enslaved ancestors and many still alive. This book is a personal attempt to help towards the exorcism of the demon of Black obsession with white deliverance and the denying of Black power rooted in the imagination of *imago Dei* with its innate powers of creation and sustenance. To quote Cone again, 'any movement of freedom that is dependent upon the oppressor's support for survival is doomed to failure from the start' (Cone 1992, p. 91). However, it is as though Black British people have become so absorbed into the orbit of white that in spite of this having been an abusive relationship, they appear incapable of envisaging a way into the future that is black- not white-dependent. This has to change!

Black British people can either spend more valuable years attempting to dismantle and eradicate racism, personal and institutional, or they reason intentionally to create their own cosmological infrastructure through a plan of action that offers an alternative to white-centred anti-African Caribbean, Euro-centric anti-African world of the past 500 years. When racism says the Black person is not good enough, or that black is inferior, the conversation should be understood as a distraction from one's purpose. As Gupta (2016) says,

> I really think that racism is a waste of time. It's a waste of energy because it distracts us from all the things we could do as human beings. We're constantly managing perceptions about us, and their presentation and performance, versus really doing what we're good at. Once I began to see that I didn't want to perform other people's expectations of me, I could really be my full self. I want to do that for other people.

African American writer Toni Morrison, in a 1975 keynote address at Portland State University, said that 'the very serious function of racism' is a distraction. 'It keeps you from doing your work. It keeps you explaining, over and over again, your reason for being' (Morrison 1975). A Jamaican folk tale tells of giving a ghost a basket to fetch water as a means of keeping them busy eternally to neutralize their malevolence. The antidote is to be self-assured concerning one's human identity and spend less or no time convincing detractors. If one lacks certitude in one's identity in the midst of threats to that identity, it heightens vulnerability. Such threats have to be transcended by a Black identity foregrounded in *imago Dei* and the incarnation. This, then, is the theological battleground in the contestation of how Black humanity engages in the struggle of good over evil and against those who attempt to contest their God-given humanity, to whom ground should never be conceded under any circumstances.

It is time for an honest conversation in the Black British community about how Black British people move beyond the gravitational pull of whiteness to truly self-understand within the vortex of their own humanity as a decisive sustainable step forward as a flourishing part of a multicultural society. Rather than attempting to dismantle racism, Black British people might usefully become preoccupied with assembling the building blocks of its own cosmology concerning African hybrid identity, a humanity living out their experience of historical realities in myriad spaces, now in Britain. Pivoting away from the learned reflex of seeing the Black self through a white lens will also provide a clear indicator that black is no 'wannabe white'; instead placing ultimate value upon African rootedness taking its place as a part of the human race. Black British recognizes the aspect, however unfortunate and undesirable, of the British contribution to my existence but most of all it clarifies and affirms the authentic historic contributories from which my identity is constructed. Black British identity therefore is held together by the strength of assurance that Black humanity is created in the image and likeness of God having creativity and moral reasoning, with agency, dignity and self-determining powers. It is less concerned with breaking down and more concerned with building up!

Andrews unapologetically states that white Western imperialist infrastructure is unchanging. This means that those who are encouraged by signs of its demise are being misled, deceived. Black British people therefore who live under or within the shadow of the infrastructure of white imperialism should know that is where they live and take necessary precautionary measures, rather than expect or depend upon the racist structure changing and granting them respite. This means that those who work in the 'race industry' should reflect upon the aims of 'Inclusion and Equality' strategy and maybe conclude that such strategies are aimed at getting Black British people a larger piece of the cake in a bad system, not aimed at dismantling a system altogether. Once they have freed themselves from the 'Black Man's Burden' – dismantling racism – recognize the context for what it really is, a super-contested space, they can go on the offensive and build their cosmological world view creating black space within a multiethnic, multipolar Britain.

I want to mention briefly a fourth 'contextual false prophetic oracle' concerning some theological-doctrinal praxis of the Black church likely to undermine Black British flourishing, such as 'It's all about Jesus'. I am an unabashed supporter and apologist of the Black church in Britain as an extension of the religiosity of people of African heritage, not just as a riposte to white racist rejection. As explained elsewhere, to see the Black church as a mere response to white behaviour is to attempt to rob Black British people of the validity to spiritual expression rooted in their beingness, not merely responding as a 'done to' people; we *have* been done to, but we are much more than that! A sense of deep appreciation for the way the Black church in Britain has provided a rich nurturing space for me and people like me, causes me to appreciate this multifaceted pluriform phenomenon and to defend it against presumptuous critique that is often ill-informed even if well-meaning.

Cone's epilogue in his co-edited tome in which he analyses key arguments between US Black theologians concerning the relational developments of the natures of and the relationship between Black Theology and Black religion interests me (Wilmore and Cone 1979, pp. 609–22). Of particular interest is the manner in which Black religiosity is at once historical and situational, global and local, so that the relationship between differently situated Black theologians is in a constant state of flux and contestation. The same is true of religious practitioners in the pew, so that no two local congregations are the same, even within one denomination; they will have developed their particular nomenclature for internal worship and external ministry. The article raises several issues, such as whether the Black church can embrace established theological values and understandings given their rootedness in Eurocentric, imperialist and racist character that has committed extensive violence and injustice against Black people. To what extent should Black British people rely upon the Christian concept of God, its religious teachings, and its theology as liberational agents? Should the Black church and Black Theology be concerned simply with the curating of black power to overthrow white imperialist power? If so, does either have a role beyond this narrow *raison d'être*? Cone examines too the relationship between liberation, reconciliation, violence and suffering as they relate to Black religion and Black Theology. As I reflect upon religious praxis as I have experienced it in my Black church tradition I wonder if the contradictions are directly linked to the complex nature of the multiple intersections between a people in transition geographically, culturally, spiritually and in multiple other ways since, as Cone says, the issues are complex and the participants do not agree (Wilmore and Cone 1979, p. 615).

I am aware that for some the conservatism of the Black church is problematic (Reddie 2006, p. 31), for others so too is their lack of national strategic political activism and clear severance from colonial influences (Beckford 2014, p. 172). These challenges, among others, have their place, and the Black church should take note, learn, adapt and develop organically, focused on Black flourishing. I continue to worry about the problems of external coercive influences even as they tend to ignore or underplay the excellent role played by the Black church in British society (Aldred 2005; Sturge 2005, Aldred 2020), yet recognize there are some areas of legitimate concerns about hindrances to Black flourishing. Notwithstanding variations in belonging and identity, these churches have much in common when popular expressions, not doctrinal and ecclesial officialdom, are looked at, and I want to explore some of the more egregious ones. The churches that make up the Black church in Britain end up with doctrinal, theological, cultural praxis that is a product of the differences that mark the ecclesial and cultural contributories.

A key strength and weakness of the Black church in Britain is its rich diversity, or fragmentation. I view these churches through ecumenical lenses as one Black church although they are a complex network of independent and denominational ecclesial bodies, some answering to headquarters overseas such as the New Testament Church of God (also known as Church of God) and the Church of God of Prophecy in the United States, or the Redeemed Christian Church of God in Nigeria. Particularly in the case of the Church of God of Prophecy and New Testament Church of God, a step that could enhance the agency of both Black British churches would be to sever the quasi-colonial link with their white southern American headquarters and become independent, Black-led and self-determined, associating with the USA as associate ecclesial bodies. Those who enable maintenance of these links should have their reasons put under scrutiny through the lens of Black agency, self-determination, humanity and dignity. Among independent churches, the likes of the Ruach Network of Churches and Kingsway International Ministries are Black British mega-churches with tentacles overseas; while others are linked to national and international networks, others still are fiercely independent local congregations. These Black-led churches would do well to foster greater ecumenical relations between themselves locally, regionally, nationally and internationally, becoming a large and strong black ecclesiological, social, economic and political influence as they interact with other entities, whether religious or secular. Those who use doctrinal differences to promote fragmentation between Black-led churches also should have their reasons subject to the lens of Black agency, self-determination and Black human dignity.

In real life since the ending of the slave trade and chattel slavery, Black communities confront oppressive situations and cannot afford the luxury of mere liberational theories, they have to choose between social, economic and political options that will effectively contribute to the struggle to transform the world they inhabit (Wilmore and Cone 1979, p. 616). Conflicting tributaries combine into an incoherent narrative and it appears that the Black church tradition I grew up in and still belong to has evolved 'oracles' that operate within and beyond written institutional dogmas, allowing for variations across zones. One saying goes, 'let Jesus fix it for you'. An immediate contradiction is that the majority of people in Black churches are achievers through hard work, dedication and thrift, as they are taught from the scriptures (Gen. 3.19; 1 Tim. 5.8). They know material things do not fall out of the sky, yet in the worship space the hegemony of ecclesial over secular roles is near absolute, and the bishop or pastor becomes the pinnacle of the church order (Edwards 1999). This *a priori* position of spiritual positional prestige usurping secular positions, no matter how lofty, escalates into the wider regional, national and international ideology too. It is not unusual to find those who deem a role in the order of the church superior to equitable or higher-ranking roles in the secular world are prepared to choose the church role should there be a choice to be made.

Some individuals are upwardly mobile simultaneously in secular and religious spheres, each helping to advance the other, but in the church, the church offices and positions and titles trump the non-religious ones. This model breaks down at points, such as when a bishop's honorary (or, unusually, earned) title of Doctor is elevated above the clerical title. What is clear is that the church space is one in which people are encouraged to do well, work hard and succeed but that secular success has little or no place in the worship space where, with few exceptions, the pastor and church officers are the revered ones. This explains why, for example, little is mentioned in the worship space about politics, as activists tend to believe worship should be front and centre of the communal life of a people still regarded as disadvantaged, and by some oppressed. The troubles of the world are mentioned but only to emphasize the power of God to change and to overcome circumstances. This spiritualized emphasis in the worship space and separation from work done in the social, economic and political realm include attributing everything to God with phrases like: 'God will make a way', 'Prayer changes things', 'It's not about us, it's all about him', 'Isn't he worthy?', 'Just pray about it', 'PUSH: pray until something happens', 'Just believe and you will receive', 'Speak it into the atmosphere' and so on. Utterances through songs, testimonies, sermons and prayer that amount to 'Let Jesus fix it for you' dominate the worship space by the same people who may have worked the night before, got little or no sleep to ensure they are in church for worship, who are used to burning the midnight oil to pursue academic degrees and who sacrifice themselves to provide for their family. I have occasionally heard recited,

> The heights by great men reached and kept
> Were not attained by sudden flight.
> But they, while their companions slept
> Were toiling upward in the night.
> (Henry Wadsworth Longfellow)

Few if any really believe that you pray all night and expect that there will be a gift-wrapped answer to prayer on your table in the morning. Where this psychological upsidedownness comes from is hard to tell. The casual onlooker may be forgiven for interpreting this behaviour as somewhat schizophrenic, as the same person gives all credit for their achievement to God, but instinctively knows that they are the ones who must expend all effort, energy, ingenuity in pursuit of the very thing. The impression given is that there is no human involvement in people's success, we just pray, believe and Jesus does the rest. If it is a job you need, if you want a partner, if you want good health, all that is needed is to trust the Lord and he will fix it for you. This underplaying – near denial – of human involvement and effort in the issues of life is, I believe, potentially detrimental and a betrayal of the image and likeness of God in human agency and self-determination. There ought to be a determined effort to bring these two facets of Black church praxis together so that the synergy between what we pray for and what we work towards are one and the same. Reflecting in the worship space the human contribution will bring much needed gravitas to the liturgy of the Black church expressed in songs, prayer and preaching. It will also demonstrate a coherent and holistic understanding of God as everywhere present in accompaniment and unity between God and human.

Beckford's recent work highlights confusing the dichotomized engagement of the Black British church with the social-historical world, biblical interpretation (Beckford 2023). I argue that while Beckford is correct in the assertion that Black church song leaders, musicians and songwriters' work continues to be informed by what Beckford calls 'colonial Christian ideas about God' this is due to the way 'worship' is proccupied with the rhetoric of 'let Jesus fix it for you'. As Beckford claims, Black British worship music continues to echo faith sentiments about the doctrine of God, biblical hermeneutics and black ontology reflecting colonized sentiments. However, this should not be confused with an absence of much hard work in the areas of social justice, economic empowerment, Black agency and politics, a fact however imperfectly undertaken (Stone 2021). Black British churches' challenge to align their liturgy in the church with their actions in the world such as establishing the Pentecostal Credit Union (https://www.pcuuk.com/), Nehemiah Housing Association (https://nehemiah.co.uk/) and much beside is a work in progress.

I am making the argument, then, that Black British Christians should desist from a simplistic notion of 'let Jesus fix it for you', since history and our own lived experience teach that Jesus doesn't behave like this. It is counterintuitive to liturgize one way and live in the world in another; the two streams must align in a coherent belief system. Those who lead us into worshipping God in ways that are counter to our experience of God must be challenged for facilitating this flawed theology. Instead, Black British Christians should liturgize through songs, scriptures and prayers that are in line with the Black African history pre-dating white European encounters resulting in the transatlantic slave trade, chattel plantation slavery, colonialism and white imperialism and racism. Black churches can praise God for who their ancestors were before European encounters (Walker 2006; Agama 2016), often cited in the Bible (Isa. 45.14; Acts 8.26–40), and in secular history. Liturgy can include lament for the transatlantic slave trade, chattel and plantation slavery, colonialism and racism and the accompanying and empowering experience of God in the midst of all this as Black British people attempted to live out their humanity as mothers, fathers, brothers, sisters, friends etc., then the meaning of God in diaspora, relating to the affairs in the world as they relate to the people of Africa and indeed the whole human race. The worship of God is misleading and superficial if it merely waxes lyrical with versions of 'let Jesus fix it for you'. The highs and lows of everyday living and the black experience of journeying with God must permeate liturgy; most of all the things that preoccupy Black British individuals, families and groups (as part of the nation and the world) need to be sung, prayed and preached about in the worship space as well as lived out in the world. The worship setting can do without the trite calling of a people who have had their humanity humbled to submit or surrender yourself to God; instead we might deal with sentiments of empowerment, enabling, raising up the fallen, self-care in the company of an enabling God. Black faith should not be an extension of the historical subservience and humbling of the past half a millennium. Religious philosophies that result in keeping the masses dependent, docile, lacking in self-belief should be regarded as counter to the best interests of Black British worshippers and removed from the liturgical frame. A deep clean of the black liturgical content is needed in prayers, songs, scripture and other readings, reflecting a God who accompanies, giving power to those who appropriate it to live triumphantly even in the valley of the shadow of death (Psalm 23). The Black Christian knows that Jesus does not fix things, Jesus empowers them to fix things for themselves. To suggest and depend on another formula is to deny lived experience, and proffer 'a contextual false prophetic oracle'.

Briefly and finally here, the Black church needs to consider further the empowering difference it might make were it to state with one voice, in spite of its pluriform nature, that God who is spirit indwells all believers, not just Pentecostals; that the presence of God is not necessarily evidenced by noise, especially as noise and power do not always go together (switching on an electric bulb, for instance). I recommend that all local and regional and national churches should scrutinize their doctrinal and cultural tenets and in the multitude of counsellors (Prov. 11.14) decide to abandon those tenets that are not spiritually and secularly life affirming. Whatever a church does it must affirm the *imago Dei* in all humanity, with a commitment to help nurture to maturity and fruitfulness all in its community to become more and more like God in the person of Christ.

In this chapter I have attempted to highlight some contextual false prophetic oracles that risk hindering the attempt of a people to flourish in 'Babylon', with imperial forces arrayed against them, at a time when they need most to know what the plan is for flourishing. I have formed a conclusion based on my experience of the Eurocentric form of Christian faith that I and people like me have imbibed, which helps us in some ways and undermines us in other ways. The good ways are good, but the bad ways undercut the good and threaten to disempower us, condemn us to underachievement and undervaluing ourselves. In the end these false prophesies may have been false not because of dishonest or malevolent intent, but because their strategy lacked rigour and deliverability. As we discover, Jeremiah's way offered a workable plan. The manner in which a community decides which voices to have regard for and which to ignore is not straightforward. Some, like Jeremiah in the sixth century, speak with a sense of assurance rooted in religious faith. Others are listened to less convincingly, while some are rejected out of hand. As much of Old Testament scripture is thought to have been 'written' retrospectively, in this time maybe the validity and effectiveness of what is written and said is what stands the test of time. I encourage all 'prophets', religious and secular, to speak and write and act what God puts in your spirit, with the aim of helping the Black British community to flourish, allowing the community to decide the value of their contribution.

Questions for intergenerational discussions

- Who in the Black British community, past and present, do you regard as a prophet and why?
- Should anybody be called a false prophet and why?
- What should happen to those who prove to be self-serving while purporting to be serving the diaspora community?

6

Flourishing in Babylon

> This is what the LORD says: 'When seventy years are completed for Babylon, I will come to you and fulfil my good promise to bring you back to this place. For I know the plans I have for you,' declares the LORD, 'plans to prosper you and not to harm you, plans to give you hope and a future. Then you will call on me and come and pray to me, and I will listen to you. You will seek me and find me when you seek me with all your heart. I will be found by you,' declares the LORD, 'and will bring you back from captivity. I will gather you from all the nations and places where I have banished you,' declares the LORD, 'and will bring you back to the place from which I carried you into exile.' (Jer. 29.10–14, NIV)

I am now a grandfather, and likely to remain in Britain for life. This chapter attempts to sum up for posterity some key reflections from my lived experience, observations and study. In sum, this is my call to the Black British community to consider that the power to flourish lies not 'out there' in the ether but 'in here' within themselves. A troubled history of lack of Black self-trust and confidence to self-determine has resulted in an ever-present danger that they might be seduced into believing that God will work things out without them, or that only 'Westerners have the unique power to uplift, edify and strengthen' Black people (Straubhaar 2015). Flourishing in Babylon based upon key principles contained in Jeremiah's letter to the exiles, as discussed above, can be entrenched and perpetuated by centring the Black British people as their own self-determining agents.

Black flourishing in Britain is a greater possibility now because of the shoulders of past and present giants from around the world upon which this and future generations stand. Black British people should take note of those who exerted their agency by opposing and resisting oppression through bloody uprisings and diplomacy that successfully ended the Arab and European slave trades, chattel plantation slavery, colonialism, Jim Crow, apartheid and racialized segregation, won civil rights, anti-racism legislation, and continue to challenge racism and pursue flourishing (Bell 2013). It falls to this and future generations of Black British people to throw off the final vestiges of racialized inferiorization, to stop seeking liberation already won, and instead take it, assume it, live it – in honour of those who secured victories over this enemy of humanity. This can be the generation of Black British people who spiritually, mentally, emotionally and legally turn the tables on the historical racist system and the individuals and groups that functionalize it, by calling time on it. Racism may not cease to exist, but it must no longer dictate the terms of engagement, even while still living in 'Babylon'. Black British people must deploy their spiritual, intellectual and physical energies in pursuit of flourishing, deploying the law, group force and any means necessary to transcend racism in all its forms, personal, group, systemic, institutional and endemic. As Douglass states, 'the limits of tyrants are prescribed by the endurance of those whom they oppress' (cited in Bell 2013, p. 34).

In this concluding chapter, I endeavour to highlight some matters that my lived experience as a pastor and bishop in the Black British church suggests are essential to flourishing in Britain. It is important to note some differences between the Jewish exiles in Babylon and my context. According to the biblical narrative, they were exiled as correctional chastisement by Yahweh, and as spoils of war by Nebuchadnezzar. The Black British community I am part of do not accept that we are here as a divine curse, although it has felt so on occasions. The Jewish exiles' odyssey was prophesied by Jeremiah as 70 years, but falsely counter-prophesied as a mere two years. While the stay of Black people in Britain has been indeterminate, the intentions of the Windrush era economic migrants can be described as a 'five-year syndrome' that was realized by few, with the majority, like those Jewish exiles, resulting in multigenerational stays, with no end dates. Both communities then found that short-termism was not a feature of migration, whether forced or voluntary, and that once transplantation has occurred, a determined resolve was needed in order to thrive in a new setting which tends towards hostility rather than warm human welcome. I found that constructing a new way of life in a new setting at the centre of empire meant encountering opportunities as well as obstacles, counterforces that create possibilities to influence my own situation, that of my family, and others including wider society and my kinfolks back home (Allen 2008, p. 136).

Reading Jeremiah's letter to the exiles, one might be forgiven for supposing that Yahweh is literally an active participant in the lives of the people. Phrases like, 'I will come to you', 'bring you back to this place', 'I know the plans I have for you', 'I will bring you back from captivity', 'I will gather you from all the nations', all sound highly present and participative in a practical way, as though expectations of a theophany may be fulfilled. My upbringing in a Black Pentecostal church encouraged this literal view of God and created an understanding that this divine activity was palpable in the experience of the Jews in Babylonian exile. Consequently, an expectation is created that God works similarly palpably in my day, except that such divinely orchestrated action requires human agency to turn divine promise into lived experience. At some point I became aware of what my elders call 'knowing the mind of God'. Jeremiah's letter to the exiles, then, may be best understood as stating what was on Yahweh's mind – the divine intention towards the exiles. Any who thought and acted as though there was some divine inevitability about the promises of God by God would be sorely disappointed because execution of the mind of God required human hands, feet, imagination, blood, sweat and tears. For me, the mind of God can be summed up as God's will that Black people would flourish, live optimally, or as Jesus put it, have life in abundance (John 10.10). However, to flourish required the Jews to heed Jeremiah's call to self-sufficiently plant, build, increase and participate, and that reality is also suggestive for Black British people.

I note that Jeremiah did not tell the Jewish exiles to wait '70 years' to flourish, but rather, to live life in Babylon to the fullest, and in the due course of time Babylon's political and economic situation would result in opportunity for them to return to their homeland. The exiles were to exercise their agency to plant and build in Babylon, bridging the gap between the present and future. Christian theology embraces eschatology as a means of focusing on the fullness of time or 'end times', usually meaning the end of the world and more broadly death, afterlife, divine judgement, heaven, hell and rapture (Hunt 2016, pp. 245–75). This futuristic idea has its place, but I align my thinking about the kingdom of God, which Jesus speaks about, with the concept of realized eschatology that advances the notion that human flourishing can be experienced in the here, not only in the hereafter. Today and tomorrow are part of one continuum (van Oudtshoorn 2021). The Black church has long been accused of being other-worldly, encouraging its members to willingly suffer any and every thing now for the prize of eternal life in heaven. Suffering is even perceived as a price worth paying to get there, correspondingly making adverse lived experience now of little consequence, a mere inconvenience. Stowe gives a glimpse of this ideology, rooted in a response to the degrading, living-death experience of enslaved African people rejoicing in adversity because of their Christian hope of 'going to glory' when they die (Stowe 1995, p. 29).

Since neither divinely promised nor hoped-for prosperity falls from the sky, it is essential for the Black British diaspora community to have an explicit and uncompromising awareness that their well-being is dependent upon themselves. While much of what is needed to flourish will come from beyond the minority community, leadership, ownership and control must be directed by Black agency. Responsibility for Black British flourishing must never be franchised; it must be owned and brought into being by the people themselves, or they risk it never happening. 'Flourishing in Babylon' insists that now is the time for Black British people to live optimally, and I want to expand this further under four headings. First, as mentioned above, I find God as an accompanying presence, not a liberator; second, I have learned that flourishing is a Promised Land with giants; third, racism is like a bully in the playground that preys on the weak and vulnerable, which means Black British people must become strong spiritually, socially, economically and politically; and fourth, 'home' is a complex thing.

An accompanying God

One of the profound realities of human existence is that I have had to learn as a Christian that beyond creation of the cosmos, as a rule of thumb, what God is credited with doing happens through human agency. This confounds our usual rhetoric that suggests otherwise. I recall that when I was a young Christian leader, a visitor started attending our local church. This man was distinguishable first by his white gown and then by his life of prayer and faith, which we knew about by his public testimonies, personal conversations and long public prayers. The visitor was soon drawn unofficially into the leadership group and given regular opportunities to preach and encourage. Gradually, his going home with the pastor and his family to Sunday lunch became the norm, and as I was a mentee to the pastor I was sometimes there too. A few weeks had elapsed, and it became clear that this brother had no reliable income. The pastor had compassion on the brother and began to give him some cash to help him along. After a few months had passed, his emphasis on prayer and faith became quite strikingly hollow as clearly he was scrounging off the pastor and other individuals he managed to solicit help from. One fateful day as we sat at a dining table, the visitor began to expound his now familiar prayer and faith mantra and to tell us how wonderful God had been to him in answering his prayers of faith, providing enough for him so that he had never gone hungry since happening upon our congregation. 'Prayer and faith work,' he said. 'You all need to trust God and he will always answer your prayer of faith. Because,' he stated, 'the Bible says whatsoever you ask in faith believing God will give it to you, I am a living testimony.' At length, the pastor could not resist the urge to respond. 'Brother X,' he started, 'it is all well and good for you to pray in faith to God week after week, month after month, and for God to answer your prayers; but do you know who is meeting the cost of your faith prayers? Me. Your faith is too expensive for me and you are going to have to find a job to support yourself, because today is the last day I will be the answer to your prayers.' You could, as the saying goes, hear a pin drop. As Yong and Alexander suggest, prayer and intercessions in Pentecostal settings can vary between encountering God and political praxis – and I will add personal gain (Yong and Alexander 2011, p. 233).

I learned a vital theological lesson that day about the relationship between God and us, between prayer, faith and action. For Brother X, God was answering his prayers, yet for the pastor this burdensome visitor was behaving quite unconscionably, taking money from his new friends while failing to understand that what he viewed as answers to his prayers of faith was a form of extortion from his increasingly reluctant hosts. The pastor's unspoken exhortation was that if Brother X was prayerfully listening, not only talking, to God, he might have heard God saying, 'Find work to earn a living.' Later, as a pastor myself, I experienced similar situations and would advise early that God's will is that all, as much as is possible, should pursue financial independence for self and family, and be able to help those who may need it. Indeed, leaving room for the occasional divinely miraculous or the humanly unexplainable event, it seems helpful for prayers in faith to remember that God does not have money, therefore if you pray for money and your prayers are answered, the money will have come at a loss to someone – it will not have dropped like manna from the clouds. God will not have accessed your bank account and deposited money or opened your wallet to put money in it. In this sense, even an omnipotent God may be said to be impotent in the material world, with human beings becoming God's hands, feet and voice. This is apparent in the ministry of

Jesus and the early Church in the writings of Luke, showing a focus upon the poor and oppressed sometimes through radical sharing of belongings as an example of God delivering ministry through human agency (Scheffler 2016). 'Impotent' may be an inappropriate term for God, but a way needs to be found to understand the nature of the God who did not intervene during murderous and dehumanising pursuits such as the Arab and European transatlantic slave trades, chattel and plantation slavery, colonialism, the Holocaust and many other atrocities over centuries. The most that I can argue for in these circumstances is that God is present, seeing and feeling – and, in Jesus, dying – but as an accompanier, empowerer and enabler. To petition God through prayer without a clear understanding that God delivers through human agency is to misunderstand, to human detriment, the way God works. Black British people may helpfully reflect upon an understanding of God as a divine presence with them at the best and worst of times, at home and in diaspora/exile, under oppression and in freedom, in life and in death. This is not a Father Christmas God bearing literal gifts, more a divine accompanying presence helping us to take direct responsibility for and be the delivery agents of God's answers to human prayers. Liberation, for example, God's will for all humanity, rarely if ever comes to the oppressed without their taking it by whatever means necessary.

The Jews in Babylonian captivity, to whom Jeremiah wrote with reassuring words about God's good intentions towards them, provide a useful object lesson concerning the nature of their relationship with God. They were a people whose ancestors endured centuries of wanderings, occupation and enslavement. After 400 years of crying to God for liberation from enslavement in Egypt, God is understood eventually to hear their groanings, yet it is evident that it took Moses' leadership to get the liberation project to happen. Having escaped Egypt, the Jews found that after 40 years of wilderness wanderings they had to fight to get into the Promised Land, and then once they were in, the battles continued until they were overrun and occupied by enemy forces, in the north then the south before some were exiled to Babylon, and finally dispersed into diaspora. Far from God saving the Jews from these woes, prophets were clear that their sufferings resulted from their disobedience, disloyalty and idolatry against God, and the injustices and oppressions perpetrated upon their own people. Somehow this topsy-turvy relationship between the Jewish people and their God survives and defines them as a people of faith, perennially embracing hopes of restoration despite all the upheaval they endured in the context of diaspora and imperial domination by hostile powers (Staples 2021). An interpretation of the relationship between God and Israel is one of near-benign divine accompaniment, so that when there was a battle to be fought, human physical and spiritual fortitude were key even as divine presence was declared by prophets and believed to be so by the people.

Although the Black British community is not identifiable as a religious group like the Jewish exiles in Babylon, it is widely accepted that they tend towards a higher rate of belief in God and religious adherence than the white British majority do. For example, while mainstream adherence to the Christian faith in Britain is in decline, Black churches have been growing (Woodhead and Catto (eds) 2012, p. 20). Why this is the case is open to conjecture, but as a participant in the life of a Black Christian community my observation is that steadfast faith praxis tends to rise with dangers and uncertainties, which has been the case for generations of Black people. Black theologians identify Black people with a history of suffering at white hands, associating them with the suffering of Jesus at Roman hands (Joseph 2020). This is undoubtedly the case, and yet I find something deeper and more profound in addition to identifying with a suffering Christ. The Black church community I have grown up in exhibit a much more theocentric than Christocentric faith, in which the abiding presence of God expressed as Jesus and the Holy Spirit come first. It is this sense of God as an accompanier and empowerer that I believe is attractive to many Black British Christians. Notwithstanding the notion of God as liberator, the Black British Christianity I belong to relates to God much more as a spirit that accompanies and empowers them as individuals and as a group, less so the God who literally delivers liberation by the mystical or miraculous. When liberation has come, it has not been delivered through some invisible agency, but by the actions of human beings who know this too is the will of God who created them in the divine image.

Because Black British people are such a God-fearing community, their understanding of God is of paramount importance. When all the razzmatazz is over in the Black church worship space, for example, what needs to be done will be done, not by an invisible God, but by human hands carrying out the will of God. This is a crucial lesson to learn – that the God Black people find accompanies them, acting through (even with) and not *for* them! Flourishing in Babylon requires a fundamental shift in their understanding or perception of God, towards one rooted in the bitter-sweet experience of the exiled or diaspora people. Teel notes a difference between (privileged) white Christian people who attend church out of custom, duty, pride or virtue, and Black Christian people who go to church out of a generational history of injustice that continues, for strength to make a way out of no way (Teel 2011, p. 2). Exiled, enslaved and diaspora people experience life with odds stacked against them and acknowledge divine strength to endure and to enable them to throw off their oppressors' yoke; a process through which they become aware over time that the God who accompanied them in ages past does so again and again. Part of what this book is about is encouraging an understanding of God based on what history and experience tell us, information that does not fit easily into neat expressions such as liberator, omnipotent, omnipresent, omniscient, or even great and worthy. Green, in an exploration of a Barthian theological concept of divine providence, shows that Barth sought to address European doubts about God in answer to questions that arose about faith following two world wars that caused people to ask where God was in their time of acute suffering (C. Green 2013). This European theological concept of a providential God addressing a European dilemma is an example of how Black British people also should see through the lens of their history and contemporary lived experience. This includes a realization that in the furnace of adversity lasting centuries, when African peoples cried out to God the slave traders prevailed and the suffering of the enslaved continued, by which the people discovered no divinely preordained plan of liberation. At length, literal freedom came at human hands with God as a spiritual presence accompanying desperate humanity, strengthening them and empowering them to discern the best way to go. We might wonder what outcomes there may have been had the enslaved realized that God was not coming to deliver them; God was right there with them and they needed to take matters fully into their own hands and in the power of God overthrow their oppressors. Some did.

Black British people should not blame God for their struggles and troubles, neither should they glory in them as though oppression can be perversely virtuous for victims. There is redemptive suffering of course, such as when undergoing persecution for your beliefs, working hard to achieve a goal or sacrificing to help others. However, after Black people's half a millennium of suffering, Black British people should reject the notion that black dehumanization is by divine permission as a curse, with religion used as a tool of subjugation as depicted in the compliant 'Uncle Tom' character (Stowe 1995). Black suffering, although not authorised by God, has been legitimized by pseudo-religious and pseudo-scientific claims about God (Fryer 1984; Yeboah 1997; Ashimolowo 2007). After suffering terrible injustices through stratified dehumanizing perpetrated upon them by fellow human beings, somehow a majority of Black British people manage to retain belief in the transcendent power that has not brought liberation to them even during the most desperate conditions. Black faith in God endures for generation after generation, as God walks with them through the valley of the shadow of death, sometimes through the valley of death itself, they find a way to interpret the promise of God to deliver and be a present help in trouble (Psalm 46). God has been and will be there willing those made in the divine image who are being sinned against to be victorious over their adversaries and aggressors through their self-determining agency. The God who continues to accompany the Black community has demonstrated divine faithfulness and well-wishing towards them in Britain and beyond. Jeremiah 29.11 should not be utilized as a direct message to Black British people, but it provides insight into how against even the worst of backgrounds the God in whose image and likeness they are made accompanies them to the umpteenth generations as they pursue flourishing in the knowledge that God is on their side. The urgent exercise of liberative agency is exemplified in the activities of the Maroons and leaders of uprisings like Sam Sharpe, Paul Bogle and countless others, and provides examples of the urgency with which Black British people should deploy their energies towards flourishing (Dick 2002). Liberation is not something to pray and wait on God for, it is something to be grasped now by any means necessary. It is the will of God.

Belief in an accompanying God on the side of Black people in historic suffering under white oppression should never camouflage the urgency of literal liberation from oppression for the people on a whole. It is better that like the Jewish cohort in exile in Babylon whom God dealt with as a group, not just as individuals, the Black British people note the imperative of the 'us' over the 'I'. It is the group that ensures intergenerational continuity, well-being and posterity and it is in the midst of the group where God can be found. Individual identity and special interests contribute to the sum of the whole, but are subservient to group identity and interests. Herein lies a reason why the British Black community needs to take group identity seriously, since without this corporeality, the welfare of the Black British people simply dissipates and become absorbed into the gravitational pull of individualism and other groups and social constructs. The Southern Africans have shared with the world the concept of *ubuntu*, 'I am because we are, and we are because I am.' Membe-Matale reminds us of the way *ubuntu* can work to ensure that the interest of the natives are not left at the mercy of foreign power and control as often is the case in Africa. It points to a holistic economy of life, intertwining the material with the spiritual in the interest of the well-being of all in society and encapsulating a transformative spirit that connects us to others, motivating us towards the common good as together the redemption of the whole earth is sought

(Membe-Matale 2015). A triune God having created humanity in the divine image models for us hybridization, incarnation, and how to flourish in a hostile imperial context, as Jesus did. The Black British community should seek to bring into lived existence the reflection of the God seen by the human gaze into the corporate nature of the divine. And the God who lives out a perfect triunity acts as encouragement to take corporeality seriously since it is as groups that humans best reflect unity in diversity in the presence of the God who wills them to flourish.

There is clearly a paradox in a God who means Black people well, yet has seemed impotent to help at the greatest point of their historical need. In the experienced reality of non-intervention by God, Black people come to one of two conclusions; either God does not exist, or God exists but is an invisible force that accompanies them through life willing them to overthrow evil powers even as Jesus symbolically overturned the money changers' tables and drove illicit cattle traders out of the temple (Matt. 21.12–13). God as an accompanying empowerer should be understood in this way, so that Black British people understand that what is most important in their relationship with God is to perceive the divine will and act upon it by the power and permission of God. In the case of ongoing racism in British and Western societies, the actions necessary emanate in the mind of a just God who means Black people well. As God's hands, feet and mouths, Black people discover how to actualize freedom from oppressive forces. As mentioned above, Black people have, in the main, concluded that God exists and accompanies them on the journey of life in all its complexities, and by divine presence has strengthened Black British people as part of the cohort of Black African heritage people around the world, in the face of past acts of enslavement and subjugation and present attempts to racialize them. This is the God Black British people find, who silently yet powerfully accompanies them generation after generation, willing Black British people to, in the words of Bob Marley, 'Get up, stand up!' To acknowledge God as accompanier is to recognize divine presence during suffering and during liberation, and accept the human agency that delivers liberation in the presence of the God who proverbially walks and talks with the oppressed and the free.

Flourishing is a Promised Land with giants

I suggest Black British people should view flourishing as a 'Promised Land', a habitation, that is not a place but is the lived actualizing of Black humanity in the image of God, even in a hostile environment. The embodiment of such lived flourishing has been challenged by a journey that includes Black British people's enslaved and colonized African ancestors, in the Caribbean and in Africa, and extended during life in Britain encountering racism and associated disadvantages. I argue that Black British people are now in danger of entrapment in a circular oppression/liberation narrative mediated through a lens of underperformance and negativity from which only they can free themselves by taking ownership of their God-given freedom to flourish. Living optimally is the Promised Land of spiritual and mental freedom in the presence of hostile giants that challenge them, based on the strong opposition to, not necessarily the extinction of, the Black British community should predicate their prosperity. Historic disadvantages rooted in past racialized legal instruments, all of which have been overturned, should not be allowed to predominate in the relationships between Black and white British people. What Black British people need are just laws, and where the laws of the land are deemed inadequate the corporate weight of community action will be deployed. They should not need to be loved or liked by their adversaries who refuse to do so, since the law, coupled with Black agency, will mediate infringements even as a coalition of the willing work together in mutual flourishing. There are risks posed by residual systemic, institutional, personal and cultural racism by some white people and systems which Black British people must make it their business to empower themselves to confront and prevail over in the shared and contested space they are determined to make their Promised Land of flourishing. Black British efforts to engage and overcome racialized inequities must be matched by Black empowerment that builds Black resilience to robustly resist hostile white oppositional forces while fostering appropriate allyship.

I have sat in many Sunday school classes, and taught a fair number too, and some lessons have stayed with me. One such is the writing of St Paul to an early church in Corinth about his plans to visit them and to take from them a much-needed collection for the church in Jerusalem (1 Cor. 16). However, Paul's departure from Ephesus was delayed because his mission there was 'going well, but was also arousing opposition' (Adeyemo 2006, p. 1423). The nature of the missionary's opportunity and opposition is not a focus here, as the Sunday School lesson's purpose was to teach the inseparability of the two interconnected forces. As a pastor, I worry that in this diasporic space, young Black British people particularly might lose sight of the ongoing coexistences of these two forces, and end up chasing opportunities, or unexpectedly encountering opposition, having assumed an opposition-free context. There are two broad points I seek to make here. First, that to flourish or have justice or be liberated does not indicate the absence of antagonisms, but rather mastery over them; and second, flourishing is less about others giving in to your demands and more about you taking your share and contributing to the whole.

Here I want to emphasize that flourishing in Babylon, or indeed anywhere, will always be accompanied by opposition that needs to be faced down in order for success to be achieved. This truism applies to the Babylonians as well as to the exiles who need to preoccupy themselves more with their self-determined destination to flourish, dealing with opposition as it is encountered, rather than be preoccupied and consumed by obstacles. An exilic minority community will find that the nature of opposition differs from that faced by members of the majority ethnic community and other minorities. However, the exiles should be neither surprised nor knocked off course by opposition, but expect it and be prepared for it. Black British people should never be tolerant, yet never surprised, and always expectant of contextual oppositional forces of all sorts.

From antiquity, mainstream cultures have existed in conflict with minority cultures for which 'utopia is a landscape of the imagination ... built on historical and futuristic ideals and based on an ideological pursuit of purity and happiness' (Neil 2020). Black British people living against a background of racialized oppression over the past half a millennium may possess a longing for better and imagine a Britain that is racism free and inequality free, and with a level playing field. This, however, is a utopian dream without any evidence for its existence anywhere in the world, in history or in the present. Words like 'flourishing', 'justice' and 'liberation' have a whiff of utopia about them, and can imply the suggestion that when arrived at you will have no lack or want of anything. Utopia, as we know, does not exist, therefore while idealism may represent aspiration, Black British people will benefit from realism in what is meant by and how they achieve and live in flourishing, justice and liberation. This should include healthy doses of realism and idealism since one without the other risks leaving Black British people hopeless, or over-hopeful; whereas together they are likely to engender lasting success.

The Jewish people were 400 years in Egyptian slavery, before liberation and their journey to the 'Promised Land' bequeathed to them by their patriarchs. Drawing a sheet over four centuries of subjugation and suffering, God appears to bear no blame for that but instead gets credit for breaking the bars of their yoke to make them walk erect and, as Stoutjesdijk argues, the Torah suggests the Jews' redemption from Egypt's service was not so much a release from slavery, as it was a change of master (Stoutjesdijk 2018). By this arrangement, Israel became slaves to God as their ultimate purpose and God became their Father and Master and so could be expected to deliver the Promised Land into their possession. With the human agency of Moses, the Jews set out from Egypt on a protracted, eventful and identity-forming 40-year journey to the Promised Land. Eventually, with the Promised Land in sight, reconnaissance was conducted with five men dispatched to spy out the land (Judg. 18). Their split report identified a fertile Promised Land that was already occupied, and some of the occupants were giants; however, four of the five viewed the task of possessing the land by subduing its inhabitants as unattainable on account of the giants.

If the Jewish people thought after 400 years of enslavement, liberation would be without hindrance or opposition, they were sorely mistaken. By the time they left Egypt as a 'mixed multitude' we may assume some of their number were so integrated into Egyptian society they did not wish to be liberated, and some native Egyptians left with them, complicating identity upon entering the Promised Land. Once there, they had challenges on a human level and in their relations with God, causing division and injustice. Pomegranates and figs may have been in abundance, but the Promised Land had giants and other occupiers vying for dominance. It is difficult for those who are situated in safe, fortified and secure spaces to understand the challenges of the often-perilous journey to a Promised Land (Groody and Campese 2008). Indeed, the Jewish people had to fight to get into the land and fight to remain there, before being taken into exile again while still under occupation by foreign forces at home. Flourishing is never without its challenges, there are always oppositional giants roaming the land even as opportunities for advancement can be found.

Experience teaches me that flourishing is less about others giving in to my demands and more about me taking my share of common resources in our communal life. The Black British community may need to acknowledge that white British people may never completely change their attitudes towards them, even were the majority to do so. The Black British community need to do their own reconnaissance to find out what opportunities and opposition there are in society so that they can build resilience rooted in knowledge gained from investigations of their own. This calls for understanding the nature, motivation and practice of racism at a personal or institutional or systemic level and therefore how to mitigate its insidious presence and effect (Yeboah 1997; Eddo-Lodge 2018; DiAngelo 2018). The struggle to eradicate racism cannot afford to neglect the reality that racism in Britain is intractably linked to racism in the Western world; it is in the fabric of western culture and mindset and has been for the past half a millennium. To expend all one's energies on a negative of eradicating racism may be best replaced by a commitment to oppose and fight racism which implies the Black British community have to consider how they can become strong enough to stand against the phenomenon. If this were a boxing match, both boxers would train hard, paying attention to diet, sleep and physical strength; they would not spend an undue amount of time and effort trying to kill their opponent. Jeremiah, in addressing the plight of Jewish exile in sixth-century Babylon, stays clear of linking their prosperity, their *shalom*, to the dismantling of the Babylonian Empire; rather, he encourages them to build the Jewish community strong enough to flourish in it, support their kinfolks in their homeland, and create a Jewish ontological infrastructure that transcends Babylon.

There is in Jeremiah an anticipation that empire endures and when the current one ends it will be replaced by another. Any prosperity predicated on end of empire is prosperity deferred. The example we have from Jeremiah's letter to the exiles is to situate the self in relation to empire so that as opportunities arise they are ready and able to capitalize. By understanding empire, its strengths, weaknesses and vulnerabilities, they empower themselves to access resources, strengthening themselves and those in their native homelands. Empire eventually morphs, just as racism has morphed, but continues chameleon-like. Black British people must de-essentialize racism, dethrone it of its demigod status, reduce it to one of the giants in the land we occupy; and as David showed, Goliath can be defeated when the intimidating giant is understood and starved of its oxygen of fear and fought not on its ground but on the ground of *imago Dei*, agency and self-determination (Gladwell 2013, p. 15).

Power: spiritual, social, economic and political

I argue that Black British flourishing is inextricably linked to power that enables and facilitates it, particularly within the communal life of Black British people in a dynamic multi-verse society that eschews weakness. The late father of Black Theology, Professor James Cone, shares that he was prompted to develop a Black Theology in response to the Black Power movement espoused in particular by Malcolm X (Cone 1969; X 1965). I believe X was right that white power had to be met with black power that showed strength. The civil rights campaign of Reverend Dr Martin Luther King achieved much in terms of legislative change, as has the anti-apartheid work of Nelson Mandela. However, I am of the conviction that African Americans could have got a better deal had the Black Power of Malcolm X and the Black Theology of Cone collaborated, and had the militancy of Steve Biko, the early Mandela in South Africa, collaborated with the advocacy and diplomacy of Archbishop Desmond Tutu and others. Calls for the unjust and unreasonable to be just and reasonable where the asker carries no threat will always fall prey to the maxim, 'power is never given, it is only ever taken', and result in minimalist concessions that are unlikely to get to the roots of inequality. As Bonilla-Silva (2003) argues, endemic racism operates in such a form that perpetuates racism without racists in which we all become actors in an ongoing process of racialization. A consequence of this is that poverty is still the lot of the Black masses in South Africa and America today since deploying the agency of the masses was never part of the agreement, just a white concession. Systemic change must of necessity include explicit application of Black agency otherwise we are back to a scenario similar to the ending of slavery with a pay-out for the slave-owners to pave their way ahead but no provision for former slaves in the arrangements. Today, black disadvantage in both settings is glaring. In the boxing ring of life, power skilfully deployed is needed to meet the power coming at you, as in the words of the hymn, 'Stand up for Jesus': 'let courage rise with danger, and strength to strength oppose' (Duffield and

Webb 1969, p. 412). There is a danger that the Black British diaspora assumes that what is required is to identify inequities, injustices and disparities, and believe that the rightness of the case automatically renders a good outcome in their favour. As everyone knows, this is often not the case since 'society' does not level the playing field, therefore the Black British community needs to deploy power and persistence to advance beyond the bumps in the road in a competitive, uneven world, making 'society' do what you will, and work to make happen.

Goodwill sentiments, making demands and speaking truth to power count for little in the real world of lived experience unless backed by a force of power to enforce or activate what is needed or that incentivises your protagonist to see things your way. As a Black Christian practitioner, it has been clear to me that we take and develop the characteristics of God we choose. Some like the 'gentle Jesus meek and mild' type, others the 'Jesus wants me for a sunbeam' type, others still, the 'turn the other cheek' type. I prefer the God who says, 'I give you power to cast out demons' (Mark 3), and we wrestle against principalities, powers, the rulers of darkness, spiritual wickedness in high places (Eph. 6). I love Jesus' words that the only way to take back what the strong man has taken from you is to be stronger than the strong man (Matt. 12.29). All these and other portrayals have their application, and right now the God who bestows irrevocable power upon humanity made in the divine image to utilize their agency, self-determination and human presence with dignity in the world is the God I work with. Given the symbiotic relationship between power and the flourishing of Black British people I want to explore briefly power in relation to the religious/spiritual, social, economic and political arenas.

Spiritual power

It is generally accepted that African people are a highly religious/spiritual people, both historically and still today. Here I make no distinction between the religious and the spiritual

– both represent human attempts to relate to the transcendent other. Black British people vary widely in forms of spirituality or religiosity and for the purposes of this book their qualifier is that they seek to enhance and uphold Black agency and self-determination as sources of Black empowerment in a space dominated by the white other. Any religion or religiosity that diminishes these God-given qualities is drawing you back into forms of colonialism in a situation where you are already subject to a superimposed imperial framework. All hands on deck must contribute to the resistance of that and other powers, and help towards flourishing, rather than establish a sub-colonial stratum that reinforces or perpetuates imperialism in any form. To pursue religious flourishing – I speak as a Christian – Black British people should consider resisting the Western trend towards secularization or humanism where this displaces or supersedes religious faith that has been a cornerstone of Black life for centuries. However, religious faith must serve practical purposes if they are to be credible aspects of Black British people's lives. As a pastor assisting in the holistic care of persons, body and spirit, I continue to struggle with the notion of spiritual power that does not affect literal human needs or that embraces a 'clientelistic nature' that requires the use of techniques to get God's attention, which becomes even more acute when a miracle is thought to be urgently needed (Davies 2010, p. 169). In my own tradition of Pentecostalism, for example, a tradition which recognizes the indwelling presence and power of God as the Holy Spirit, the idea that it requires particular techniques to get through to God brings into serious question the very nature of God. A people in diaspora can ill afford a God you need a special password to access – such a God opens the door to exploitation. Spiritual power worth having is that which connects you direct to God who accompanies and empowers and guides.

Jeremiah's letter to the exiles told them to pray for Babylon – that is, take the place to your spiritual concern and seek God for its betterment for everyone's benefit. People of African heritage living in the Western world have a rich history rooted in the concept of a Creator of the cosmos and all within and even beyond it, whatever other peoples do; and where there are shared heritages they should not abandon one to the exclusion of what has been integral to the well-being of the other. Just because the majority culture backslides in belief in God and church attendance does not mean Black British people automatically follow, and indeed Black churches have demonstrated this in many inner cities where previously white churches predominated but are now peopled by Black and other minority ethnic congregations.

Black Pentecostal churches in Britain have made significant contributions to the flourishing of Black British people, but have made insufficient practical links between its pneumatic claims and the lived experiences of its people in the real world. Consequently, too many Pentecostals live in poverty in the world and too many who do well do not sufficiently make the link between their material success and their belief in the transformational power of the Holy Spirit in the literal world. Since a key aspect of Pentecostal beliefs is the empowerment of believers through what is called baptism with or in the Holy Spirit, you should expect to do exploits once that power accompanies you. Acts 2 provides a key reference for this teaching; however, Black Pentecostals define this experience narrowly and this results in exclusivity rather than inclusivity, so some believers are not filled with the Holy Spirit. Since God is Spirit and it is by Spirit that one becomes a Christian (what Jesus calls being 'born again of the Spirit'), it is scarcely credible that any Christian believer can be without the Spirit (Aldred 2020). Scripture is clear that the Spirit blows like wind, catching everything and everyone in its path – at times as a cool breeze, or a violent storm or even a hurricane (John 3). However, instead of this understanding of the Spirit blowing upon the people of God made in the divine image and likeness, Pentecostals too often view the Spirit as theirs with specifically predetermined ways of experiencing the phenomenon known only to them. In this way people and groups are denominationalized, sectarianized, weakened and devalued unless their particular formula is satisfied. An outstanding challenge to flourishing is bridging the gap between the spiritual and material by which the impact of spiritual power extends beyond 'self-help' economics to transformation on the scale being claimed in the spiritual involving miracles of healing for example (Barnes 2012, p. 143).

In the quest to flourish spiritually, congregations should reject any theology, doctrine or practice that characterizes them as without the Holy Spirit, and therefore disempowered and lacking in agency; instead, they should live their lives in the surety of the innate image and likeness of God, and being followers who are doubly assured of the Comforter's presence as he promised (John 14). Here a key issue is training in Black British Pentecostal churches where every youth pastor or leader should have adequate mandatory training in children's and youth work and, crucially, theology – given the importance of younger generations to future spiritual flourishing. Equally, every Christian congregation should understand itself as part of the *koinonia* made up of individuals in whom the Holy Spirit lives and, like bricks or stones in a house, building up a spiritual house for the habitation of God and in service to God and in mission in the world. If there needs to be a test or evidence of the Spirit's presence, then rather than some esoteric demonstration of a 'gift' it could be the abiding test posited by Jesus, love (*agape*). Beginning with love of self and neighbour, then being empowered to unselfishly serve others, being filled with the Spirit of Christ enables the people of God to love, care for and minister to all humanity. In this way, love is dynamic, wholesome and transformative (1 Cor. 13). When organized religion is a hindrance to flourishing in spiritual power through unhelpful dogma, Black British people should reserve their right to desist from adhering to them. It is possible to belong to communities of faith while reserving the right to unsubscribe from unhelpful and unhealthy dogmas, as we sometimes need to within families. However, because of the importance of community especially for a people in diaspora, before walking away from faltering churches or other faith groups, seeking to help to transform those institutions may be more beneficial to the Black British community on a whole since the aim of individuals is not merely self-preservation but the spiritual and literal enrichment of the group. Imagine a Black British community marked by love and that love extended towards all others! The Black British Pentecostal Church with an established tradition of sensitivity to the dynamism of the Holy Spirit might lead on what it means to be spiritually powerful by acknowledging the Spirit as indwelling all believers, churches, denominations or ecclesial streams; the only reliable evidential identifying mark is that of unselfish love for self and other. Profoundly, spiritual power is predicated upon the connectivity with the divine that informs the communal and individual lives of the Black British community; in this the Black British church might be a leader.

Social power

Social power in a diasporic context relates to having accumulated influence in interconnecting areas such as education, health, housing, criminal justice, the arts and many more. This can be understood through the lens of social capital, which, like money, speaks of an accumulation to the point where it amounts to something capable of having currency beyond itself such as prestige, honour and the right to be listened to (Byfield 2008, p. 13). When seeking to purchase property or other highly priced items it requires an accumulation of funds to the level where the sum of the capital can be exchanged for the property or goods. Social power, then, in the context of diaspora, accumulates in the Black British community, acquiring credibility first among Black British people before impacting wider society. For social power to be effective in delivering self-respect and feelings of integrity, it needs to be rooted and validated within the social spheres of the community, rather than be handed it by 'white society' as bait for inclusion. Indeed, social power is best acquired by being rooted and centred in the Black British community and distinguishable as such; only then can its identity be discerned by the people themselves as well as wider society. The Black British people then need to build upon social capital through their contribution and presence, self-validation, irrefutable work in the social realms, and becoming visible to the mainstream.

This is observable in institutions like Black churches and other community organizations, whose leaders and other significant persons emerge as champions of their people and wider community through their dedication and success at supporting the flourishing of their community. These champions of their people in 'exile' are not always the ones favoured by 'Babylon's' powerbrokers as social connectors for their communities from which they emerge. Some who have not been approved and affirmed by their community for their work and value to them, cultivate other means of attracting attention and approval from the mainstream and are made leaders of their community by the mainstream, and superimposed upon the Black British community as their representatives. It is therefore common to find that the publicly recognizable 'faces' in press and media, civic and political agencies have little to no Black community approval and acclaim. However, the community has little to no choice other than to live with those created by imperial power and who operate without community approval or affirmation, driven instead from another power base within Babylon. The majority culture has multiple ways of conjuring up the outcomes it desires by appointments to prestigious positions, and other social constructs like King's honours, honorary degrees, public appointments and such like. This does represent a form of social power that may even contribute to the Black British public good, in small or great ways, but effective social power needs to operate through connectivity to the main arteries of the Black British community. Or it may end up serving only or mainly the purposes of the imperial forces.

The cause of social power is served when various community needs are legitimately met from within it, addressing what is in their public good. Jeremiah's call to the Jewish exiles to throw their lot in with the Babylonian society comes after they are instructed to build various areas of their communal lives. People have first to build and strengthen their own internal social fabric before they possess what can be contributed to 'Babylon', not through integration of their weakness and vulnerabilities, but through contribution and involvement, and through their strengths as they bring their profound social history developed over centuries to the table of communal life. As mentioned above, in Black British social spheres, authentic and effective contributions to black power are often wielded by operatives unrecognized by wider Black British society. For example, in the various congregations and denominations I have served in or been associated with, if the mainstream community are aware of anyone it will only be aware of the leader and one or two others. However, to make a local church of 200 run smoothly and effectively there will be approximately a third of that congregation in leadership positions, usually as volunteers. The congregations will be aware of them, as they will be of those who operate district, regional, national and international functions. However, those contributing to making strong the social fabric of churches and community projects, as happens in the majority culture, are largely unknown to the outside world beyond their operational boundaries.

My observation is that for the foreseeable future a combination of those approved by 'Babylon' and those approved by the 'exiles' need to work together to hold real social power in Britain, the one having access to the inner contours of white majority British society, the other having access to the real issues and priorities of the community. The one is better able to unlock resources of state, the other has knowledge of what is actually required by the community. This prototype of malfunction is mirrored by the Western education received by the children of wealthy leaders in so-called developing countries, who after studying return to their countries of origin to take up leadership meant to benefit their citizens. Often, however, social expertise is Westernized, the persons return with privileged status but removed from the challenges they now attempt to address. Although communities have a divine and legal right to development, it means little unless embraced and actualized by the people themselves (Igbinedion 2019).

Social power in the Black British context needs hybridity, incarnational structure and working together across a spectrum of expertise, favour and need. Just because someone has the ears, even heart, of British society and can manipulate it effectively does not guarantee that what is done is to the benefit of the Black British community on whose behalf they purport to act. Similarly, just because someone's heart and ears and sight are located in the Black British community does not mean they have the wherewithal to address those legitimate concerns without access to the levers of power in the wider society. Regrettably the power of the media is such that those it holds up as Black British power brokers are the ones who are publicly acclaimed by wider society; their appearance on TV screens, newspapers and magazines proves irresistible. The majority Black British community should never be duped by this public acclaim, but be aware who are the people in their corner and insist that those held up by the press and media locate their work not in the approval of wider society but in the interest of the Black British community; finding ways to hold them to account. From my own place in the Pentecostal Church, it remains an unanswered question whether the leitmotif of faith can help deliver 'dynamics of popular social mobilization' in the lived experience of Black British people, equivalent to claims made concerning power in the invisible spiritual realm (Wilson 2010).

Economic power

Wisdom literature offers us a pithy, 'money is the answer for everything' (Eccl. 10.19). The sense here is that most things – feasting and wine are mentioned for example – have their limited applicability, but money has near unlimited applicability; with love being one of the exceptions some have suggested (for example, the Beatles' 'money can't buy you love'). As far back as the sixth century BC, Jeremiah encouraged economic growth as a way to flourish and to stamp the community's presence upon their exilic situation. Economic power enables a community to manoeuvre in ways that are impossible without that economic power, so they are rendered susceptible to multiple vulnerabilities and dependent upon external forces often antagonistic towards the exile – it is they who have usually precipitated the situation. Economic power is important for countries, regions, organizations, families and individuals because it facilitates autonomy and options (Bento 2023). The Black British community has to become recognizable for being economically strong or they will be known as poor, disadvantaged, oppressed, as they are now. The current situation is unsurprising given the historic context: the Black British community started from a place of relative poverty, arriving in Britain as enslaved people, servants, entertainers, servicemen and women and low skilled workers against a background of societal racism that further limited their prospects with mainstream white society viewing them as inferior. While some have been able to progress economically, such progress has been slow as a group, as shown by data related to home ownership, employment, education and training, and qualifications. By one measure, income poverty rate in Britain shows White British people at 20%, Bangladeshi 65%, Black Africans 45% and Black Caribbeans 30% (https://www.jrf.org.uk/race-and-ethnicity/poverty-rates-among-ethnic-groups-in-great-britain). Another source shows that a typical White British person has wealth of £197,000 while a Black African person in Britain has wealth of £24,000, and Black Caribbean £41,800 (https://www.resolutionfoundation.org/press-releases/wealth-gaps-between-different-ethnic-groups-in-britain-are-large-and-likely-to-persist/). This aptly demonstrates that the Black British person and community have a long way to go to claim to have economic power in Britain.

By contrast, the Black church as a diverse brand of several unconnected charities and businesses constitute multimillion-pound enterprises and are an example of what is possible. Were these churches to link their bank balances and property portfolios across denominations and across African and Caribbean ethnic identities the possibilities of what such leveraging could drive may be astonishing. Additionally, were the various economic initiatives owned by Black British people to be index-linked in ways that make them transparent to the community and wider society, the wealth of Black British people would be made evident. From my observation, there are also numerous Black British individuals and unincorporated groups with significant portfolios of property existing under the public radar because they don't want 'people to know we business'. Currently the perception and working assumption about the Black British community is that they are economically deprived and weak, although with Black sports people, actors and musicians becoming more openly philanthropic, the Black British reputation for self-improvement is beginning to change. We may assume much good work is done discreetly, but three examples are footballer Marcus Rashford's contribution to providing free meals for school children (fareshare.org.uk); musician Stormzy's Cambridge University scholarship for Black UK students (undergraduate.study.com.ac.uk); and Formula 1 driver Lewis Hamilton's foundation supporting children and young people (totalgiving.co.uk).

The perception of Black British people as 'poor and oppressed' needs to change, and there are steps that can be taken, among which are the following. First, quality intelligence that provides informed analysis and publication of the economic state of the Black British community. Second, the use of such information to build upon existing enterprises, or to identify gaps and to exploit for new economic initiatives, particularly for entrepreneurs in the Black British community. Key also to moving to a stronger economic position is the awareness that as a small percentage of the British population, Black British people need to do business within and beyond their own ethnic community. Also, a reason so many migrate from Africa and Caribbean countries to Britain for economic betterment has to do with the exploitation of those countries by Britain and other European countries that operated slave and free colonies for the benefit of their imperial systems. This points to the call for reparations from these countries, a call being made louder and more strategic than before, such as CARICOM's Ten Point Plan for Reparatory Justice (https://caricom.org/caricom-ten-point-plan-for-reparatory-justice/). And while the Black British community as the descendants of enslaved and colonized peoples cannot afford to sit and wait for reparations to come, it does not mean the call is not just. The aim, then, of a flourishing Black British community calls for economic power that enables them to answer all calls with autonomy and integrity, at least on a par with other communities with respect to per capita wealth. This economic power is never going to be handed to the community on a plate; such power needs to be cultivated by the community at all levels and spheres, individual and corporate, and in respect of reparations fought for by the exilic Black British community in partnership both with kinfolk back home and with allies in Britain and Europe. Such Black British-led initiative-taking will usher in the day when the community is known as one having economic power. Where there is a will there is a way.

Political power

A further sign of flourishing is political power, as important in homelands as well as in exile or diaspora. When Jeremiah told Jewish exiles to increase and not decrease, I read this as a call to political action and participation that can affect local and national politics. Politics is about people, numbers and attributes, content of character and thinking. Operation Black Vote (OBV) has long promoted the idea of how numbers can shape political debate and exercise of political power (Woolley 2022). Where politicians feel a people pose no threat to their election prospects, the needs of those people tend to be put further down the pecking order in favour of those believed to know their political numerical weight and who are prepared to vote politicians out of office. In addition to mobilizing Black people to register to vote and exercise their franchise, the encouragement is to synchronize their political compound weight by casting their votes in accord with their personal and group interests. Clearly a minority community has a relatively small and finite number of votes but when coordinated they maximize the impact of the casting of those votes. This kind of politics aims to be non-slavishly party-politically or ideologically aligned, and instead aligned to the imperatives of the community. Political power should be wielded wisely by minority communities in their own interest and not a party political interest that can miss what is important to them. This is the aim of the National Church Leaders Forum Political Manifesto (https://blackgifted.app/nclf-manifesto).

While participating in political franchise is important, what is also of great significance is that Black British people seek elected office for political parties or as independents. This can run counter to the party line of politics, yet that tension can be creative. A Black voter may or may not vote for a Black candidate, but it is important that Black British people run for office, and given the fact that independent candidates struggle to progress as candidates in a strong party political system those who will run successfully will almost always belong to a political party. A challenge for those elected is to have regard to doing good by their electorate who will be a cross-section of the population, while also serving their ethnic group's welfare and flourishing.

A minimum signifier of political power might be equilibrium of the Black British percentage of the population against the percentage of elected politicians, as in other civic and political spheres; so that 5% of the population aims for a minimum 5% of MPs, councillors, JPs, across all strata of life in Britain. Politics exist beyond organized politics too, in the form of protests and behind-the-scenes manoeuverings. Black British people should seek to be involved in all forms of politics and campaigning in the interests of their community and country. Currently the Black British community is viewed as politically weak and underperforming; this needs to change. Punching their weight politically, Black British people will need to encourage political interest and engagement and thereby increase representation across the political and civic spectrum. Some may be apathetic about political involvement but the more effective participation at all levels, the greater the returns are likely to be to the community, as the rest of the political fraternity view Black British people as active, effective, a threat to their prospects if they do not do good by them, and as key political allies in the interest of the whole of society. Significantly, by having a sense of self-determining direction, and driving forward their self-interested agenda, all will note that the Black British people are not hanging back expecting others to invite them; rather, it will be clear this community operates not by beseeching or even demanding inclusion – where necessary they will create their own political vehicles if the ones that exist are inaccessible. It ought to be obvious, but clearly is not always, that political decisions ostensibly made in the interest of all in society will almost always be made with the interests of a majority paramount. This means that inevitably all political projects will have downsides for some minorities as they aim at a powerful majority, therefore particularly ethnic minorities like the Black British community must ensure they have political formations in place to address blind spots that miss some discrete needs of minority communities. Political power for Black British people exists as they put a high value on their participation and votes, making clear to seekers of those votes that they cannot be taken for granted by tradition. The right to vote is therefore guided by 'here are our priorities, persuade us why we should vote for you'.

Home

A fourth and final facet of flourishing I look at is home. Jeremiah's letter to the exiles promised that after 70 years, or in the fullness of time, they would return home, exile over, all will be well. If only! We know that by the time the Babylonian Empire was overthrown by the Persian Empire, much had changed. In an introduction to an edited work, Greenspoon reminds us that the Jews have had multiple exiles and returns home, of which the Babylonian experience was one. This complexifies exile and home in the imagination even as Jerusalem occupied a central, 'geographically cosmic' idea of home for exiled Jews and those in Judah (Greenspoon 2019, p. 19). Exile, like return, represents a protracted concept in which the meaning of home has to be reconceptualized and reconfigured. When the time comes to go home, 'Jerusalem' may hold spiritual resonance, yet some may never leave 'Babylon' to live there. Even the concept of how to flourish in Babylon may not hold true for other generations who consider it home.

My concept of 'home' is informed by my reality of having lived in 20 addresses in my lifetime, with the longest – almost 16 years – being the tiny unsophisticated family home where I was born in Jamaica before moving to England. Three-quarters of these have been since being married and raising a family which means my wife and our three daughters have shared substantially in my nomadic existence. Each move carried with it a mix of excitement, drama and sometimes trauma to add to the challenge of turning house into home. This frequency of house moves has largely nullified the fear of moving, arduous though each move has been. I identify with scripture when I read, 'Here we do not have an enduring city' (Heb. 13.14), or 'the Son of Man has nowhere to lay his head' (Matt. 8.20). Yet I have made and remade house into home time and time again. Home for me therefore has lacked permanence and entrenched my ability to settle into wherever I am. On occasions while visiting my birth island of Jamaica I am called a 'foreigner'! I feel Jamaica is home when I am in England, but England feels like home when I am in Jamaica. Having lived in hope and expectation that I would retire to Jamaica, I find myself embedded into Britain as 'home' having lived here for most of my life, with consequential outcomes of rootedness, particularly in relation to family. Living in diaspora means reconceptualizing 'home' as something at once definable and nebulous, literal and spiritual. Expectation of going home to heaven as a final destination remains a Christian hope, yet beyond conceptualizing as being in the presence of God not much is clear to me. Flourishing here feels like a divine command, and home is, conceptually and literally, the epicentre of this world.

The concept of 'home' is crucial to the concept of flourishing. One definition of 'home' I stumbled upon on the internet is, 'The place in which one's domestic affections are centred'. For me, home is where I am at my most comfortable, feel safest, feel like I belong. I recall returning home after attending a night-time church meeting to find we had been burgled and ransacked. It was a feeling of my family being violated and that we were vulnerable in our home in a manner I had never known before. Home, therefore, is not always comfortable or safe, it is more than that: more the aforementioned centre of one's world. Home, though, is more than a house and may best be understood through practices, rituals and an emotional attachment to an ideal existence rooted in one's heart. The tangible and the intangible may be inseparably intertwined and at times one may feature more prominently than the other.

As I have been developing in this book, the meaning of home has changed since the millions having perished under the cruel weight of capture, chattel slavery and colonialism, millions more dispersed across the Americas and Caribbean, and after generations many have undergone further removal, such as from the Caribbean to the USA, Canada, Britain and elsewhere. Where home is therefore is not straightforward and consequently a return home is also a complex matter. The alluring text in Jeremiah 29.11 much loved by the Black Christian community feels more like a spiritual ideal than a literal aspiration. Home, then, is a sphere of beingness out of which one abides among one's people and from which one relates to the immediate context and the wider world. Home, while also a place in time, is also transitory and transcendent, centred on where I live among my people in ever-increasing circles until it includes all of humanity and beyond. Home is the United Kingdom, the Caribbean, especially Jamaica, and Africa, for Black British people the original motherland.

For Black British people, dignity, agency and self-determination all help to make home wherever they are. Black people create and recreate home in spite of the existence of oppositional forces not because they cease to exist. Once Black British people recognize that power to be at home rests in their hands, they also discover the many white and other British allies who adopt a pragmatism that makes neighbourliness possible. What is more, none in the Black community needs to be left homeless since strong bonds of family and community structure allied with awareness of state provision and connectedness with Africans around the globe make strong and powerful partners for themselves and wider society. The home Black British people need to settle in most of all is the one in their own selves, with, for a Christian like me, knowledge that God in whose image I am made accompanies me on the journey of life.

This idea of home everywhere means Africa, the Caribbean, Britain, America and the rest of the world. This wider existence means taking an active interest in the affairs and well-being of kinfolks in the homelands and in diaspora. The freeing up of hard and fast ideas about where is home permit creative acts that take flourishing as their *raison d'être*. Key to flourishing, as I have been discussing above, is that Black British people, by deployment of their agency, self-determination, with dignity in the *imago Dei*, under God alone determine where and how they live their life within and beyond any context. Liberation is not something they seek, it is what they live! The empowerment of Black British people should be a key objective because only by strength can they flourish in Babylon. In the end, Black British people being strong in their God-imaged likeness, agency and self-determination is the foundation upon which they can bring into being the changes they want in areas of justice, peace and flourishing, since nothing will be achieved by wishing well, and power is never given, it is only ever taken whether at home or in diaspora. As I came to the end of this book, I came across a work that speaks a helpful truth in its topic, 'flourish by design' (Dunn, Cruickshank, Coupe 2023). It is the only way, wherever we find ourselves, to set about designing the flourishing we seek that is in the mind of almighty God in whose image and likeness we are made!

Questions for intergenerational discussions

- Why are Black people so religious?
- In addition to racism, what are some of the giants in the way of Black flourishing?
- What will it take for Black British people to have power: spiritual, social, economic, political?
- Where really is home for Black British people ... Africa, Britain, or the Caribbean?

Bibliography

Ackroyd, Peter, 1968, *Exile and Restoration*, London: SCM Press.

Adamo, David T., 2018, 'The Portrayal of Africa and Africans in the Book of Jeremiah', *In die Skriflig*, Vol. 52, No. 1.

———, 2021, 'The African Background of the Prosperity Gospel', *Theologia Viatorum*, Vol. 45, No. 1, pp. 1–10.

Adams, Scott Lewis, 2021, 'The Rhetorical Function of Petitionary Prayer in Revelation', *Neotestamentica*, Vol. 55, No. 1, pp. 1–22, doi: 10.10520/ejc-neotest_v55_n1_a1.

Adedibu, Babatunde, 2012, *Coat of Many Colours: The Origin, Growth, Distinctives and Contributions of Black Majority Churches to British Christianity*, London: Wisdom Summit.

Aderibigbe, Ibigbolade S., 2016, 'Religion', in Abdul Karim Bangura, *Culpability of the Trans-Atlantic Slave Trade: A Multidisciplinary Primer*, Falls Village, CT: Hamilton Books, pp. 227–43.

Adeyemo, Tokunboh, 2006, *Africa Bible Commentary*, Nairobi, Kenya: WordAlive Publishers.

Afari, Yasus, 2007, *Overstanding Rastafari: Jamaica's Gift to the World*, Jamaica: Senya-Cum.

Agama, Doye T., 2016, *Africa, Christianity and the Bible – Our Global Destiny*, Peterborough: FastPrint Publishing.

Akala, 2018, *Natives: Race and Class in the Ruins of Empire*, Great Britain: Two Roads.

Aldred, Genelle, 2021, *Communicate for Change: Creating Justice in a World of Bias*, London: SPCK.

Aldred, Joe, 2000, *Sisters with Power*, London: Bloomsbury.

———, 2005, *Respect: Understanding Caribbean British Christianity*, Peterborough: Epworth.

———, 2013, *Thinking Outside the Box: On Race, Faith and Life*, Hertford: Hansib Publications.

———, 2015, *From Top Mountain: an Autobiography*, Hertford: Hansib Publications.

———, 2020, 'The Holy Spirit and the Black Church' in Joe Aldred and Keno Ogbo (eds), *The Black Church in the 21st Century*, revised ed., London: Darton, Longman and Todd, pp. 45–62.

———, 2022, 'The Flourishing of the UK African and Caribbean Diaspora', *Black Theology*, Vol. 20, No. 2, pp. 198–210.

——— (ed.), 1999, *Preaching with Power: Sermons by Black Preachers*, London: Cassell.

——— (ed.), 2000, *Praying with Power*, London: Bloomsbury Continuum.

Aldrich, Robert, and Andreas Stucki, 2023, *The Colonial World: A History of European Empires, 1780s to the Present*, London: Bloomsbury Academic.

Ali, Grace Aneiza, 2019, 'The Ones Who Leave ... the Ones Who Are Left: Guyanese Migration Story' in Deborah Willis, Ellyn Toscano, Kalia Brooks Nelson (eds), *Women and Migration: Responses in Art and History*, Cambridge, UK: Open Book Publishers, pp. 473–90.

Allen, Leslie C., 2008, *Jeremiah: A Commentary*, Louisville, KY: Westminster John Knox Press.

Alpers, Edward A., 1975, *Ivory and Slaves: Changing Pattern of International Trade In East Central Africa to the Later Nineteenth Century*, Berkeley, CA: University of California Press.

Altman, Neil, 2020, *White Privilege: Psychoanalytic Perspectives*, London: Routledge.

Anderson, Victor, 1999, *Beyond Ontological Blackness*, New York: Continuum.

Andrews, Kehinde, 2013, *Resisting Racism: Race, Inequality and the Black Supplementary School Movement*, London: Institute of Education Press.

———, 2018, *Back to African Caribbean: Retelling Black Radicalism for the 21st Century*, London: Zed Books.

Arnold, S. E., 1992, *From Scepticism to Hope: One African Caribbean-Led Church's Response to Social Responsibility*, Nottingham: Grove Books.

Ashimolowo, Matthew, 2007, *What is Wrong with Being Black? Celebrating our Heritage, Confronting our Challenges*, Shippensberg, PA: Destiny Image.

Attanasi, Katy, and Amos Yong, 2012, *Pentecostalism and Prosperity: The Socio-economics of the Global Charismatic Movement*, New York: Palgrave Macmillan.

Augustine, Daniela C., 2019, *The Spirit and the Common Good: Shared Flourishing in the Image of God*, Grand Rapids, MI: Eerdmans.

Baillie Abidi, Catherine, 2018, *Pedagogies for Building Cultures of Peace: Challenging Constructions of an Enemy*, Boston, MA: Brill.

Baimbridge, M., P. B. Whyman and B. Brian, 2011, *Britain in a Global World: Options for a New Beginning*, Luton: Andrews UK.

Bakan, Abigail B., 1990, *Ideology and Class Conflict in Jamaica: The Politics of Rebellion*, Montreal, Quebec: McGill-Queen's University Press.

Baker-Fletcher, G., 2009, *Bible Witness in Black Churches*, London: Palgrave Macmillan.

Balentine, Samuel E., 1981, 'Prophet of Prayer', *Review & Expositor*, Vol. 78, No. 3, pp. 331–44.

Bantum, Brian, 2010, *Redeeming Mulatto: A Theology of Race and Christian Hybridity*, Waco, TX: Baylor University Press.
Barber, Leroy, 2016, *Embrace: God's Radical Shalom for a Divided World*, Westmont, IL: InterVarsity Press.
Barnes, Sandra L., 2012, *Live Long and Prosper: How Black Megachurches Address HIV/AIDS and Poverty in the Age of Prosperity Theology*, New York: Fordham University Press.
Bartleman, Frank, 1980, *Azusa Street: The Roots of Modern-Day Pentecost,* South Plainfield, NJ: Bridge Publishing.
Barton, Mukti, 2005, *Rejection, Resistance and Resurrection: Speaking Out on Racism in the Church*, London: Darton, Longman and Todd.
Beach, Lee, 2015, *The Church in Exile: Living in Hope after Christendom*, Foreword by Walter Brueggemann, London: InterVarsity Press.
Beckford, Robert, 1999, 'Black Pentecostals and Black Politics', in Allan H. Anderson and Walter J. Hollenweger, *Pentecostals After a Century: Global Perspectives on a Movement*, Sheffield: Sheffield Academic Press, pp. 48–59.
———, 2000, *Dread and Pentecostalism: A Political Theology for the Black Church in Britain*, London: SPCK.
———, 2001, *God of the Rahtid*, London: Darton, Longman and Todd.
———, 2014, *Documentary as Exorcism: Resisting the Bewitchment of Colonial Christianity*, London: Bloomsbury.
———, 2023, *Decolonizing Contemporary Gospel Music Through Praxis*, Handsworth Revolutions, London: Bloomsbury.
Beckles, Hilary McD., 2013, *Britain's Black Debt: Reparations for Caribbean Slavery and Native Genocide*, Kingston, Jamaica: University of the West Indies Press.
Bell, Alton, 2013, *Breaking the Chains of Mental Slavery: Practical Tools to Bring Freedom to You and Your Descendants*, London: A & M Publishing.
Bellagamba, Alice, et al., 2013, *African Voices on Slavery and the Slave Trade*: *Volume 1, The Sources,* New York: Cambridge University Press.
Bento, Vitor, 2023, *Strategic Autonomy and Economic Power: The Economy as a Strategic Theatre*, Abingdon: Routledge.
Bertocci, Peter A., 2004, *The Person God Is*, London: Routledge.
Bhopal, Kalwant, 2018, *White Privilege: The Myth of a Post-racial Society*, Bristol: Policy Press.
Boal, Augusto, 2006, *The Aesthetics of the Oppressed*, London: Routledge.
Boer, Roland, 2009, 'Resistance Versus Accommodation: What to do with Romans 13?' in Tat-siong Benny Liew (ed.), *Postcolonial Interventions: Essays in Honour of R. S. Sugirtharajah*, Sheffield: Sheffield Phoenix Press, pp. 109–22.

———, 2018, 'Nehemiah' in Hemchand Gossai (ed.), *Postcolonial Commentary and the Old Testament*, London: Bloomsbury, pp. 195–208.

Boff, Leonardo and Clodovis Boff, 1987, *Introducing Liberation Theology*, Maryknoll, NY: Orbis Books.

Bogues, Anthony, 2010, *Empire of Liberty: Power, Desire, and Freedom*, Lebanon, NH: University Press of New England.

Bonilla-Silva, Eduardo, 2003, *Racism Without Racists: Colour-Blind Racism and the Persistence of Racial Inequality in the United States*, Lanham, MD: Rowman and Littlefield.

Bowers Du Toit, Nadine, 2018, 'Decolonising Development? Re-Claiming Biko and a Black Theology of Liberation Within the Context of Faith Based Organisations in South Africa, Missionalia', *Southern African Journal of Mission Studies*, Vol. 46, No. 1, pp. 24–35.

Bowes, Elaine, 2023, 'Section 3, Economic Development in Black Church Political Mobilisation, A Manifesto for Action', London: National Church Leaders Forum.

Brazelton, J. Henry Augustus (ed.), 1918, *Self-determination: The Salvation of the Race*, Oklahoma City, OK: The Educator.

Brennan, R., 2015, *Describing the Hand of God: Divine Agency and Augustinian Obstacles to the Dialogue between Theology and Science*, Eugene, OR: Wipf and Stock.

Brooks, Ira, 1970, *In Chains They Shall Come Over*, Birmingham: New Testament Church of God.

———, 1982, *Where do we go from here? A history of 25 years of the New Testament Church of God in the United Kingdom 1955–1980*, London: Charles Raper.

———, 1985, *Another Gentleman to the Ministry*, Birmingham: Compeer Press.

Brooten, Bernadette J., and Jacqueline L. Hazelton (eds), 2010, *Beyond Slavery: Overcoming Its Religious and Sexual Legacies*, New York: Palgrave Macmillan.

Brueggemann, Walter, 1991, *Jeremiah: To Build, to Plant, Jeremiah 26–52*, Grand Rapids, MI: Eerdmans.

Buffel, O. A., 2010, 'Black Theology and the Black Masses: The Need of an Organic Relationship Between Black Theology and the Black Masses', *Scriptura*, Vol. 105.

Bullard, Robert D., 2008, *Dumping in Dixie: Race, Class, and Environmental Quality*, 3rd edition, New York: Westview Press.

Burrell, Barrington O., 2011, *African-Caribbean Church Culture: The Evolution of Black Majority Churches in Britain*, London: Grosvenor House.

Burrell, David, and Elena Malits, 1997, *Original Peace: Restoring God's Creation*, New York: Paulist Press.

Butler, Lee H., 2016, 'The Power of a Black Christology: Africana Pastoral Theology Reflects on Black Divinity', in Jawanza Eric Clark (ed.), *Albert Cleage Jr and the Black Madonna and Child*, New York: Palgrave Macmillan, pp. 157–69.

Byfield, Cheron, 2008, *Black Boys Can Make It: How they Overcome the Obstacles to University in the UK and USA*, Stoke-on-Trent: Trentham Books.

Cabral, Amber, 2020, *Allies and Advocates: Creating an Inclusive and Equitable Culture*, New York: Wiley.

Campbell-Stephens, Rosemary M., 2021, *Educational Leadership and the Global Majority: Decolonising Narratives*, Cham, Switzerland: Palgrave Macmillan.

Carnegie, Charles V. (ed.), 1987, *Afro-Caribbean Villages in Historical Perspective*, Kingston, Jamaica: Institute of Jamaica Publications.

Cartledge, M. J., and D. Cheetham (eds), 2012, *Intercultural Theology*, London: SCM Press.

Castillo, Jason, et al., 2022, 'Failing to Bend the Arc of the Moral Universe? Dr. King, Newton, Piaget, and Social Work', *Critical Social Work*, Vol. 23, No. 1, doi: 10.22329/csw.v23i1.7590.

Channer, Yvonne, 1995, *I am a Promise: the School Achievement of British African Caribbeans*, Stoke-on-Trent, UK: Trentham Books.

Clark, J., 2012, *Indigenous Black Theology: Toward an African-Centered Theology of the African American Religious Experience*, London: Palgrave Macmillan.

Clark, Keturah, 2018, 'Black Hair and the Imago Dei: An Embodiment for God's Vision of Wholeness, A Thesis in the Field of Multicultural Studies for the Degree of Master of Arts in Theological Studies, Colgate Rochester Crozer Divinity School.

Clay, Elonda, 2010, 'A Black Theology of Liberation or Legitimation: A Postcolonial Response to Cone's Black Theology and Black Power at Forty', *Black Theology: An International Journal*, Vol. 8, No. 3, Sheffield: Equinox Publishing Group.

Coleman, Will, 2000, *Tribal Talk: Black Theology, Hermeneutics, and African/American Ways of 'Telling the Story'*, University Park, PA: Pennsylvania State University Press.

Commission on Race and Ethnic Disparities, 2021, *Report*, https://www.gov.uk/government/publications/the-report-of-the-commission-on-race-and-ethnic-disparities

Cone, James H., 1969, 1989, *Black Theology and Black Power*, New York: Seabury Press, reissued 1989 with introduction by James H. Cone, New York: Harper and Row.

———, 1975, *God of the Oppressed*, San Francisco, CA: Harper San Francisco.

———, 1984, 1992, *For My People: Black Theology and the Black Church: Where Have we Been and Where are we Going?*, Maryknoll, NY: Orbis Books.

———, 1993, *My Soul Looks Back*, Maryknoll, NY: Orbis Books.

———, 2022, *The Cross and the Lynching Tree*, Maryknoll, NY: Orbis Books.

Coogan, Michael D. (ed.), 1999, *The Oxford History of the Biblical World*, Oxford: Oxford University Press.

Cornelius, Elma M., 2022, 'Can the New Testament Be Blamed for Unfair Discrimination or Domination in Modern Societies?', *Die Skriflig*, Vol. 56, No. 1.

Csinos, David M., 2020, 'From Pioneer to Partner: Dismantling White Normativity in Ethnographic Theology', *Religious Educator Journal of the Religious Education Association*, Vol. 115, Issue 4, pp. 400–42.

Cummings, Elijah, and Hilary Beard, 2021, *We're Better than This: My Fight for the Future of Democracy*, New York: HarperCollins.

Dabydeen, David, John Gilmore and Cecily Jones (eds), 2007, *The Oxford Companion to Black British History*, Oxford: Oxford University Press.

D'Aguiar, Fred, 1999, 'Home is Always Elsewhere: Individual and Communal Regenerative Capacities of Loss' in Kwesi Owusu (ed.), *Black British Culture and Society: A Text-Reader*, London: Routledge, pp. 209–20.

Davidson, Steed V., 2011, *Empire and Exile: Postcolonial Readings of the Book of Jeremiah*, London; New York: Continuum.

Davies, Omar, and Michael Witter, 1989, 'The Development of the Jamaican Economy since Independence' in Rex Nettleford (ed.), *Jamaica in Independence: Essays on the Early Years*, Kingston, Jamaica: Heinemann Publishers (Caribbean), pp. 75–101.

Davies W., 2010, *The Embattled but Empowered Community: Comparing Understandings of Spiritual Power in Argentine Popular and Pentecostal Cosmologies*, Boston, MA: Brill.

Davis, Kortright, 1990, *Emancipation Still Comin': Explorations in Caribbean Emancipatory Theology*, Maryknoll, NY: Orbis Books.

DiAngelo, Robin, 2018, *White Fragility: Why It's So Hard for White People to Talk about Racism*, London: Beacon Press.

Dick, Devon, 2002, *Rebellion to Riot: The Jamaican Church in Nation Building*, Kingston: Ian Randle Publishers.

Domeris, W. R., 1993, 'Honour and Shame in the New Testament', *Neotestamentica*, Vol. 27, No. 2, pp. 283–97.

Douglass, Frederick, 1995, *Narrative of the Life of Frederick Douglass*, Garden City, NY: Dover.

Downs, Gregory P., 2011, *Declarations of Dependence: The Long Reconstruction of Popular Politics in the South, 1861–1908*, Chapel Hill, NC: University of North Carolina Press.

Drever, James, 1966, *A Dictionary of Psychology*, Harmondsworth, Middlesex: Penguin Books.

Duffield, George, and George J. Webb, 1969, 'Stand up for Jesus' in

Hymns of Glorious Praise, Church of God of Prophecy, USA: Gospel Publishing House.

Dumbuya, Peter A., 2016, 'Reverse Migration and State Formation in West Africa', in Abdul Karim Bangura, *Culpability of the Trans-Atlantic Slave Trade: A Multidisciplinary Primer*, Falls Village, CT: Hamilton Books, pp. 245–60.

Dunkley, D. A., 2012, *Agency of the Enslaved: Jamaica and the Culture of Freedom in the Atlantic World*, Lanham, MD: Lexington Books/ Fortress Academic.

Dunn, Nick, Leon Cruickshank and Gemma Coupe (eds), 2023, *Flourish by Design*, Abingdon: Routledge.

Dwyer, Philip, and Amanda Nettelbeck, 2017, *Violence, Colonialism and Empire in the Modern World*, New York: Springer.

Eddo-Lodge, Reni, 2018, *Why I'm No Longer Talking To White People About Race*, London: Bloomsbury.

Edwards, Joel, 1999, *Lord Make Us One But Not All The Same: Seeking Unity in Diversity*, London: Hodder & Stoughton.

——— (ed.), 1992, *Let's Praise Him Again!: An African-Caribbean Perspective on Worship*, Eastbourne: Kingsway.

Elliott, Steve, 2012, *Thriving in Exile: How to Build, Plant, Bless and Pray through Tough Times*, Maxwell, IA: Grassfire Nation.

Erskine, N. L., 1998, *Decolonizing Theology: A Caribbean Perspective*, Asmara, Eritrea: Africa World Press.

——— 2008, *Black Theology and Pedagogy*, New York: Palgrave Macmillan US.

Equiano, Olaudah, 1995, *The Interesting Narrative and Other Writings*, London: Penguin.

Felder, Cain Hope, 1991, *Stony the Road We Trod: African American Biblical Interpretation*, Minneapolis, MN: Fortress Press.

Fisher, Earle J., 2018, 'A Close Reading of Albert Cleage's The Black Messiah: A study in rhetorical hermeneutics, Black prophetic and radical Black politics', Dissertation, University of Memphis.

Foblets, Marie-Claire, Michele Graziadei and Alison Dundes Renteln, 2018, *Personal Autonomy in Plural Societies: A Principle and its Paradoxes*, Abingdon: Routledge.

Freire, Paulo, 2017, *Pedagogy of the Oppressed*, translated by M. B. Ramos, London: Penguin Books.

Fryer, Peter, 1984, *Staying Power: The History of Black People in Britain*, London: Pluto Press.

Gates, Henry Louis, Jr (ed.), 1987, *The Classic Slave Narratives*, New York: New American Library.

Gentleman, Amelia, 2019, *The Windrush Betrayal: Exposing the Hostile Environment*, London: Guardian Faber.

George, Karl, 2003, *Most people only try – I make sure*, Birmingham: Andersons KBS.

Gerloff, Roswith H., 1992, *A Plea for British Black Theologies: The Black Church Movement in Britain in its Transatlantic Cultural and Theological Interaction*, Vol. 1, New York: Peter Lang.

Getachew, Adom, 2019, *Worldmaking after Empire: The Rise and Fall of Self-Determination*, Princeton, NJ: Princeton University Press.

Gibellini, Rosino, 1986, *The Liberation Theology Debate*, London: SCM Press.

Gilroy, Paul, 2000, *Between Camps: Nation, Cultures and the Allure of Race*, London: Penguin Books.

Gladwell, Malcolm, 2013, *David and Goliath: Underdogs, Misfits and the Art of Battling Giants*, London: Penguin.

Glen, Jason T., 2005, 'Black Theology, Western Epistemology, and the Image of God, A Paper Submitted To Dr Liederbach For Partial Fulfilment Of The Requirements, Ethnic And Race Relations T3330A', Wake Forest, North Carolina: Southeastern Baptist Theological Seminary, available from https://liberty.academia.edu/JTruettGlen, accessed 22/11/2023.

Goodfellow, Maya, 2019, *Hostile Environment: How Immigrants Became Scapegoats*, London: Verso Books.

Gordon-Carter, Glynne, 2003, *An Amazing Journey: The Church of England's Response to Institutional Racism*, London: Church House Publishing.

Görlach, Manfred, and John Holm (eds), 1986, *Focus on the Caribbean*, Amsterdam: John Benjamins.

Gossai, Hemchand, 2009, 'Challenging the Empire: The Conscience of the Prophet and Prophetic Dissent From a Postcolonial Perspective' in Tat-siong Benny Liew (ed.), *Postcolonial Interventions: Essays in Honour of R. S. Sugirtharajah*, Sheffield: Sheffield Phoenix Press, pp. 98–108.

———, 2018, 'Jeremiah's Welfare Ethic: Challenging Imperial Militarism' in Hemchand Gossai (ed.), *Postcolonial Commentary and the Old Testament*, London: Bloomsbury, pp. 258–74.

Grant, Jacquelyn, 1989, *White Women's Christ and Black Women's Jesus*, Atlanta, GA: Scholars Press.

Grant, Paul, and Raj Patel, 1990, *A Time to Speak: Perspectives of Black Christians in Britain*, Birmingham: Black Theology Working Group.

Green, Barbara, 2013, *Jeremiah and God's Plans of Well-Being*, Columbia, SC: University of South Carolina Press.

Green, Christopher C., 2013, *Doxological Theology: Karl Barth on Divine Providence, Evil, and the Angels*, London: Bloomsbury.

Greenspoon, Leonard J. (ed.), 2019, *Next Year in Jerusalem: Exile and Return in Jewish History*, West Lafayette, IN: Purdue University Press.

Gregory, Steven, and Roger Sanjek, 1994, *Race*, New Brunswick, NJ: Rutgers University Press.

Grizzle, Trevor L., 2021, 'The Bible and Racial Justice' in Clifton R. Clarke and Wayne C. Solomon (eds), *Skin Deep: Pentecostalism, Racism and the Church*, Cleveland, TN: Seymour Press, pp. 73–96.

Groody, Daniel G., and Gioacchino Campese, 2008, *A Promised Land, a Perilous Journey: Theological Perspectives on Migration*, Notre Dame, IN: University of Notre Dame Press.

Gul, Malik, 2012, 'From Hard to Reach to Within Reach – the "How" of Community Engagement in the Era of the Big Society' in *Better Health in Harder Times: Active Citizens and Innovation on the Frontline*, ed. Celia Davies, Jan Walmsley, Mike Hales and Ray Flux, Bristol, UK: Policy Press, pp. 153–6, https://doi.org/10.51952/9781447306955-041.

Gupta, Anurag, 2016, https://www.facebook.com/echoinggreen/photos/i-really-think-that-racism-is-a-waste-of-our-time-its-a-waste-of-our-energy-beca/10154271240220923/ accessed 04/01/2024.

Gutiérrez, Gustavo, 1984, *We Drink from our own Wells: The Spiritual Journey of a People*, Maryknoll, NY: Orbis Books.

Hall, Delroy, 2021, *A Redemption Song: Illuminations on Black Pastoral Theology and Culture*, London: SCM Press.

Hall, Stuart, 2017, *The Fateful Triangle: Race, Ethnicity, Nation*, Cambridge, MA: Harvard University Press.

Halvorson-Taylor, Martien, 2010, *Enduring Exile: The Metaphorization of Exile in the Hebrew Bible*, Boston, MA: Brill.

Hampton, Ellen, 2013, '"Lawdy! I Was Sho' Happy When I Was a Slave!": Manipulative Editing in the Wpa Former-Slave Narratives from Mississippi', *L'Ordinaire des Amériques*, 215, doi: 10.4000/orda.522.

Hannaford, Ivan, 1996, *Race: The History of an Idea in the West*, Baltimore, MD: Johns Hopkins University Press.

Harmon-Jones, Eddie (ed.), 2019, *Cognitive Dissonance: Reexamining a Pivotal Theory in Psychology*, Washington, DC: American Psychological Association.

Hass, Kristin Ann (ed.), 2021, *Being Human During Covid*, Ann Arbor, MI: University of Michigan Press.

Hayes, Diana L., 1996, *And Still We Rise: An Introduction to Black Liberation Theology*, New York: Paulist Press.

Hejzlar, Pavel, 2010, *Two Paradigms for Divine Healing: Fred F. Bosworth, Kenneth E. Hagin, Agnes Sanford, and Francis MacNutt in Dialogue*, Boston, MA: Brill.

Henry-Robinson, Tessa, 2017, 'Blackness, Black Power and God-talk: A Reflection', *Black Theology: An International Journal*, Vol. 15, Issue 2, pp. 117–35.

Hicks, Shari Renee, 2015, *A Critical Analysis of Post Traumatic Slave Syndrome: A Multigenerational Legacy of Slavery*, San Francisco, CA: California Institute of Integral Studies.

Hill, Clifford and Monica Hill, 2016, *Living in Babylon*, Haddington, East Lothian: Handsel Press.

Hill, Johnny Bernard, 2013, *Prophetic Rage*, Grand Rapids, MI: Eerdmans.

Hinson, David F., 1990, *History of Israel: Old Testament Introduction 1* (revised edition), London: SPCK.

Hirsh, Afua, 2018, *Brit(ish): On Race, Identity and Belonging*, London: Jonathan Cape.

Hollenweger, Walter J., 1997, *Pentecostalism: Origins and Developments Worldwide*, Peabody, MA: Hendrickson.

hooks, bell, 1993, *Sisters of the Yam: Black Women and Self-discovery*, London: Turnaround.

Hopkins, Dwight N., 1993, *Shoes That Fit Our Feet: Sources for a Constructive Black Theology*, Maryknoll, NY: Orbis Books.

Hudson, Simon, 2021, *History Through the Black Experience*, Vols 1 & 2, London: New Generation Publishing.

Hunt, Stephen, 2016, *Handbook of Global Contemporary Christianity: Movements, Institutions, and Allegiance*, Leiden: Brill.

Igbinedion, Simeon A., 2019, 'Finding Value for the Right to Development in International Law', *African Human Rights Law Journal*, Vol. 19, No. 1, pp. 395–417.

Ikeanyibe, Okechukwu Marcellus, Chuka E. Ugwu, Ifeoma Florence Nzekwe and Josephine Obioji, 2021, 'The United Nations, the Political Economy of International Organisations, and Managing Self-Determination in Africa', *International Journal of Renaissance Studies*, Vol. 16, No. 1, doi.org/10.1080/18186874.2021.1950558.

Isasi-Díaz, Ada María, 1996, *Mujerista Theology: A Theology for the Twenty-first Century*, Maryknoll, NY: Orbis Books.

Jackson, Jonathan, 2021, *The Power of Agreement: Understanding Covenant Theology*, West Bromwich: Marcia M Publishing.

Jacques-Garvey, Amy (ed.), 1977, *Philosophy and Opinions of Marcus Garvey*, New York: Atheneum.

Jagessar, Michael N., and Anthony Reddie (eds), 2007a, *Postcolonial Black British Theology: New Textures and Themes*, Peterborough: Epworth.

———, 2007b, *Black Theology in Britain: A Reader*, London: Equinox.

Jeffries, Bayyinah S., 2014, *A Nation Can Rise No Higher Than Its Women: African American Muslim Women in the Movement for Black Self-Determination, 1950–1975*, New York: Lexington Books/Fortress Academic.

———, 2020, 'Prioritizing Black Self-Determination: The Last Strident Voice of Twentieth-Century Black Nationalism', *Genealogy*, Vol. 4, No. 4, https://doi.org/10.3390/genealogy4040110.

John, Gus, 2006, *Taking a Stand – Gus John Speaks on Education, Race, Social Action and Civil Unrest 1980–2005*, Gus John Partnership.

Johnson-Fisher, Angela, 2008, *Afristocracy: Free Women of Color and the Politics of Race, Class, and Culture*, Saarbrücken VDM Verlag: Dr. Müller.

Jones, Sarah Catherine, 2020, 'Interview with Tony Kelly, Diabetes Advocate', https://www.unsungheroawards.com/interview-with-tony-kelly-diabetes-advocate/ accessed 02/05/2023.

Jones, William, 1971, 'Theodicy and Methodology in Black Theology: A Critique of Washington, Cone and Cleage', *The Harvard Theological Review*, Vol. 64, No. 4, pp. 541–57.

Joseph, Celucien L., 2019, 'Theodicy and Black Theological Anthropology in James Cone's Theological Identity', *Toronto Journal of Theology*, Vol. 35, Issue 1, pp. 83–111.

——— 2020, 'The Meaning of James H. Cone and the Significance of Black Theology: Some Reflections on His Legacy', *Black Theology An International Journal*, Vol. 18, Issue 2, pp. 112–43.

Kabongo, Kasebwe T. L., 2020, 'Migration to South Africa: A Missional Reflection of a Refugee Using Jeremiah 29.4–12 as an Interpretive Framework', *Theologia Viatorum Journal*, Vol. 44, No. 1.

——— 2021, 'Making Sense of the COVID-19 Disruptions in Incarnational Ministry Using Micah 6:8 as an Interpretive Framework', *Verbum et Ecclesia*, Vol. 42, Issue 1.

Kahane, Adam, 2017, *Collaborating with the Enemy: How to Work with People You Don't Agree with or Like or Trust*, Oakland, CA: Berrett-Koehler Publishers.

Katho, R. B., 2021, *Reading Jeremiah in Africa: Biblical Essays in Socio-political Imagination*, Bukuru, Plateau State, Nigeria: Hippo Books.

Kay, William K., 2009, *Pentecostalism*, London: SCM Press.

Kelly, Kenneth G., 1997, 'The Archaeology of African-European Interaction: Investigating the Social Roles of Trade, Traders, and the Use of Space in the Seventeenth- and Eighteenth-Century Hueda Kingdom, Republic of Benin', *World Archaeology*, Vol. 28, No. 3, pp. 351–69.

Kendi, Ibram X., 2019, *How to Be an Antiracist*, London: Penguin Random House.

Kgatla, Selaelo T., 2023, 'Allan Anderson: African Pentecostalism, Theology and the Othering', *HTS Theological Studies*, Vol. 79, No. 1.

Killen, Melanie, and Audun Dahl, 2021, 'Moral Reasoning Enables Developmental and Societal Change', *Sage Journal*, Vol. 16, Issue 6.

King, Sam, 2004, *Climbing up the Rough Side of the Mountain*, London: FastPrint Publisher.

Kotsko, Adam, 2010, *The Politics of Redemption: The Social Agency of Redemption*, London: T&T Clark.

Kufour, Karen St-Jean, 1999, 'Black Britain's Economic Power, Myth, or Reality? An Empirical Review and Analysis of the Economic Reality of Black Britain' in Kwesi Owusu (ed.), *Black British Culture and Society: A Text-Reader*, London: Routledge.

Kwiyani, Harvey C., 2014, *Sent Forth: African Missionary Work in the West*, Maryknoll, NY: Orbis Books.

Lartey, Emmanuel Y., 1998, 'Editorial', *Black Theology in Britain: A Journal of Contextual Praxis*, Issue 1, Sheffield: Sheffield Academic Press.

——— 2015, *Postcolonializing God: New Perspectives on Pastoral and Practical Theology*, London: SCM Press.

Laubscher, M., 2022, 'The (Demanding) History of South African Public Theology as Prophetic Theology', *In die Skriflig*, Vol. 56, No. 1, doi: 10.4102/ids.v56i1.2856.

Lestar, Tamas, 2022, 'A Seventh-Day Adventist Farm Community in Tanzania and Vegetarianism As a Social Practice', *Journal of Organizational Ethnography*, Vol. 11, Issue 3, pp. 294–315.

Levy, Horace (ed.), 2009, *Black Worldview and the Making of Caribbean Society, History, Biology, Culture*, Jamaica: University of the West Indies Press.

Lindsay, Ben, 2019, *We Need To Talk About Race: Understanding The Black Experience in White Majority Churches*, London: SPCK.

Loba-Mkole, Jean-Claude, 2019, 'Interculturality in Peace-Building and Mutual Edification (Rm 14:19)', *Theological Studies*, Vol. 75, No. 4, pp. 1–8.

Lorde, Audre, 2018, *The Master's Tools Will Never Dismantle the Master's House*, London: Penguin Random House.

Louw, Daniel J., 2017, '"Black Pain is a White Commodity": Moving beyond postcolonial theory in practical theology: #CaesarMustFall!', *HTS Teologiese Studies/Theological Studies*, Vol. 73, No. 4.

Lovejoy, Paul E., 2011, *Transformations in Slavery: A History of Slavery in Africa*, Cambridge: Cambridge University Press.

Lynch, Hollis R., 1967, *Edward Wilmott Blyden: Pan-Negro Patriot 1832–1912*, London: Oxford University Press.

Lyseight, Oliver A., 1995, *Forward March (An Autobiography)*, West Midlands: George S. Garwood.

Magezi, V., 2019, 'Pastoral Care to Migrants as Care at the "in-between" and "liminal" Home away from Home: Towards Public Pastoral Care to Migrants', *Verbum et Ecclesia*, Vol. 40, No 1.

Maier, Christl M., and Carolyn J. Sharp (eds), 2015, *Prophecy and Power: Jeremiah in Feminist and Postcolonial Perspective*, London: Bloomsbury.

Manley, Michael, 1983, *Up the Down Escalator: Development and the International Economy – A Jamaican Case Study*, Washington, DC: Howard University Press.

Marley, Bob, 2002, *Legend: The Best of Bob Marley and the Wailers*, reissued by Tuff Gong Records.

Masango, Maake J., 2019, 'The Pain of Migrants in a Strange Land', *HTS Theological Studies*, Vol. 75, No. 1.

Matthews, David, 2018, *Voices of the Windrush Generation: The Real Story Told by the People Themselves*, London: Blink Publishing.

Mbiti, John S., 1969, *African Religions and Philosophy*, second edition, Oxford: Heinemann International Literature.

Mbubaegbu, Chine, 2013, *Am I Beautiful? Finding Freedom in the Answer*, Milton Keynes: Authentic Media.

McCalla, Doreen (ed.), 2003, *Black Success in the UK: Essays in Racial and Ethnic Studies,* Birmingham: DMee: Vision Learning.

McCloughry, Roy, 1992, *Men and Masculinity: From Power to Love*, Sevenoaks, Kent: Hodder and Stoughton.

McFarland, Ian A., et al. (eds), 2011, *The Cambridge Dictionary of Christian Theology*, Cambridge: Cambridge University Press.

McGrath, Alister, 1988, *NIV Bible Commentary*, London: Hodder and Stoughton.

McKenzie, Everal, 2002, *Jamaica Proverbs and Culture Explained*, Padstow: TJ International.

McMillan, Michael, 2005, *The Front Room: Migrant Aesthetics in the Home*, London: Black Dog Publishing.

McRorie, Christina G., 2021, 'Moral Reasoning in "the World"', *Theological Studies*, Vol. 82, no. 2, pp. 213–37.

Mdingi, H. M., 2022, 'Prevent the Rise of a Black Messiah: Madness or Revolution', *HTS: Theological Studies*, Vol. 78 No. 1, doi: 10.4102/hts, v78i1.7816.

Membe-Matale, Suzanne, 2015, 'Ubuntu Theology', *Ecumenical Review*, Vol. 67, Issue 2, pp. 273–323, https://doi.org/10.1111/erev.12159.

Michelle, Lecia, 2022, *The White Allies Handbook: 4 Weeks to Join the Racial Justice Fight for Black Women*, First Kensington hardcover edition, New York, NY: Dafina.

Miles, B. A., 2006, *When the Church of God Arises: A History of the Development of the Church of God of Prophecy in the Midlands and More Widely*, Birmingham: History into Print.

Miles-Tribble, Valerie, 2017, 'Restorative justice as a public theology imperative', *Sage Journals*, Vol. 114, Issue 3.

Milton, Grace, 2015, *Shalom, the Spirit and Pentecostal Conversion, a Practical-Theological Study Guide*, Leiden: Brill.

Mohabir, Philip, 1988, *Building Bridges: A Dramatic Personal Story of Reconciliation and Evangelism*, London: Hodder and Stoughton.

Mohdin, Aamna, and Carmen Aguilar García, 2023, 'Black people in England and Wales three times as likely to live in social housing', *Guardian* (15 March), https://www.theguardian.com/society/2023/mar/15/census-black-britons-social-housing-ons

Morrison, Doreen, 2014, *Slavery's Heroes: George Liele and the Ethiopian Baptists of Jamaica 1783–1865*, Birmingham: Liele Books.

Morrison, Toni, 1975, in a sound recording of Portland State

Black Studies Center public dialogue, Pt. 2, available at https://soundcloud.com/portland-state-library/portland-state-black-studies-1?fbclid=IwAR1eh1xHKqm3zvG9Y4NMAMvWkFTle4-4uFhY4dahEFJQUrA2wCwjLVtwBNc (accessed 29/12/2023).

Mosala, I. J., 1989, *Biblical Hermeneutics and Black Theology in South Africa*, Grand Rapids, MI: Eerdmans.

Mos-Shogbamimu, Shola, 2021, *This is Why I Resist: Don't Define My Black Identity*, London: Headline.

Moyo, Anderson, 2017, 'Church-Planting Considerations for African Reverse Missionaries in Britain in the Postmodern Era' in Israel Oluwole Olofinjana (ed.), *African Voices – Towards African British Theologies*, Carlisle: Langham Global Library, pp. 63–82.

Mukwashi, Amanda Khozi, 2020, *But Where Are You Really From?: On Identity, Humanhood and Hope*, London: SPCK.

Nathan, Ronald A., 2000, 'Praying from the Underside: Breaking Forth into Liberation' in Aldred, Joe (ed.), *Praying with Power*, London: Bloomsbury Continuum, pp. 90–101.

Navigators, 2018, *Jeremiah and Lamentations*, Carol Stream, IL: NavPress Publishing Group.

Nehl, Markus, 2016, 'Transnational Black Dialogues: Re-Imagining Slavery in the Twenty-First Century', *Postcolonial Studies*, Vol. 28, No. 1.

Neil, Bronwen, 2020, 'Curating the Past: The Retrieval of Historical Memories and Utopian Ideals' in Bronwen Neil and Kosta Simic (eds), *Memories of Utopia: The Revision of Histories and Landscapes in Late Antiquity*, London: Routledge, pp. 3–19.

Newsom, Carol A., et al., 2012, *Women's Bible Commentary*, third edition revised and updated, Louisville, KY: Westminster John Knox Press.

Niemandt, Cornelius J. P., 2019, 'Rooted in Christ, Grounded in Neighbourhoods – A Theology of Place', *Verbum et Ecclesia*, Vol. 40, No. 1.

Nilsen, Micheline, 2014, *The Working Man's Green Space: Allotment Gardens In England, France, and Germany, 1870–1919*, Charlottesville, VA: University of Virginia Press.

Nogalski, James D., 2018, *Introduction to the Hebrew Prophets*, Nashville, TN: Abingdon.

O'Connor, Kathleen M., 2012, 'Jeremiah' in Carol A. Newsom, Sharon H. Ringe and Jacqueline E. Lapsley, *Women's Bible Commentary*, third edition revised and updated, twentieth anniversary edn, Louisville, KY: Westminster John Knox Press, pp. 267–77.

Olofinjana, Israel, 2010, *Reverse in Ministry and Missions: Africans in the Dark Continent of Europe, An Historical Study of African Churches in Europe*, Milton Keynes: AuthorHouse.

Olofinjana, Israel Oluwole (ed.), 2017, *African Voices: Towards African British Theologies*, Carlisle: Langham Global Library.

Olusoga, David, 2016, *Black and British: A Forgotten History*, London: Macmillan.

Oosthuizen, Gerhardus C., 1992, *The Healer-Prophet in Afro-Christian Churches*, Leiden: Brill.

Osborne, Larry, et al., 2015, *Thriving in Babylon: Why Hope, Humility, and Wisdom Matter in a Godless Culture*, Colorado Springs, CO: David C. Cook.

Overholt, Thomas W., 1970, *The Threat of Falsehood: A Study in the Theology of the Book of Jeremiah*, London: SCM Press.

Owusu, Kwesi (ed.), 1999, *Black British Culture and Society: A Text-Reader*, London: Routledge.

Pareles, Jon, 2000, 'Calypso Songwriter Who Mixed Party Tunes With Deeper Messages', *New York Times* (14 Feb.).

Parks, Edd Winfield, 1937, 'Plantation Prayer (Poem)', *The Sewanee Review*, Vol. 45, No. 3.

Pemberton, P., E. Pemberton and J. R. Maxwell-Hughes (eds), 1983, *History of the Wesleyan Church in the British Isles*, Birmingham: Wesleyan Holiness Church.

Perry, Kennetta Hammond, 2016, *London Is the Place for Me: Black Britons, Citizenship and the Politics of Race*, Oxford: Oxford University Press.

Petersen, David, 1981, *The Roles of Israel's Prophets*, London: Bloomsbury.

Phillips, Mike and Trevor Phillips, 1998, *Windrush: The Irresistible Rise of Multi-Racial Britain*, London: HarperCollins Publishers.

Pieterse, Alex L., Jione A. Lewis and Matthew J. Miller (eds), 2023, 'Dismantling and Eradicating Anti-Blackness and Systemic Racism', *American Psychological Association*, Vol. 70, No. 3.

Punt, Jeremy, 2009, 'Postcolonial Theory as Academic Double Agent? Power, Ideology and Postcolonial Biblical Hermeneutics in South Africa' in Liew, Tat-siong Benny (ed.), *Postcolonial Interventions: Essays in Honour of R. S. Sugirtharajah*, Sheffield: Sheffield Phoenix Press, pp. 274–95.

Ramsey, Bradley D., 2021, 'Bridging the Divide: The Racial Ecclesiology of the Church of God' in Clarke, Clifton R., and Wayne C. Solomon (eds), *Skin Deep: Pentecostalism, Racism and the Church*, Lanham, MD: Seymour Press.

Rashidi, Runoko, 2011, *Black Star: The African Presence in Early Europe*, London: Books of Africa.

Reddie, Anthony, 2003, *Nobodies to Somebodies: A Practical Theology for Education and Liberation*, Peterborough: Epworth.

———, 2006, *Black Theology in Transatlantic Dialogue*, New York: Palgrave Macmillan.

———, 2014, *Working Against the Grain: Re-Imaging Black Theology in the 21st Century*, London: Routledge.

——, 2019, *Theologising Brexit: A liberationist and postcolonial critique*, Abingdon, Oxon: Routledge.

—— (ed.), 2012, *SCM Core Text Black Theology*, London: SCM Press.

Reddie, Richard S., 2007, *Abolition!: The Struggle to Abolish Slavery in the British Colonies*, Oxford: Lion.

——, 2012, *From an Acorn to an Oak Tree: The History of the New Testament Assembly in the UK*, London: New Testament Assembly.

Reid-Salmon, Delroy A., 2012, *Burning for Freedom: A Theology of the Black Atlantic Struggle for Liberation*, Kingston, Jamaica: Ian Randle Publishers.

——, 2014, *Home Away from Home: The Caribbean Diasporan Church in the Black Atlantic Tradition*, London: Taylor & Francis.

Reif, Stefan C. and Renater Egger-Wenzel (eds), 2015, *Ancient Jewish Prayers and Emotions: Emotions Associated with Jewish Prayer in and Around the Second Temple Period*, Berlin/Boston: De Gruyter, Inc.

Roach, Jason, and Jessamin Birdsall, 2022, *Healing the Divides: How every Christian can Advance God's Vision for Racial Unity and Justice*, London: The Good Book Company.

Roberts, Anthony Richard, 2014, '"Say It Loud!"' – Black Power Ideology Within the Theological Anthropology of James H. Cone: Being Human in the Modern World', Academia.eu.

Rodney, Walter, 1988, *How Europe Underdeveloped Africa*, London: Bogle-L'Ouverture.

Rollock, Nicola, 2015, *The Colour of Class: The Educational Strategies of the Black Middle Classes*, London: Routledge.

Rowland, Chris, and John Vincent (eds), 1995, *Liberation Theology UK*, Sheffield: Urban Theology Unit.

Sánchez, Ruben, Ramon Gelabert, Yasna Badilla and Carlos Del Valle, 2016, 'Feeding Holy Bodies: A Study on the Social Meanings of a Vegetarian Diet to Seventh-Day Adventist Church Pioneers', *HTS Theological Studies*, Vol. 72, No. 3, pp. e1–e8.

Sanghera, Sathnam, 2021, *Empireland: How Imperialism Has Shaped Modern Britain*, London: Penguin Books.

Scheffler, Eben, 2016, 'Caring for the Needy in the Acts of the Apostles', *Neotestamentica Journal*, Vol. 50, No. 3, pp. 131–66.

Schefold, R., and Peter J. M. Nas, 2008, *Indonesian Houses: Volume 2: Survey of Vernacular Architecture in Western Indonesia*, Leiden: Brill.

Scobie, Edward, 1994, *Global African Presence*, Brooklyn, NY: A&B Books Publishers.

Sealey-Skerritt, Dianne, 2018, *When God Calls: Listening, Hearing and Responding*, Ely: Melrose Books.

Senokoane, B. B., 2022, 'Witchcraft That Comes with the Bible', *HTS Theological Studies*, Vol. 78, No. 1, doi: 10.4102/hts.v78i1.7869.

Serequeberhan, Tsenay, 2015, *Existence and Heritage: Hermeneutic Explorations in African and Continental Philosophy*, New York: State University of New York Press.

Sewell, Tony, 2009, *Generating Genius: Black Boys in Search of Love, Ritual and Schooling*, Stoke-on-Trent: Trentham Books.

Seymour, Michael, 2014, *Babylon: Legend, History and the Ancient City*, London: I. B. Tauris.

Shemesh, Abraham O., 2018, 'Let Us Be Given Vegetables to Eat and Water to Drink: The Diet Consumed by Daniel and His Friends As Clarified in the Commentary of Abraham Ibn Ezra', *HTS Theological Studies*, 74, no. 1, pp. 1–7.

Shepherd, David, 2013, 'Is the Governor Also among the Prophets? Parsing the Purposes of Jeremiah in the Memory of Nehemiah' in Mark J. Boda and Lissa Wray Beal (eds), *Prophets, Prophecy, and Ancient Israelite Historiography*, University Park, PA: Pennsylvania State University Press, pp. 209–28.

Simopoulos, Nicole M., 2007, 'Who Was Hagar? Mistress, Divorcee, Exile, or Exploited Worker: An Analysis of Contemporary Grassroots Readings of Genesis 16 by Caucasian, Latina, and Black South African Women' in Gerald O. West (ed.), *Reading Other-Wise: Socially Engaged Biblical Scholars Reading with Their Local Communities*, Atlanta, GA: Society of Biblical Literature.

Singleton, Harry H., 2012, *White Religion and Black Humanity*, Lanham, MD: University Press of America.

Smith, Io, with Wendy Green, 1989, *An Ebony Cross: Being a Black Christian in Britain Today*, London: Marshall, Morgan and Scott.

Solomon, Wayne C., 2021, 'Black Pain, God's Pain: A Black Pentecostal's Reading of Dorothee Solle's theology for Skeptics and Bonhoeffer's Black Jesus' in Clifton R. Clarke and Wayne C. Solomon (eds), *Skin Deep – Pentecostalism, Racism and the Church*, Lanham, MD: Seymour Press, pp. 23–46.

Sowell, Thomas, 2019, *Discrimination and Disparities*, New York: Basic Books.

Speed, Francesca, and Anastasia Kulichyova, 2021, 'The Role of Talent Intermediaries in Accessing and Developing Refugee Talent Pools', *Journal of Organizational Effectiveness: People and Performance*, Vol. 8, No. 4, pp. 407–26, Bingley, UK: Emerald Publishing.

Spleth, Janice, 2017, 'An Inescapable Network of Mutuality: the Conversation between Senghor's Philosophy and King's Vision in the "Elegy for Martin Luther King"', *Journal of the African Literature Association*, Vol. 11, No. 3, pp. 269–78.

Staples, Jason A., 2021, *The Idea of Israel in Second Temple Judaism: A New Theory of People, Exile, and Jewish Identity*, Cambridge: Cambridge University Press.

Stone, Selina Rachael, 2021, 'Holy Spirit, Holy Bodies?: Pentecostal

Spirituality, Pneumatology and the Politics of Embodiment,' unpublished PhD thesis, University of Birmingham.

Stoutjesdijk, Martijn, 2018, 'God As Father and Master', *NTT Journal for Theology and the Study of Religion*, Vol. 72, Issue 2, pp. 121–35.

Stowe, Harriet Beecher, 1995, *Uncle Tom's Cabin*, Ware: Wordsworth Editions.

Straubhaar, Rolf, 2015, 'The Stark Reality of the "White Saviour" Complex and the Need for Critical Consciousness: a Document Analysis of the Early Journals of a Freirean Educator', *Compare: A Journal of Comparative and International Education*, Vol. 45, Issue 3, pp. 381–400.

Streeter, Gary (ed.), 2002, *There Is Such a Thing as Society: Twelve Principles of Compassionate Conservatism*, London: Politico's Publishing.

Strine, C. A., 2018, 'Embracing Asylum Seekers and Refugees: Jeremiah 29 as Foundation for a Christian Theology of Migration and Integration', *Political Theology*, Vol. 19, Issue 6, pp. 478–96.

Strong, James, 1990, *The New Strong's Exhaustive Concordance of the Bible*, Nashville, TN: Nelson.

Sturge, Mark, 2005, *Look What the Lord had Done: An Exploration of Black Christian Faith in Britain*, Bletchley: Scripture Union.

———, 2019, 'Pentecostalism and Prosperity Theology: A Call for Reappraisal of Acceptance and Rejection' in Joe Aldred (ed.), *Pentecostals and Charismatics in Britain: An Anthology*, London: SCM Press.

Sugirtharajah, R. S., 2002, *Postcolonial Criticism and Biblical Interpretation*, Oxford: Oxford University Press.

Tarrer, Seth B., 2013, *Reading with the Faithful: Interpretation of True and False Prophecy in the Book of Jeremiah from Ancient to Modern Times*, University Park, PA: Pennsylvania State University Press.

Tarus, David Kirwa, and Stephanie Lowery, 2017, 'African Theologies of Identity and Community: The Contributions of John Mbiti, Jesse Mugambi, Vincent Mulago, and Kwame Bediako', *Open Theology*, Vol. 3, pp. 305–20.

Teel, K., 2011, *Racism and the Image of God*, New York: Palgrave Macmillan.

Tha God, Charlamagne, 2017, *Black Privilege: Opportunity Comes to Those who Create It*, New York: Touchstone.

Thomas, Hugh, 1997, *The Slave Trade: the History of the Atlantic Slave Trade 1440–1870*, London: Macmillan.

Tjørhom, Ola, 2021, 'The Early Stages: Pre-1910' in Geoffrey Wainwright and Paul McPartlan (eds), *The Oxford Handbook of Ecumenical Studies*, Oxford Handbooks, Oxford: Oxford Academic.

Tomlin, Carol, 2019, *Preach It: Understanding Black Preaching*, London: SCM Press.

Torino, G. C., et al. (eds), 2019, *Microaggression Theory: Influence and Implications*, Hoboken, NJ: Wiley.

Trafford, James, 2020, *The Empire at Home: Internal Colonies and the End of Britain*, London: Pluto Press.

Trotman, Arlington, 1992, 'Black, Black-led, or What?' in Joel Edwards, *Let's Praise Him Again!: An African-Caribbean Perspective on Worship*, Eastbourne: Kingsway, pp. 12–35.

Trueland, Jennifer, 2014, 'Eating for health', *Nursing Standard*, Vol. 29, No. 5 (201410), pp. 24–5.

Tschuy, Theo, 1997, *Ethnic Conflict and Religion: Challenge to the Churches*, Geneva: WCC Publications.

Usongo, Kenneth, 2018, 'The Politics of Migration and Empire in Sam Selvon's The Lonely Londoners', *Journal of the African Literature Association*, Vol. 12, No. 2, pp. 180–200.

van Aarde, Timothy, 2016, 'Black Theology in South Africa – A Theology of Human Dignity and Black Identity', *HTS Teologiese Studies/ Theological Studies*, 72(1), a3176.

Van Eck, Ernest, and Meshack Mandla Mashinini, 2015, 'The Parables of Jesus as Critique on Food Security Systems for Vulnerable Households in Urban Townships', *HTS Theological Studies*, Vol. 72, No. 3.

van Oudtshoorn, Andre, 2021, 'The Insignificant Impact of the Historical Jesus', *In Die Skriflig*, Vol. 55, No. 1.

Van Sertima, Ivan (ed.), 1985, *African Presence in Early Europe* (*Journal of African Civilizations* Vol. 7, No. 2), New Brunswick, NJ: Transaction Books.

van Wyk, Tanya, 2019, 'Redressing the Past, Doing Justice in the Present: Necessary Paradoxes', *HTS Theological Studies*, Vol. 75, No 4.

Vellem, Vuyani S., 2017, 'Un-thinking the West: The Spirit of Doing Black Theology of Liberation in Decolonial Times', *HTS Teologiese Studies/Theological Studies*, Vol. 73, No. 3.

Vondey, Wolfgang (ed.), 2020, *The Routledge Handbook of Pentecostal Theology*, Abingdon: Routledge.

Vondey, Wolfgang and Mittelstadt, M. (eds), 2013, *The Theology of Amos Yong and the New Face of Pentecostal Scholarship: Passion for the Spirit*, Crownhill: Brill.

Wade, Tony, 2005, *Black Enterprise in Britain*, 2nd ed., London: TCS.

Walker, Robin, 2006, *When We Ruled*, London: Every Generation Media.

Walker, Theodore, 2004, *Mothership Connections: A Black Atlantic Synthesis of Neoclassical Metaphysics and Black Theology*, New York: State University of New York Press.

Wallace, Derron, and Remi Joseph-Salisbury, 2022, 'How, Still, is the Black Caribbean Child Made Educationally Subnormal in the English School System?', *Ethnic and Racial Studies*, Vol. 45, Issue 8, pp. 1426–52.

Wallerstein, Immanuel, 1988, 'The Construction of Peoplehood: Racism, Nationalism, Ethnicity' in Etienne Balibar and Immanuel Wallerstein, *Race, Nation, Class: Ambiguous Identities*, London: Verso.

Walters, Wendy W., 2005, *At Home in Diaspora: Black International Writing*, Minneapolis, MA: University of Minnesota Press.

Wariboko, Nimi, 2014, *Nigerian Pentecostalism*, Rochester, NY: University of Rochester Press.

———, 2015, 'Political Theology from Paul Tillich to Pentecostalism in Africa' in Nimi Wariboko and Amos Yong (eds), *Paul Tillich and Pentecostal Theology: Spiritual Presence and Spiritual Power*, Bloomington, IN: Indiana University Press, pp. 128–251.

Warren, Calvin L., 2018, *Ontological Terror: Blackness, Nihilism, and Emancipation*, Durham, NC: Duke University Press.

Washington, Booker T., 1901, *Up From Slavery*, New York: Doubleday, Page & Co. (and many recent editions).

Watson, Dyan, Jesse Hagopian and Wayne Au, 2018, *Teaching for Black Lives*, Milwaukee, WI: Rethinking Schools.

Weaver, Darlene Fozard, 2002, *Self Love and Christian Ethics*, Cambridge, UK: Cambridge University Press.

Weissman, D., 2020, *Agency: Moral Identity and Free Will*, Cambridge: Open Book Publishers.

Werbner, Pnina, 2002, *The Migration Process: Capital, Gifts and Offerings among British Pakistanis*, London: Routledge.

Wessels, W. J., 2016, 'Patience, Presence and Promise: a Study of Prophetic Realism in Jeremiah 29:4–7', *Verbum et Ecclesia*, Vol. 37, Issue 1, a1584.

West, Cornel, 1999, *The Cornel West Reader*, New York: Basic Civitas Books.

West, G. O., 2018, 'The Bible and/as the Lynching Tree: A South African Tribute to James H. Cone', *Missionalia: Southern African Journal of Mission Studies*, Vol. 46, No. 2, pp. 236–54.

Widmer, Michael, 2015, *Standing in the Breach: An Old Testament Theology and Spirituality of Intercessory Prayer*, University Park, PA: Pennsylvania State University Press.

Wilkinson, John, 1993, *Church in Black and White*, Edinburgh: St Andrew Press.

Williams, Eric, 1993, *From Columbus to Castro – The History of the Caribbean 1492–1969*, London: Andre Deutsch.

Williams, Martin, 2011, *The Doctrine of Salvation in the First Letter of Peter*, Cambridge: Cambridge University Press.

Williams, Michael, and Manyoni Amalemba, 2015, *Black Scientists and Inventors in the UK*, UK: BIS Publications.

Williams, Wendy, 2020, *Windrush Lessons Learned Review*, London: House of Commons.

Wilmore, Gayraud S., and James H. Cone, 1979, *Black Theology – A Documentary History, 1966–1979*, Maryknoll, NY: Orbis Books.

Wilson, Everett A., 2010, 'Redemption from Below: The Emergence of the Latin American Popular Pentecostals' in Calvin Smith (ed.), *Pentecostal Power: Expressions, Impact and Faith of Latin American Pentecostalism*, Boston, MA: Brill, pp. 9–36.

Wilson, Gerald H., 1990, *The Prayer of Daniel 9: Reflection on Jeremiah 29*, Newberg, OR: George Fox College.

Wirzba, Norman, 2019, *Food and Faith: A Theology of Eating*, Cambridge: Cambridge University Press.

Wittenberg, Günther, 2002, '"... To Build and to Plant" (Jer. 1:10) The Message of Jeremiah as a Source of Hope for the Exilic Community and its Relevance for Community Building in South Africa', *Journal of Theology for Southern Africa*, pp. 57–67.

Wolff, Ernst, 2021, *Between Daily Routine and Violent Protest: Interpreting the Technicity of Action*, Boston, MA: Walter de Gruyter GmbH.

Wood, Wilfred, 1994, *Keep the Faith Baby!: A Bishop Speaks on Faith, Evangelism, Race Relations and Community*, Oxford: The Bible Reading Fellowship.

Woodhead, Linda, and Rebecca Catto (eds), 2012, *Religion and Change in Modern Britain*, London: Routledge.

Woolley, Simon, 2022, *Soar: My Journey from Council Estate to House of Lords*, London: Manilla.

Wright, N. T., 2014, *Finding God in the Psalms: Sing, Pray*, London: SPCK.

X, Malcolm, 1963, *The Race Problem, African Students Association and NAACP Campus Chapter*, East Lansing: Michigan State University; (speech) quoted at https://ccnmtl.columbia.edu/projects/mmt/mxp/speeches/mxt17.html.

———, 1965, *Malcolm X: The Autobiography of Malcolm X*, London: Penguin Books.

Yeboah, Samuel Kennedy, 1997, *The Ideology of Racism*, London: Hansib Publishing.

Yong, Amos, 2010, *In the Days of Caesar: Pentecostalism and Political Theology*, Grand Rapids, MI: Eerdmans.

———, and Estrelda Y. Alexander (eds), 2011, *Afro-Pentecostalism: Black Pentecostal and Charismatic Christianity in History and Culture*, New York: New York University Press.

Zimmerman, Gregory M., 2008, 'Beyond Legal Sanctions: The Correlates of Self-imposed and Socially Imposed Extralegal Risk Perceptions', *Deviant Behaviour*, Vol. 29, Issue 2, pp. 157–90.

About the Author

Bishop Dr Joseph (Joe) Aldred is a retired broadcaster, ecumenist, speaker and writer. He is an Honorary Research Fellow at Roehampton University, a bishop in the Church of God of Prophecy, a director of the National Church Leaders Forum – A Black Christian Voice, a member of the Order of St Leonard's Faith Authority Council for King Solomon International Business School, and a former member of the Windrush Cross-Government Working Group.

For 18 years until 2020 Joe worked as an ecumenist at Churches Together in England, with responsibility for supporting intercultural, Pentecostal and Charismatic relations. Before that, for six years he was Director of the Centre for Black and White Christian Partnership. Prior to this he served for 13 years as pastor and bishop in the Church of God of Prophecy in Ashford, Oxford and Sheffield; as well as an Associate Pastor at Cannon Street Memorial Baptist Church, Handsworth, Birmingham from 2003 to 2005.

Joe has been a broadcaster on BBC Radio 4's Daily Service, Prayer for the Day and Pause for Thought, and for ten years he presented a weekly show aimed at the African and Caribbean community on BBC Local Radio in the West Midlands, in addition to regular appearances on Premier Radio, UCB Christian Radio and other broadcasters. Joe has served as Chair of an NHS Primary Care Trust and on strategic councils, boards and committees mainly in the areas of faith, education, health and community relations as trustee, board member and patron.

Joe is a recipient of several awards and commendations, including NSPCC Safety Award, Mighty Men of Valour Award for Community Achievement, Association of Jamaican National Community Award, Apostolic Congress' Order of Companion of St Aiden, Companion of the Order of St Leonard, Windrush Legacy Lifetime Award, Lambeth Palace Langton Award for Community Service, Windrush 75th Anniversary Inspirational Leadership Award, and Black Story Partnership's Windrush 75 Certificate for services to broadcasting.

In addition to undergraduate studies, Joe has a Master's Degree (with Distinction) and a PhD in Theology from Sheffield University, and he is a Faith in Leadership Alumnus (Oxford University/Windsor Castle). Joe is author and editor of several books and articles, including *Preaching with Power* (1998), *Praying with Power* (2000), *Sisters with Power* (2000), *Respect: Understanding Caribbean British Christianity* (2005), *The Black Church in the 21st Century* (2010, 2020), *Thinking outside the box – on race, faith and life* (2013), *From Top Mountain – An Autobiography* (2015), *Pentecostals and Charismatics in Britain* (2019) and 'The Flourishing of the UK African and Caribbean Diaspora in the 21st Century, with reference to Jeremiah's Letter to Jewish exiles in Babylon, 6th Century BCE' in *Black Theology: An International Journal* (2022, Vol. 20, Issue 2). He contributes to magazines and periodicals including *Keep the Faith* and *The Preacher*.

Joe is married, since 1974, to Novelette, a psychotherapist and NHS Chaplain. They have three daughters and five grandchildren. He is an incurable West Indies cricket supporter, and a Chelsea FC fan. And yes, blue is his favourite colour!

Index

www.ingramcontent.com/pod-product-compliance
Lightning Source LLC
Chambersburg PA
CBHW021811211224
19184CB00009B/33